Jodorowsky & Mœbius Present THE INCAL

PSYCHOVERSE

By MARK RUSSELL, YANICK PAQUETTE & DAVE McCAIG

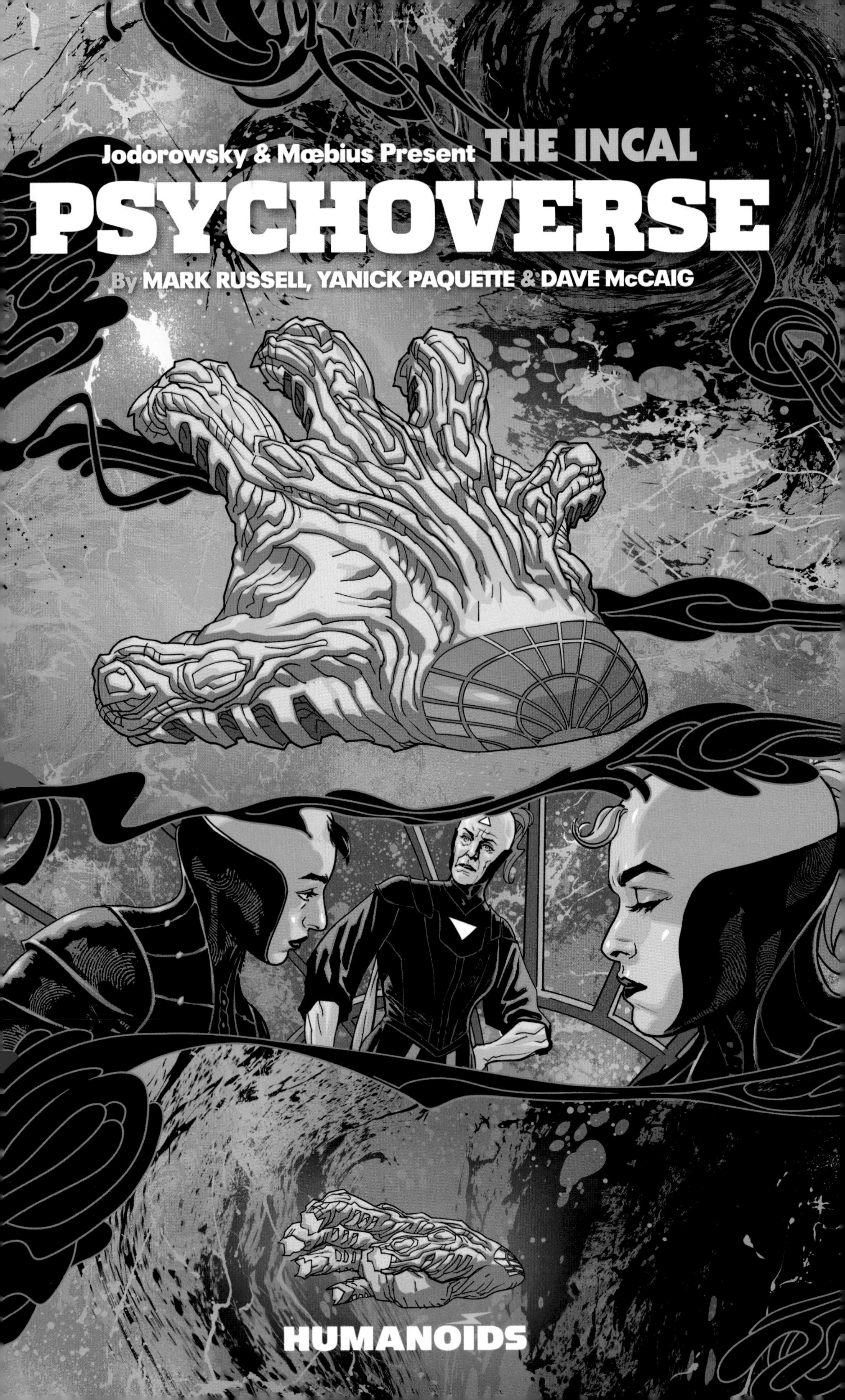

HUMANOIDS

Mark Russell
WRITER

Yanick Paquette
ARTIST

Dave McCaig
COLOR ARTIST

Troy Peteri
LETTERER

Jake Thomas, Rob Levin
EDITORS

Sandy Tanaka
DESIGNER

Jerry Frissen
SENIOR ART DIRECTOR

Fabrice Giger
PUBLISHER

Rights and Licensing
licensing@humanoids.com

Press and Social Media
pr@humanoids.com

Based on characters and universe created
by Mœbius and Alejandro Jodorowsky.

THE INCAL: PSYCHOVERSE. First Printing.
This book is a publication of Humanoids,
Inc. 8033 Sunset Blvd, #628, Los Angeles,
CA 90046. Copyright Humanoids, Inc.,
Los Angeles (USA). All rights reserved.
Humanoids® and the Humanoids logo are
registered trademarks of Humanoids, Inc.
in the U.S. and other countries.

Library of Congress Control Number:
2022945217

(RE)-INTRODUCING
THE INCAL

Exploding onto the pages of the cult sci-fi anthology *Métal Hurlant* in 1980, *The Incal*, by multifaceted Chilean-French creator Alejandro Jodorowsky and legendary French artist Jean "Mœbius" Giraud, has continuously topped lists as the best-selling science fiction graphic novel of all time and been cited as influential and inspirational by numerous comic creators, writers, and filmmakers.

[The Incal is] quite simply one of the most perfect comics ever conceived.
— **Mark Millar**

The Incal is a mind-bending, galaxy-spanning comedic adventure about the tribulations of John Difool, a low-class detective in a degenerate dystopian world who finds his life turned upside down when he discovers an ancient, mystical artifact called the Incal. While the Incal sends Difool on a journey full of sex, violence, action, and intrigue, the story is, at its heart, a tale of philosophical, spiritual exploration filled with humor and love.

Thank you [Jodorowsky and Mœbius] for literally decades of inspiration and showing all my peers and me what the graphic novel is capable of.
— **Brian Michael Bendis**

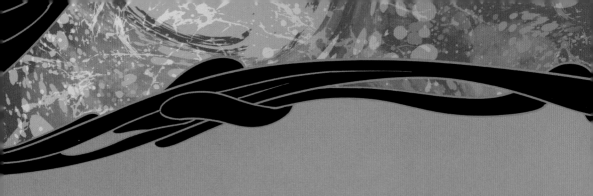

That sense of awakening fueled Jodorowsky to expand the world of *The Incal* into other books like *Before The Incal*, *Final Incal*, *The Metabarons*, and *The Technopriests*. For the first time ever, Jodorowsky is opening up the core epic, *The Incal* itself, for an infusion of new blood.

Jodorowsky, himself a cult film director of such movies as *The Holy Mountain*, has officially passed the baton to Taika Waititi to adapt *The Incal*. "If I were forty years old and it was proposed that someone other than me adapt *The Incal* to film, I'd go crazy," said Jodorowsky. "But I'm not forty anymore; I'm 93." The auteur added that Waititi will make "Waititi's *The Incal*, not Jodorowsky's," curious to see other talents bringing their personal paints to the canvas with complete creative freedom.

The Metabarons cycle is, to my mind, the greatest work of graphic fiction ever produced.
— David S. Goyer

In a process that continues this philosophy, Jodorowsky has granted the writer and artist of *Psychoverse*, Mark Russell and Yanick Paquette, the same creative freedom—not because it's certain that they will follow the canon to the letter, but precisely because they have been entrusted to shake it up, reinterpret it with talent and love.

If this is your first visit to the universe of *The Incal*, you are lucky. You have an entire world to discover forty years in the making. If you are already an initiate, welcome back, you're about to traverse some thrilling uncharted territories of *The Incal*.

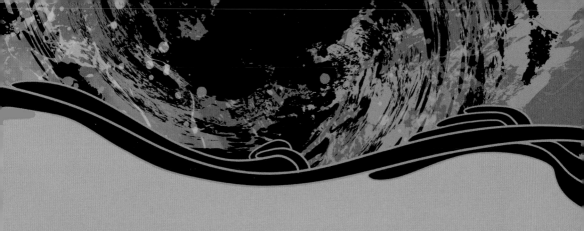

CHAPTER 1

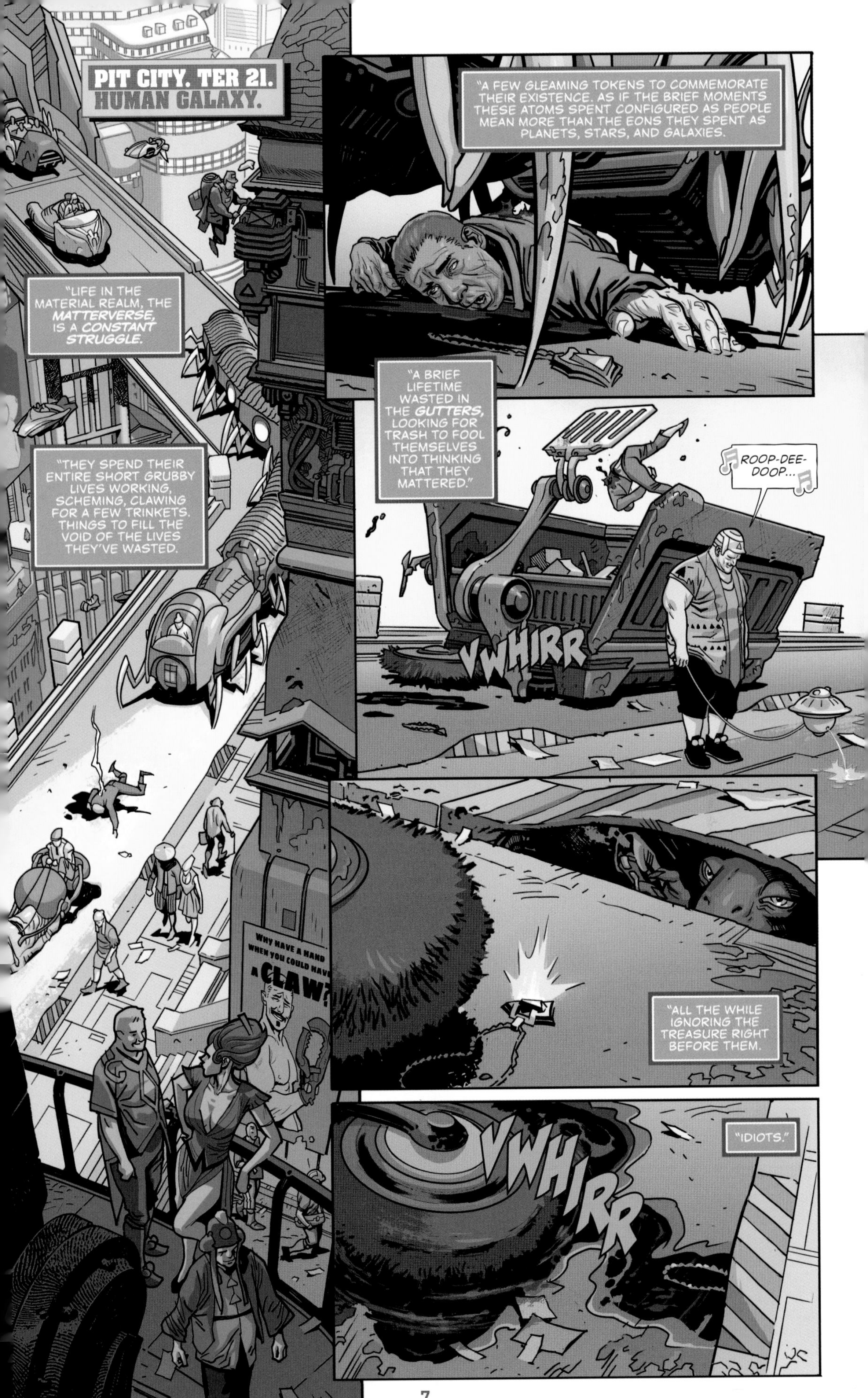
PIT CITY. TER 21. HUMAN GALAXY.
"LIFE IN THE MATERIAL REALM, THE *MATTERVERSE,* IS A *CONSTANT STRUGGLE.*
"THEY SPEND THEIR ENTIRE SHORT GRUBBY LIVES WORKING, SCHEMING, CLAWING FOR A FEW TRINKETS. THINGS TO FILL THE VOID OF THE LIVES THEY'VE WASTED.
WHY HAVE A HAND WHEN YOU COULD HAVE A CLAW?
"A FEW GLEAMING TOKENS TO COMMEMORATE THEIR EXISTENCE. AS IF THE BRIEF MOMENTS THESE ATOMS SPENT CONFIGURED AS PEOPLE MEAN MORE THAN THE EONS THEY SPENT AS PLANETS, STARS, AND GALAXIES.
"A BRIEF LIFETIME WASTED IN THE *GUTTERS,* LOOKING FOR TRASH TO FOOL THEMSELVES INTO THINKING THAT THEY MATTERED."
ROOP-DEE-DOOP...
VWHIRR
"ALL THE WHILE IGNORING THE TREASURE RIGHT BEFORE THEM.
"IDIOTS."
VWHIRR

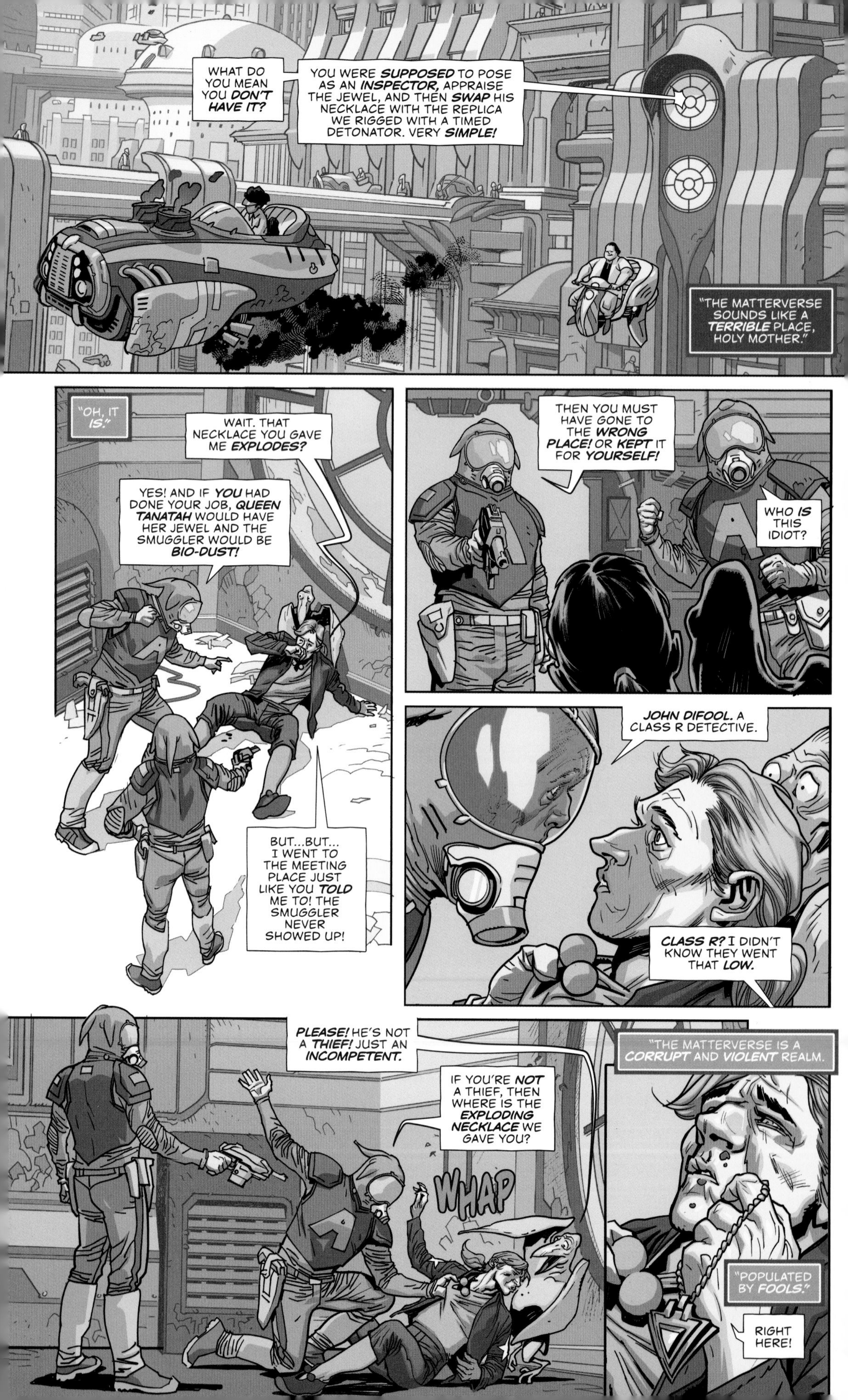
WHAT DO YOU MEAN YOU DON'T HAVE IT?
YOU WERE SUPPOSED TO POSE AS AN INSPECTOR, APPRAISE THE JEWEL, AND THEN SWAP HIS NECKLACE WITH THE REPLICA WE RIGGED WITH A TIMED DETONATOR. VERY SIMPLE!
"THE MATTERVERSE SOUNDS LIKE A TERRIBLE PLACE, HOLY MOTHER."
"OH, IT IS."
WAIT. THAT NECKLACE YOU GAVE ME EXPLODES?
YES! AND IF YOU HAD DONE YOUR JOB, QUEEN TANATAH WOULD HAVE HER JEWEL AND THE SMUGGLER WOULD BE BIO-DUST!
BUT...BUT... I WENT TO THE MEETING PLACE JUST LIKE YOU TOLD ME TO! THE SMUGGLER NEVER SHOWED UP!
THEN YOU MUST HAVE GONE TO THE WRONG PLACE! OR KEPT IT FOR YOURSELF!
WHO IS THIS IDIOT?
JOHN DIFOOL. A CLASS R DETECTIVE.
CLASS R? I DIDN'T KNOW THEY WENT THAT LOW.
PLEASE! HE'S NOT A THIEF! JUST AN INCOMPETENT.
IF YOU'RE NOT A THIEF, THEN WHERE IS THE EXPLODING NECKLACE WE GAVE YOU?
WHAP
"THE MATTERVERSE IS A CORRUPT AND VIOLENT REALM.
"POPULATED BY FOOLS."
RIGHT HERE!

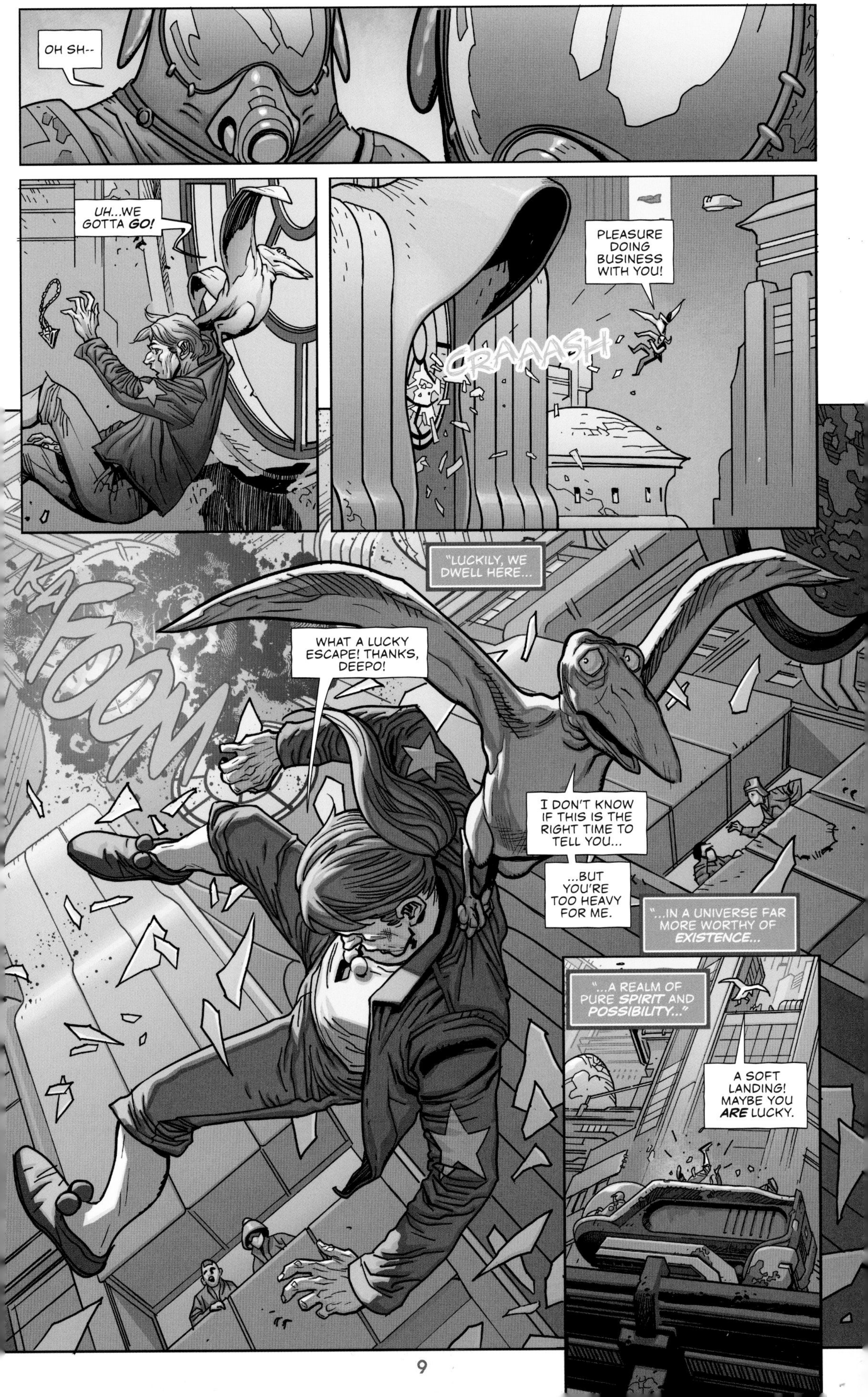
OH SH--
UH...WE GOTTA GO!
PLEASURE DOING BUSINESS WITH YOU!
CRAAASH
KA FOOM
"LUCKILY, WE DWELL HERE...
WHAT A LUCKY ESCAPE! THANKS, DEEPO!
I DON'T KNOW IF THIS IS THE RIGHT TIME TO TELL YOU...
...BUT YOU'RE TOO HEAVY FOR ME.
"...IN A UNIVERSE FAR MORE WORTHY OF EXISTENCE...
"...A REALM OF PURE SPIRIT AND POSSIBILITY..."
A SOFT LANDING! MAYBE YOU ARE LUCKY.

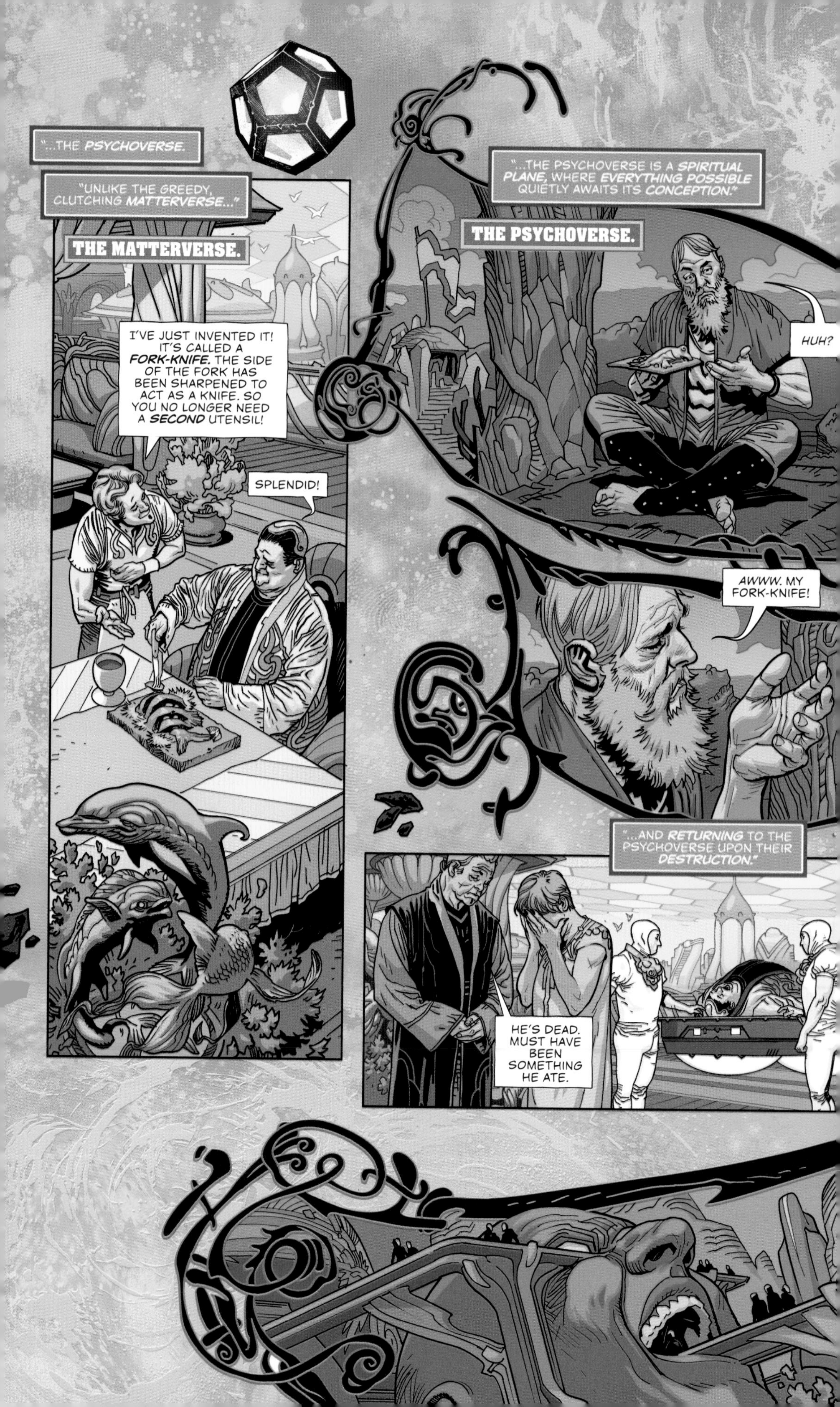

"...THE PSYCHOVERSE.
"UNLIKE THE GREEDY, CLUTCHING MATTERVERSE..."
THE MATTERVERSE.
I'VE JUST INVENTED IT! IT'S CALLED A FORK-KNIFE. THE SIDE OF THE FORK HAS BEEN SHARPENED TO ACT AS A KNIFE. SO YOU NO LONGER NEED A SECOND UTENSIL!
SPLENDID!
"...THE PSYCHOVERSE IS A SPIRITUAL PLANE, WHERE EVERYTHING POSSIBLE QUIETLY AWAITS ITS CONCEPTION."
THE PSYCHOVERSE.
HUH?
AWWW. MY FORK-KNIFE!
"...AND RETURNING TO THE PSYCHOVERSE UPON THEIR DESTRUCTION."
HE'S DEAD. MUST HAVE BEEN SOMETHING HE ATE.

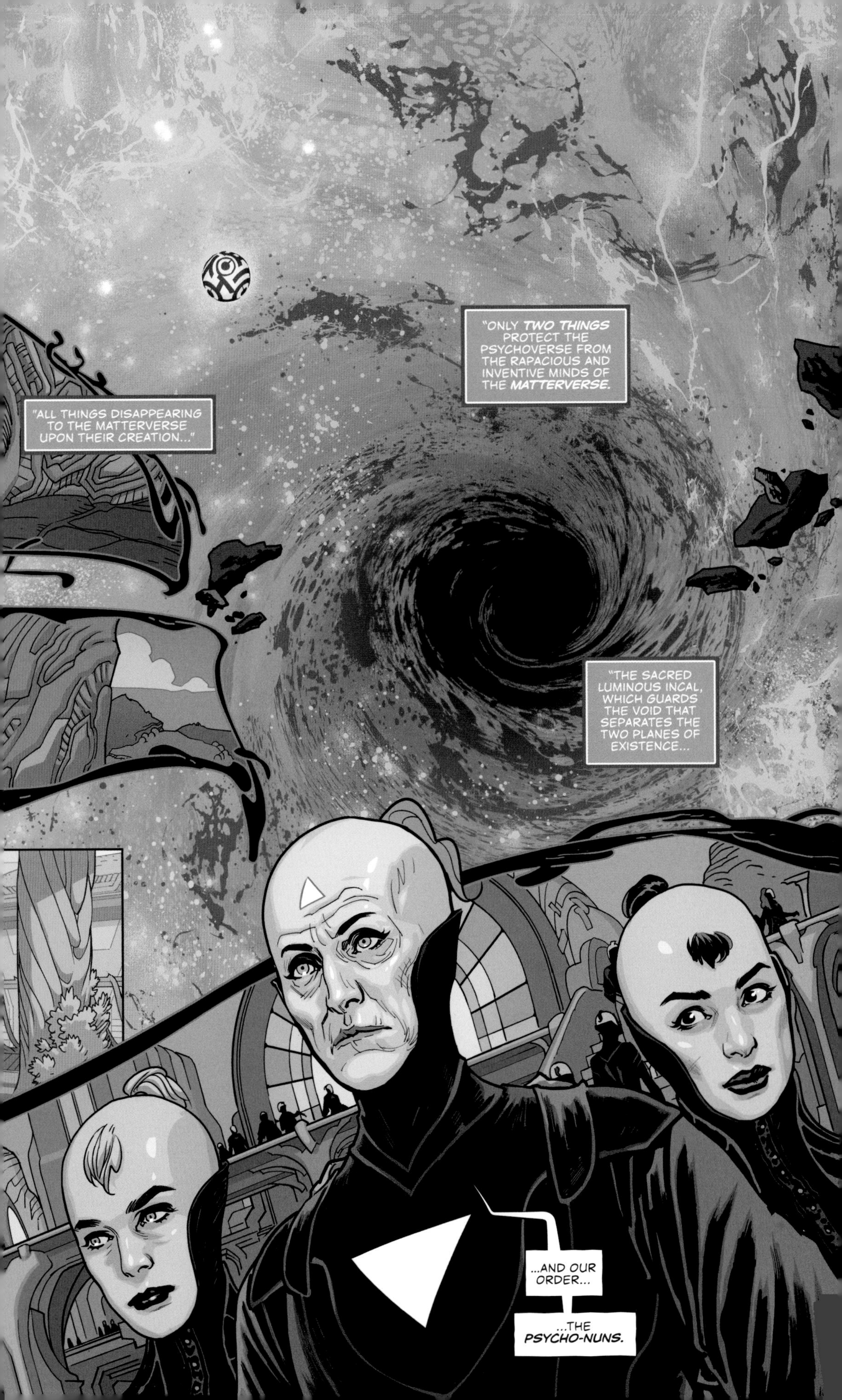
"ALL THINGS DISAPPEARING TO THE MATTERVERSE UPON THEIR CREATION..."
"ONLY *TWO THINGS* PROTECT THE PSYCHOVERSE FROM THE RAPACIOUS AND INVENTIVE MINDS OF THE *MATTERVERSE*.
"THE SACRED LUMINOUS INCAL, WHICH GUARDS THE VOID THAT SEPARATES THE TWO PLANES OF EXISTENCE...
...AND OUR ORDER...
...THE *PSYCHO-NUNS.*

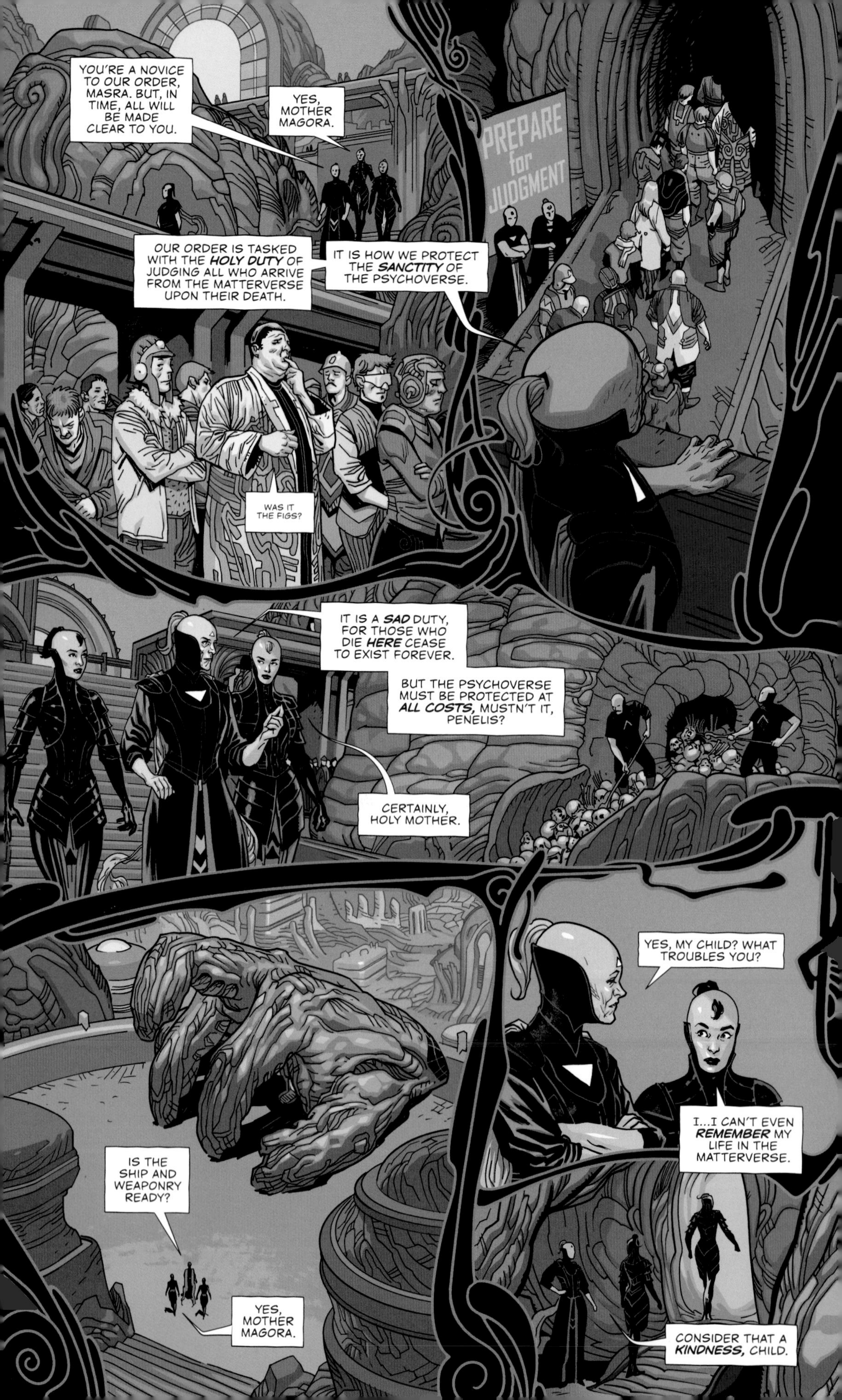
YOU'RE A NOVICE TO OUR ORDER, MASRA. BUT, IN TIME, ALL WILL BE MADE CLEAR TO YOU.
YES, MOTHER MAGORA.
PREPARE for JUDGMENT
OUR ORDER IS TASKED WITH THE **HOLY DUTY** OF JUDGING ALL WHO ARRIVE FROM THE MATTERVERSE UPON THEIR DEATH.
IT IS HOW WE PROTECT THE **SANCTITY** OF THE PSYCHOVERSE.
WAS IT THE FIGS?
IT IS A **SAD** DUTY, FOR THOSE WHO DIE **HERE** CEASE TO EXIST FOREVER.
BUT THE PSYCHOVERSE MUST BE PROTECTED AT **ALL COSTS,** MUSTN'T IT, PENELIS?
CERTAINLY, HOLY MOTHER.
IS THE SHIP AND WEAPONRY READY?
YES, MOTHER MAGORA.
YES, MY CHILD? WHAT TROUBLES YOU?
I...I CAN'T EVEN **REMEMBER** MY LIFE IN THE MATTERVERSE.
CONSIDER THAT A **KINDNESS,** CHILD.

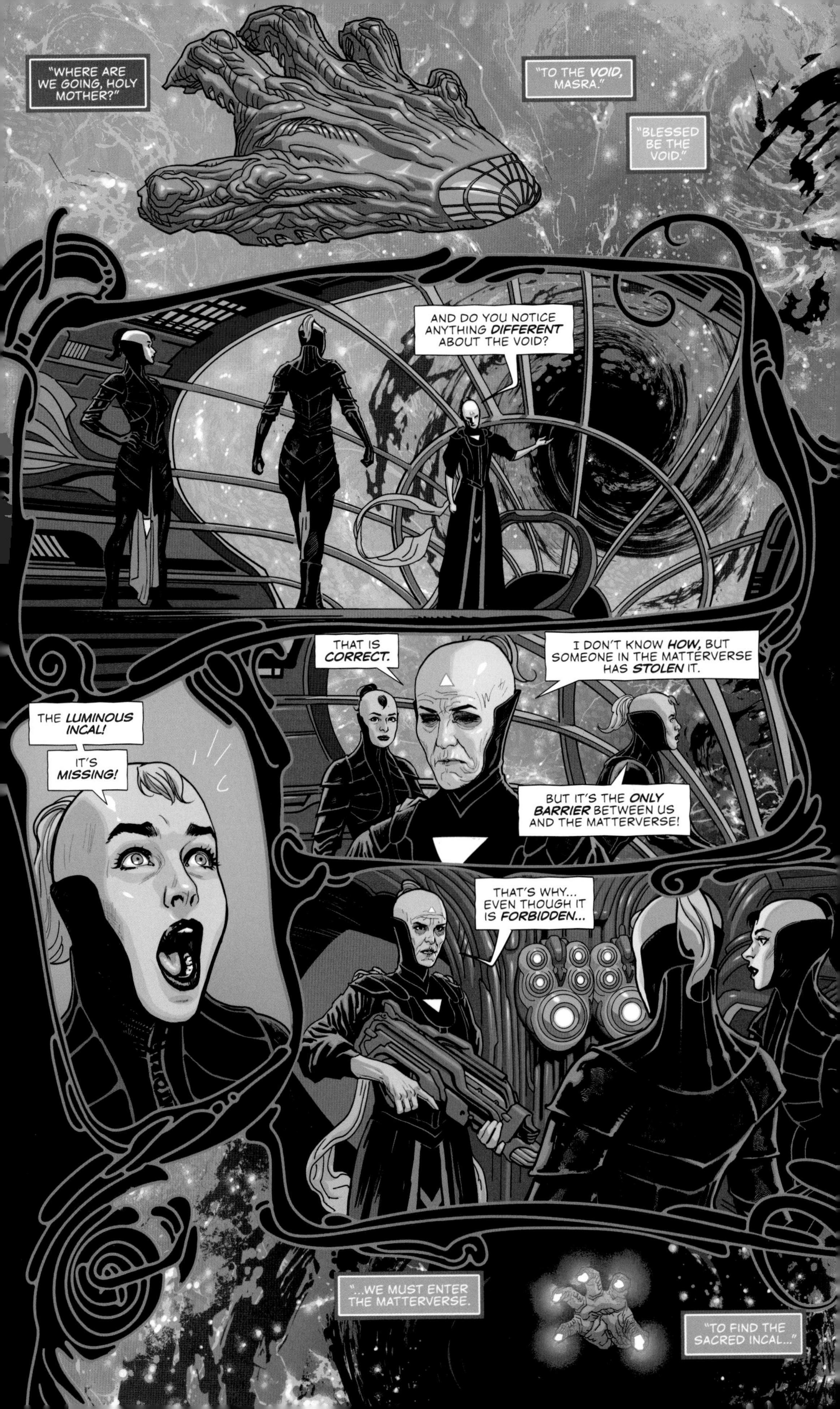
"WHERE ARE WE GOING, HOLY MOTHER?"
"TO THE VOID, MASRA."
"BLESSED BE THE VOID."
AND DO YOU NOTICE ANYTHING DIFFERENT ABOUT THE VOID?
THE LUMINOUS INCAL!
IT'S MISSING!
THAT IS CORRECT.
I DON'T KNOW HOW, BUT SOMEONE IN THE MATTERVERSE HAS STOLEN IT.
BUT IT'S THE ONLY BARRIER BETWEEN US AND THE MATTERVERSE!
THAT'S WHY... EVEN THOUGH IT IS FORBIDDEN...
"...WE MUST ENTER THE MATTERVERSE.
"TO FIND THE SACRED INCAL..."

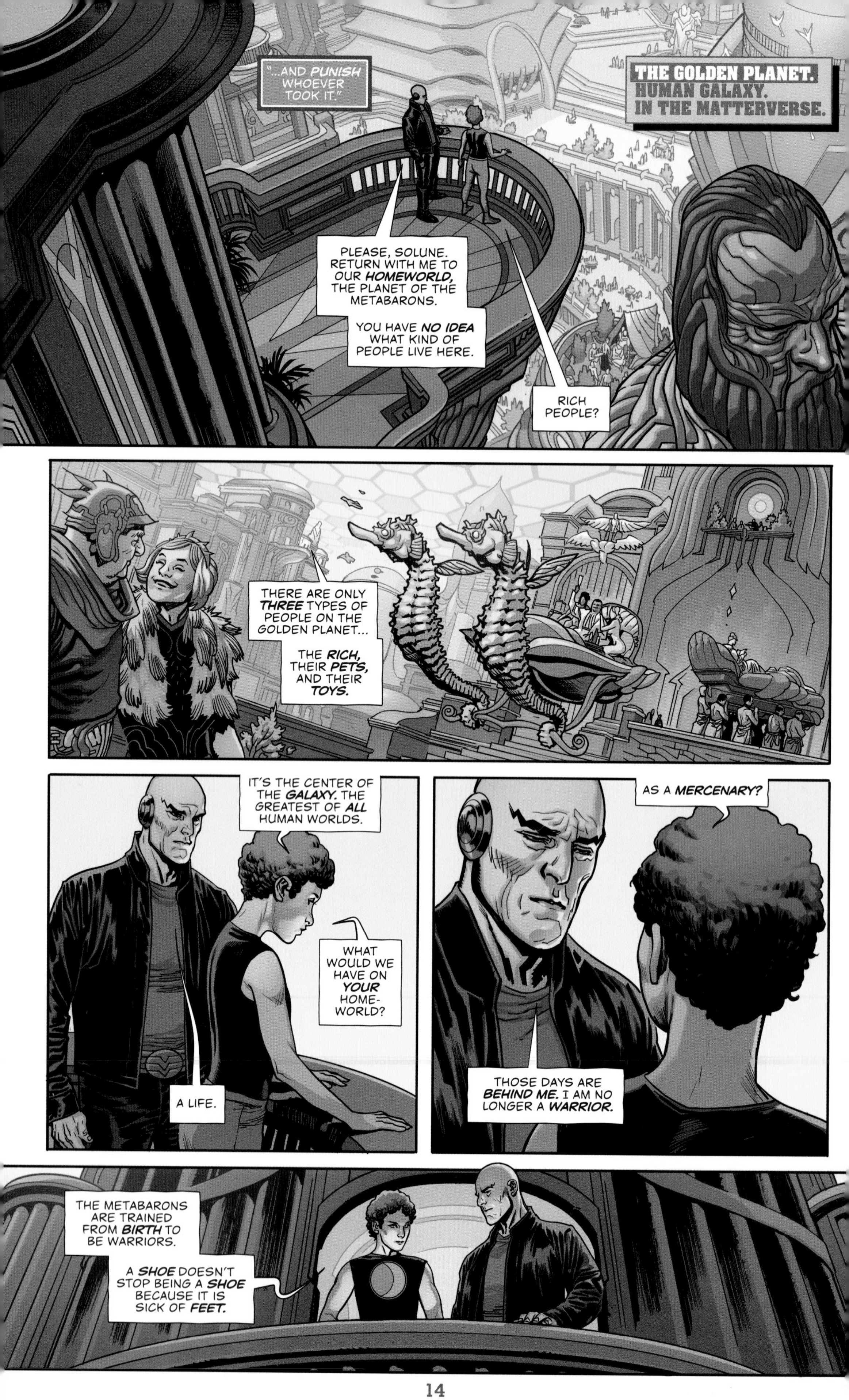

"...AND *PUNISH* WHOEVER TOOK IT."
THE GOLDEN PLANET. HUMAN GALAXY. IN THE MATTERVERSE.
PLEASE, SOLUNE. RETURN WITH ME TO OUR *HOMEWORLD,* THE PLANET OF THE METABARONS.
YOU HAVE *NO IDEA* WHAT KIND OF PEOPLE LIVE HERE.
RICH PEOPLE?
THERE ARE ONLY *THREE* TYPES OF PEOPLE ON THE GOLDEN PLANET...
THE *RICH,* THEIR *PETS,* AND THEIR *TOYS.*
IT'S THE CENTER OF THE *GALAXY.* THE GREATEST OF *ALL* HUMAN WORLDS.
WHAT WOULD WE HAVE ON *YOUR* HOME-WORLD?
A LIFE.
AS A *MERCENARY?*
THOSE DAYS ARE *BEHIND ME.* I AM NO LONGER A *WARRIOR.*
THE METABARONS ARE TRAINED FROM *BIRTH* TO BE WARRIORS.
A *SHOE* DOESN'T STOP BEING A *SHOE* BECAUSE IT IS SICK OF *FEET.*

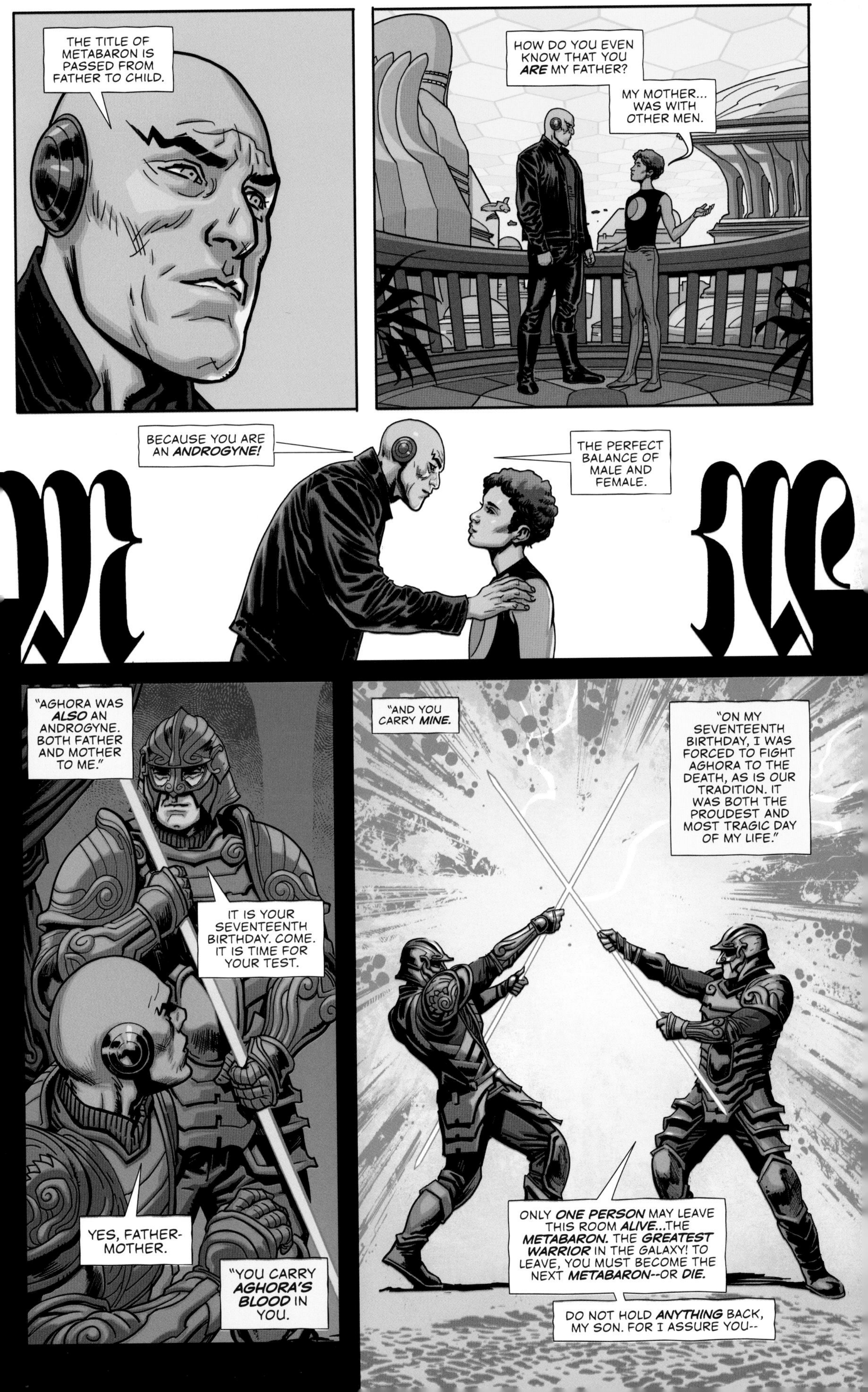
THE TITLE OF METABARON IS PASSED FROM FATHER TO CHILD.
HOW DO YOU EVEN KNOW THAT YOU ARE MY FATHER?
MY MOTHER... WAS WITH OTHER MEN.
BECAUSE YOU ARE AN ANDROGYNE!
THE PERFECT BALANCE OF MALE AND FEMALE.
"AGHORA WAS ALSO AN ANDROGYNE. BOTH FATHER AND MOTHER TO ME."
IT IS YOUR SEVENTEENTH BIRTHDAY. COME. IT IS TIME FOR YOUR TEST.
YES, FATHER-MOTHER.
"YOU CARRY AGHORA'S BLOOD IN YOU.
"AND YOU CARRY MINE.
"ON MY SEVENTEENTH BIRTHDAY, I WAS FORCED TO FIGHT AGHORA TO THE DEATH, AS IS OUR TRADITION. IT WAS BOTH THE PROUDEST AND MOST TRAGIC DAY OF MY LIFE."
ONLY ONE PERSON MAY LEAVE THIS ROOM ALIVE...THE METABARON. THE GREATEST WARRIOR IN THE GALAXY! TO LEAVE, YOU MUST BECOME THE NEXT METABARON--OR DIE.
DO NOT HOLD ANYTHING BACK, MY SON. FOR I ASSURE YOU--

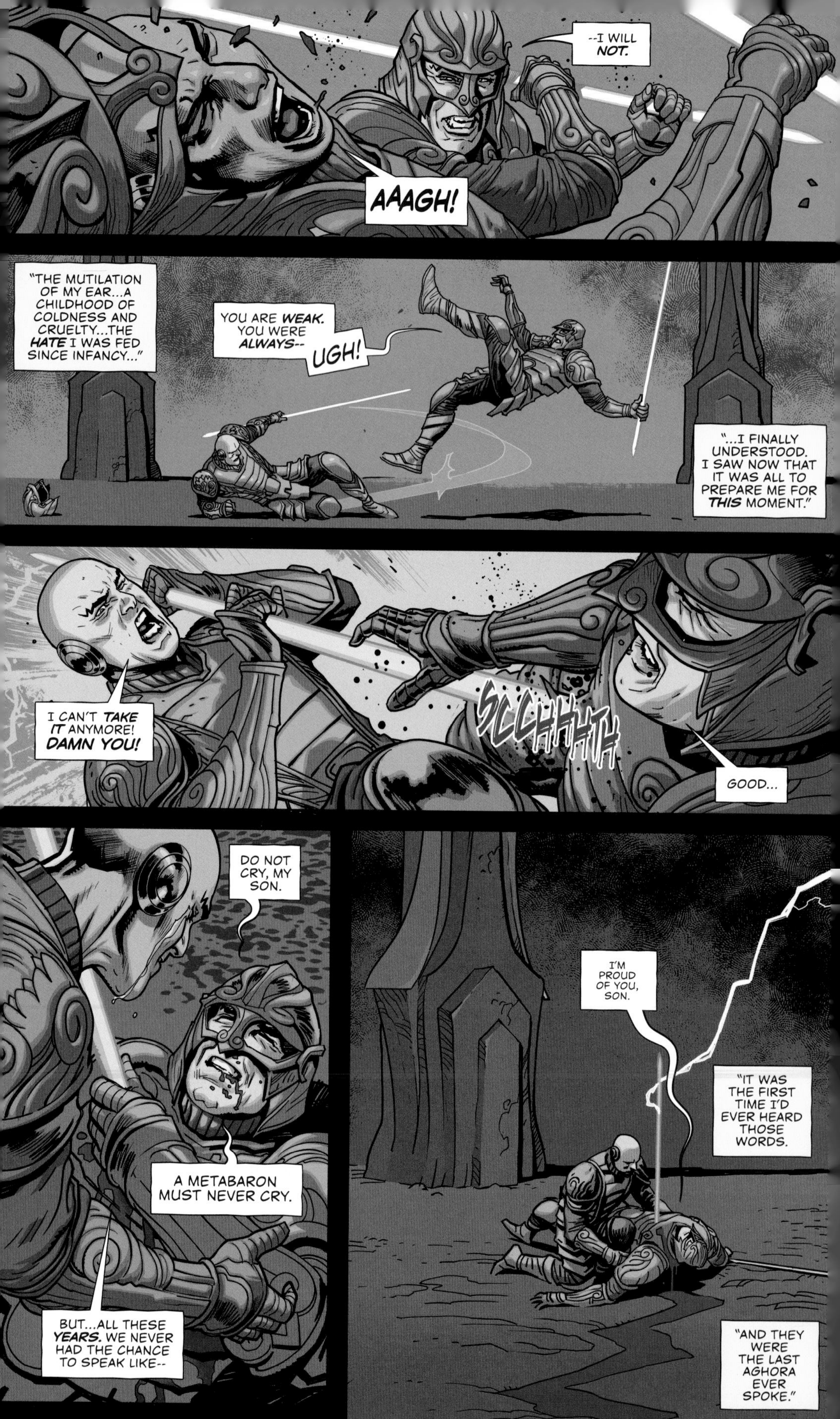
--I WILL *NOT.*
AAAGH!
"THE MUTILATION OF MY EAR...A CHILDHOOD OF COLDNESS AND CRUELTY...THE *HATE* I WAS FED SINCE INFANCY..."
YOU ARE *WEAK.* YOU WERE *ALWAYS--*
UGH!
"...I FINALLY UNDERSTOOD. I SAW NOW THAT IT WAS ALL TO PREPARE ME FOR *THIS* MOMENT."
I CAN'T *TAKE IT* ANYMORE! *DAMN YOU!*
SCCHHTH
GOOD...
DO NOT CRY, MY SON.
A METABARON MUST NEVER CRY.
BUT...ALL THESE *YEARS.* WE NEVER HAD THE CHANCE TO SPEAK LIKE--
I'M PROUD OF YOU, SON.
"IT WAS THE FIRST TIME I'D EVER HEARD THOSE WORDS.
"AND THEY WERE THE LAST AGHORA EVER SPOKE."

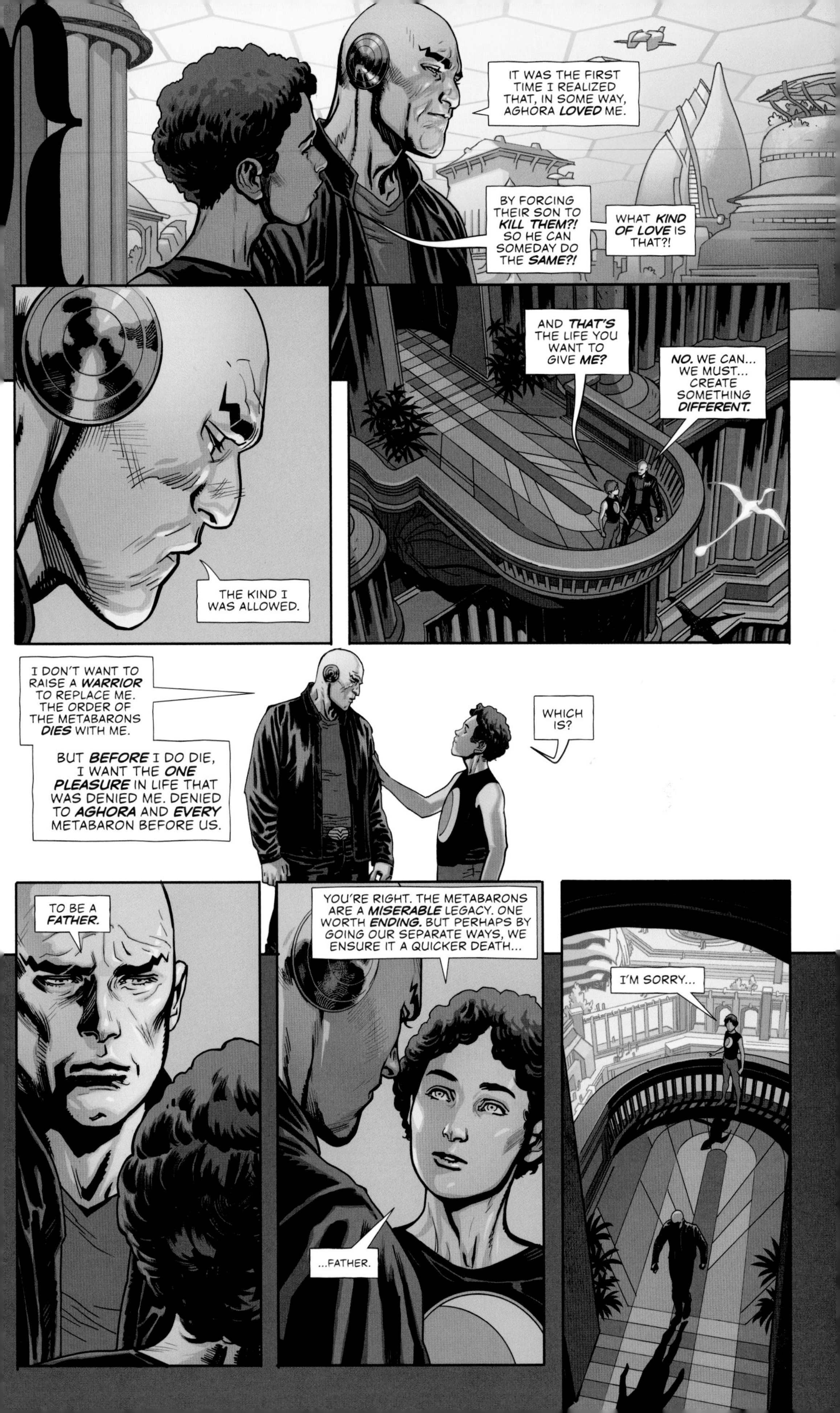
IT WAS THE FIRST TIME I REALIZED THAT, IN SOME WAY, AGHORA LOVED ME.
BY FORCING THEIR SON TO KILL THEM?! SO HE CAN SOMEDAY DO THE SAME?!
WHAT KIND OF LOVE IS THAT?!
THE KIND I WAS ALLOWED.
AND THAT'S THE LIFE YOU WANT TO GIVE ME?
NO. WE CAN... WE MUST... CREATE SOMETHING DIFFERENT.
I DON'T WANT TO RAISE A WARRIOR TO REPLACE ME. THE ORDER OF THE METABARONS DIES WITH ME.
BUT BEFORE I DO DIE, I WANT THE ONE PLEASURE IN LIFE THAT WAS DENIED ME. DENIED TO AGHORA AND EVERY METABARON BEFORE US.
WHICH IS?
TO BE A FATHER.
YOU'RE RIGHT. THE METABARONS ARE A MISERABLE LEGACY. ONE WORTH ENDING. BUT PERHAPS BY GOING OUR SEPARATE WAYS, WE ENSURE IT A QUICKER DEATH...
...FATHER.
I'M SORRY...

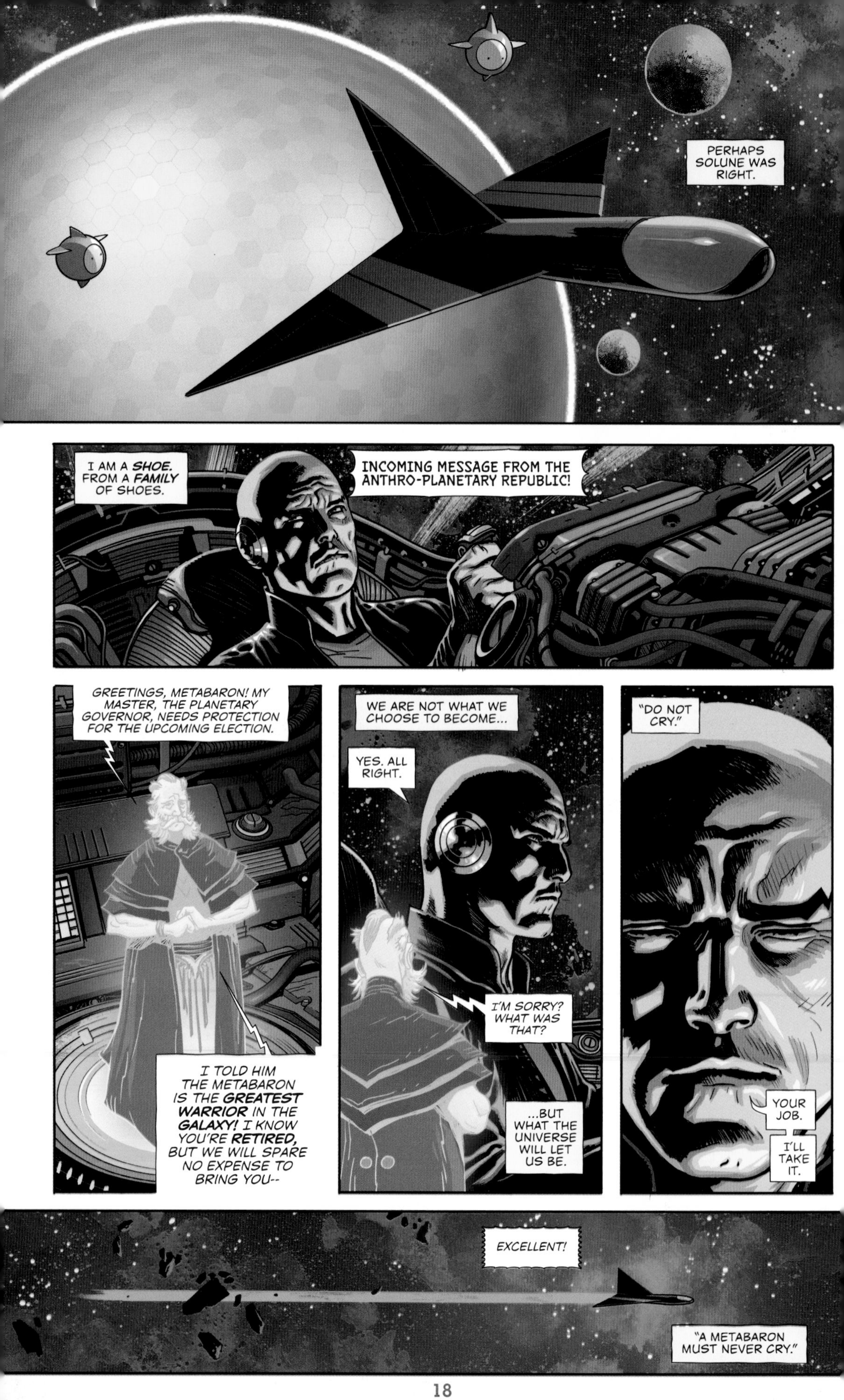

PERHAPS SOLUNE WAS RIGHT.
I AM A SHOE. FROM A FAMILY OF SHOES.
INCOMING MESSAGE FROM THE ANTHRO-PLANETARY REPUBLIC!
GREETINGS, METABARON! MY MASTER, THE PLANETARY GOVERNOR, NEEDS PROTECTION FOR THE UPCOMING ELECTION.
I TOLD HIM THE METABARON IS THE GREATEST WARRIOR IN THE GALAXY! I KNOW YOU'RE RETIRED, BUT WE WILL SPARE NO EXPENSE TO BRING YOU--
WE ARE NOT WHAT WE CHOOSE TO BECOME...
YES. ALL RIGHT.
I'M SORRY? WHAT WAS THAT?
...BUT WHAT THE UNIVERSE WILL LET US BE.
"DO NOT CRY."
YOUR JOB.
I'LL TAKE IT.
EXCELLENT!
"A METABARON MUST NEVER CRY."

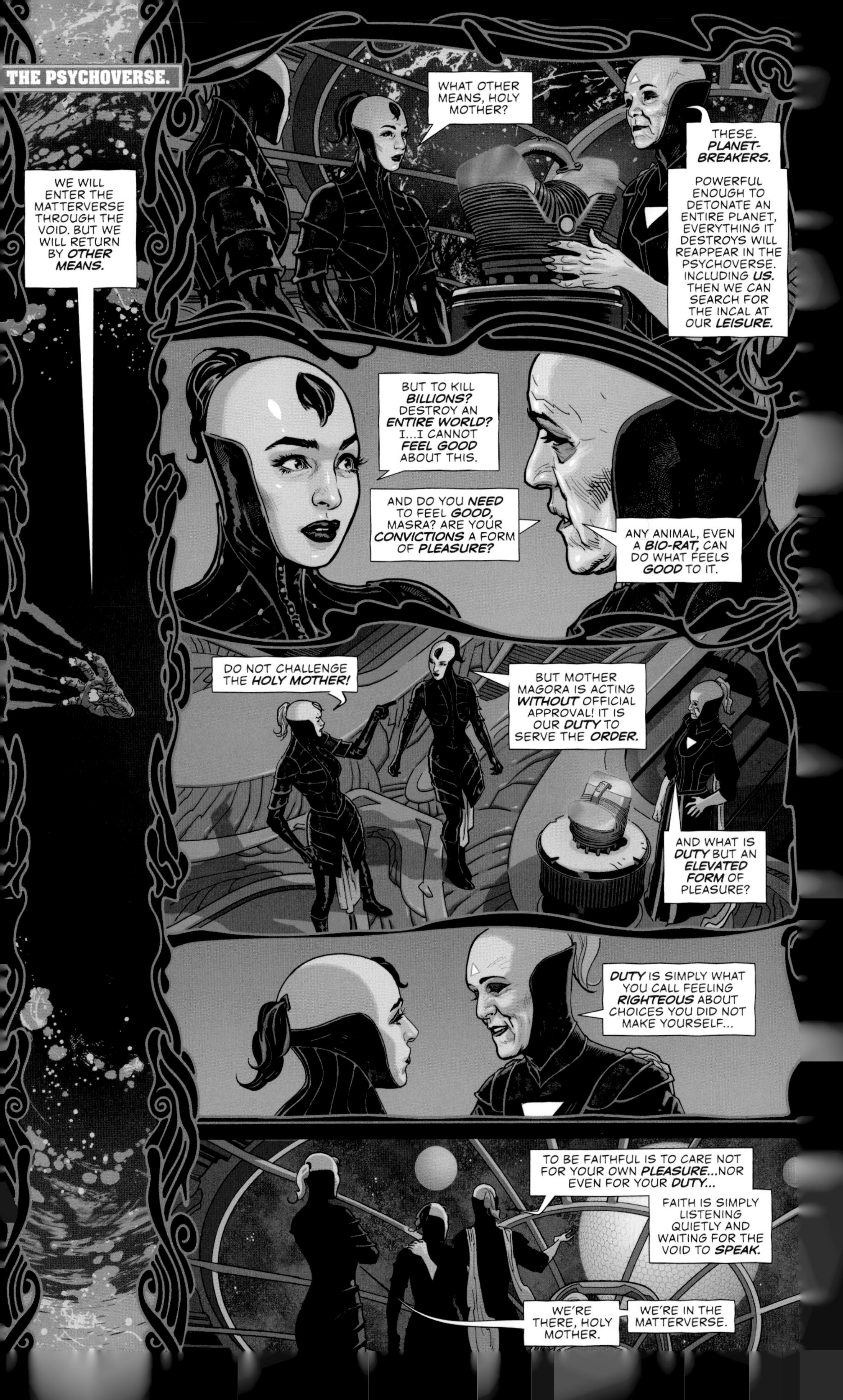
THE PSYCHOVERSE.
WE WILL ENTER THE MATTERVERSE THROUGH THE VOID. BUT WE WILL RETURN BY OTHER MEANS.
WHAT OTHER MEANS, HOLY MOTHER?
THESE. PLANET-BREAKERS.
POWERFUL ENOUGH TO DETONATE AN ENTIRE PLANET, EVERYTHING IT DESTROYS WILL REAPPEAR IN THE PSYCHOVERSE. INCLUDING US. THEN WE CAN SEARCH FOR THE INCAL AT OUR LEISURE.
BUT TO KILL BILLIONS? DESTROY AN ENTIRE WORLD? I...I CANNOT FEEL GOOD ABOUT THIS.
AND DO YOU NEED TO FEEL GOOD, MASRA? ARE YOUR CONVICTIONS A FORM OF PLEASURE?
ANY ANIMAL, EVEN A BIO-RAT, CAN DO WHAT FEELS GOOD TO IT.
DO NOT CHALLENGE THE HOLY MOTHER!
BUT MOTHER MAGORA IS ACTING WITHOUT OFFICIAL APPROVAL! IT IS OUR DUTY TO SERVE THE ORDER.
AND WHAT IS DUTY BUT AN ELEVATED FORM OF PLEASURE?
DUTY IS SIMPLY WHAT YOU CALL FEELING RIGHTEOUS ABOUT CHOICES YOU DID NOT MAKE YOURSELF...
TO BE FAITHFUL IS TO CARE NOT FOR YOUR OWN PLEASURE...NOR EVEN FOR YOUR DUTY...
FAITH IS SIMPLY LISTENING QUIETLY AND WAITING FOR THE VOID TO SPEAK.
WE'RE THERE, HOLY MOTHER.
WE'RE IN THE MATTERVERSE.

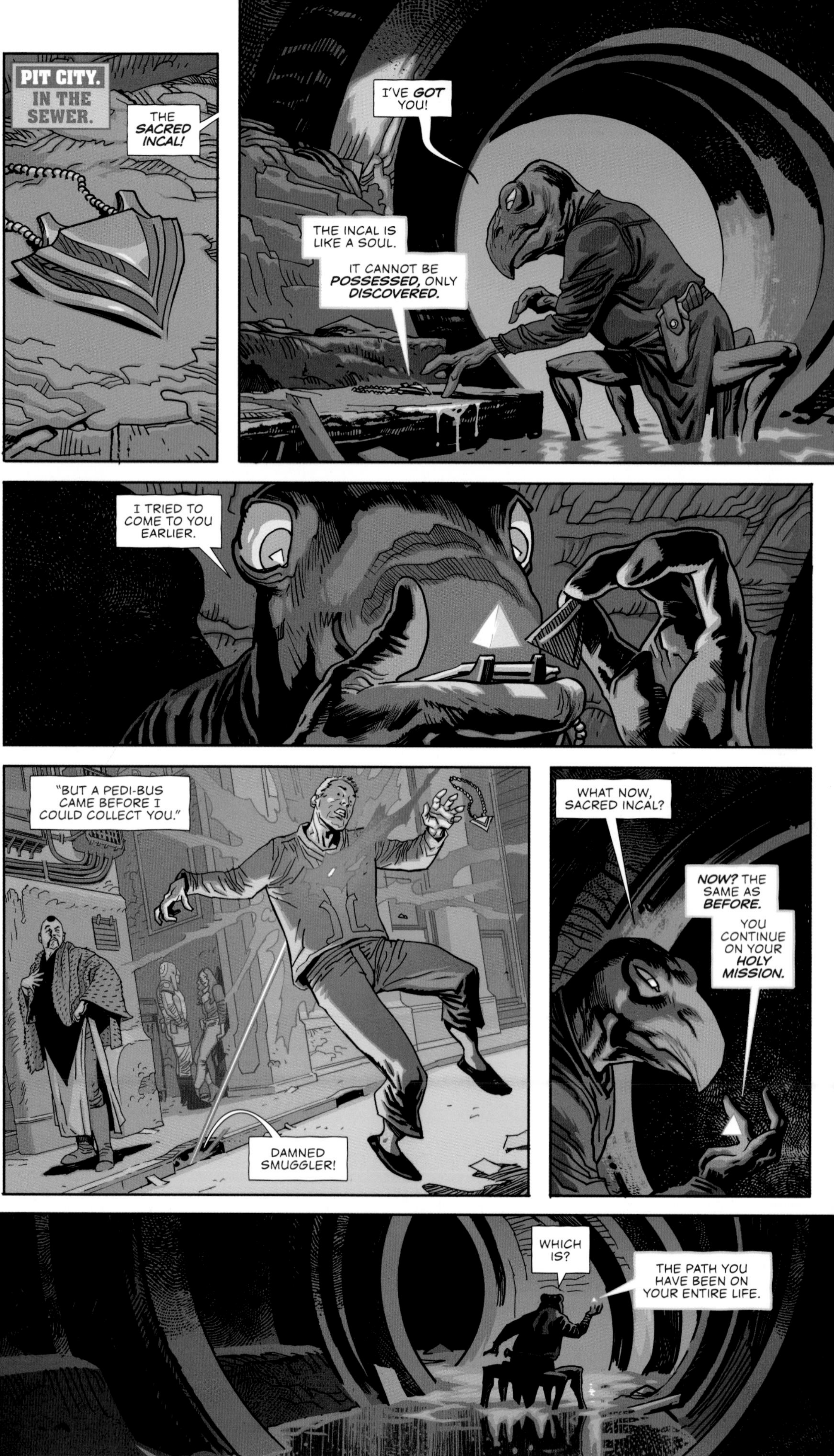
PIT CITY. IN THE SEWER.
THE SACRED INCAL!
I'VE GOT YOU!
THE INCAL IS LIKE A SOUL.
IT CANNOT BE POSSESSED, ONLY DISCOVERED.
I TRIED TO COME TO YOU EARLIER.
"BUT A PEDI-BUS CAME BEFORE I COULD COLLECT YOU."
DAMNED SMUGGLER!
WHAT NOW, SACRED INCAL?
NOW? THE SAME AS BEFORE.
YOU CONTINUE ON YOUR HOLY MISSION.
WHICH IS?
THE PATH YOU HAVE BEEN ON YOUR ENTIRE LIFE.

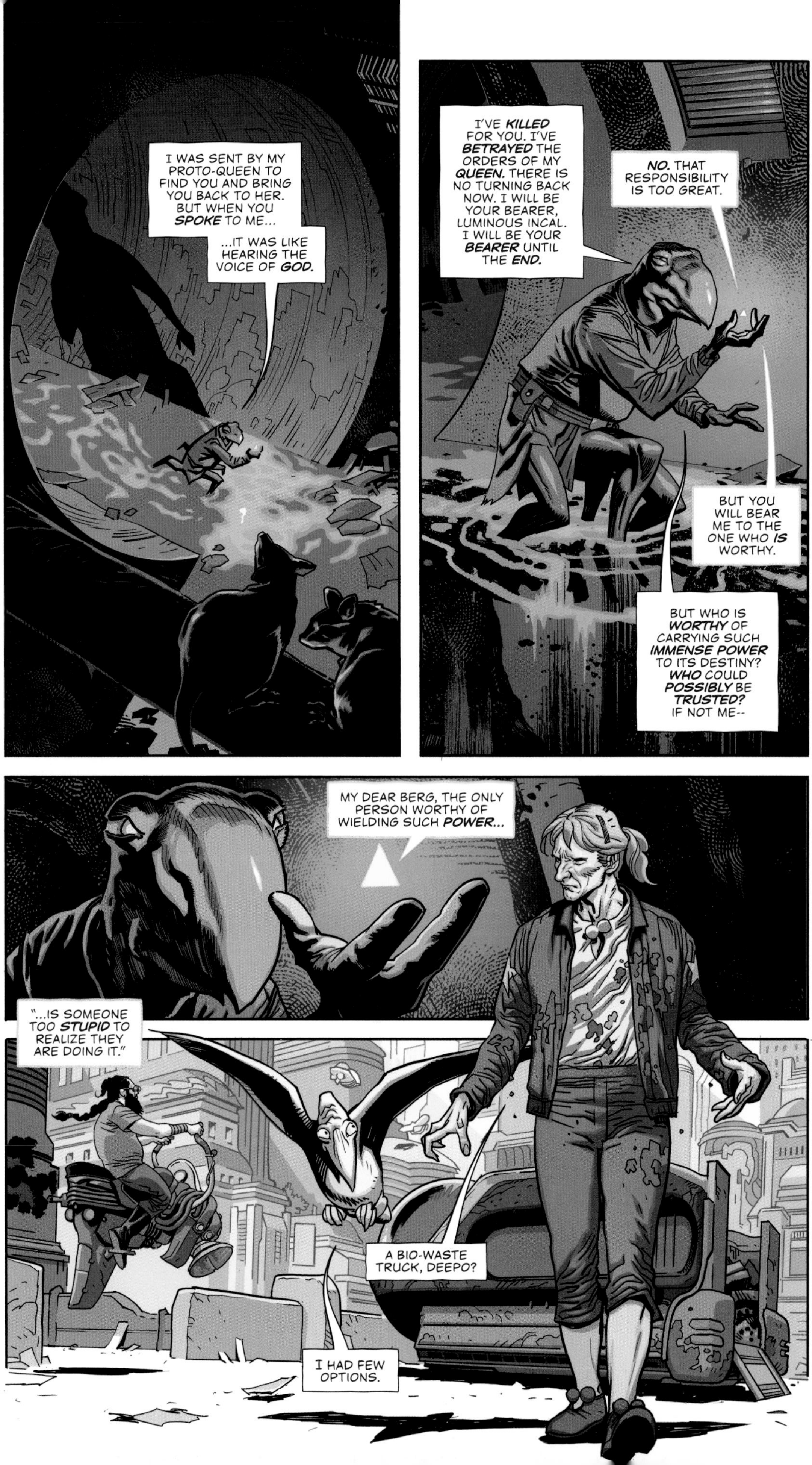
I WAS SENT BY MY PROTO-QUEEN TO FIND YOU AND BRING YOU BACK TO HER. BUT WHEN YOU SPOKE TO ME...
...IT WAS LIKE HEARING THE VOICE OF GOD.
I'VE KILLED FOR YOU. I'VE BETRAYED THE ORDERS OF MY QUEEN. THERE IS NO TURNING BACK NOW. I WILL BE YOUR BEARER, LUMINOUS INCAL. I WILL BE YOUR BEARER UNTIL THE END.
NO. THAT RESPONSIBILITY IS TOO GREAT.
BUT YOU WILL BEAR ME TO THE ONE WHO IS WORTHY.
BUT WHO IS WORTHY OF CARRYING SUCH IMMENSE POWER TO ITS DESTINY? WHO COULD POSSIBLY BE TRUSTED? IF NOT ME--
MY DEAR BERG, THE ONLY PERSON WORTHY OF WIELDING SUCH POWER...
"...IS SOMEONE TOO STUPID TO REALIZE THEY ARE DOING IT."
A BIO-WASTE TRUCK, DEEPO?
I HAD FEW OPTIONS.

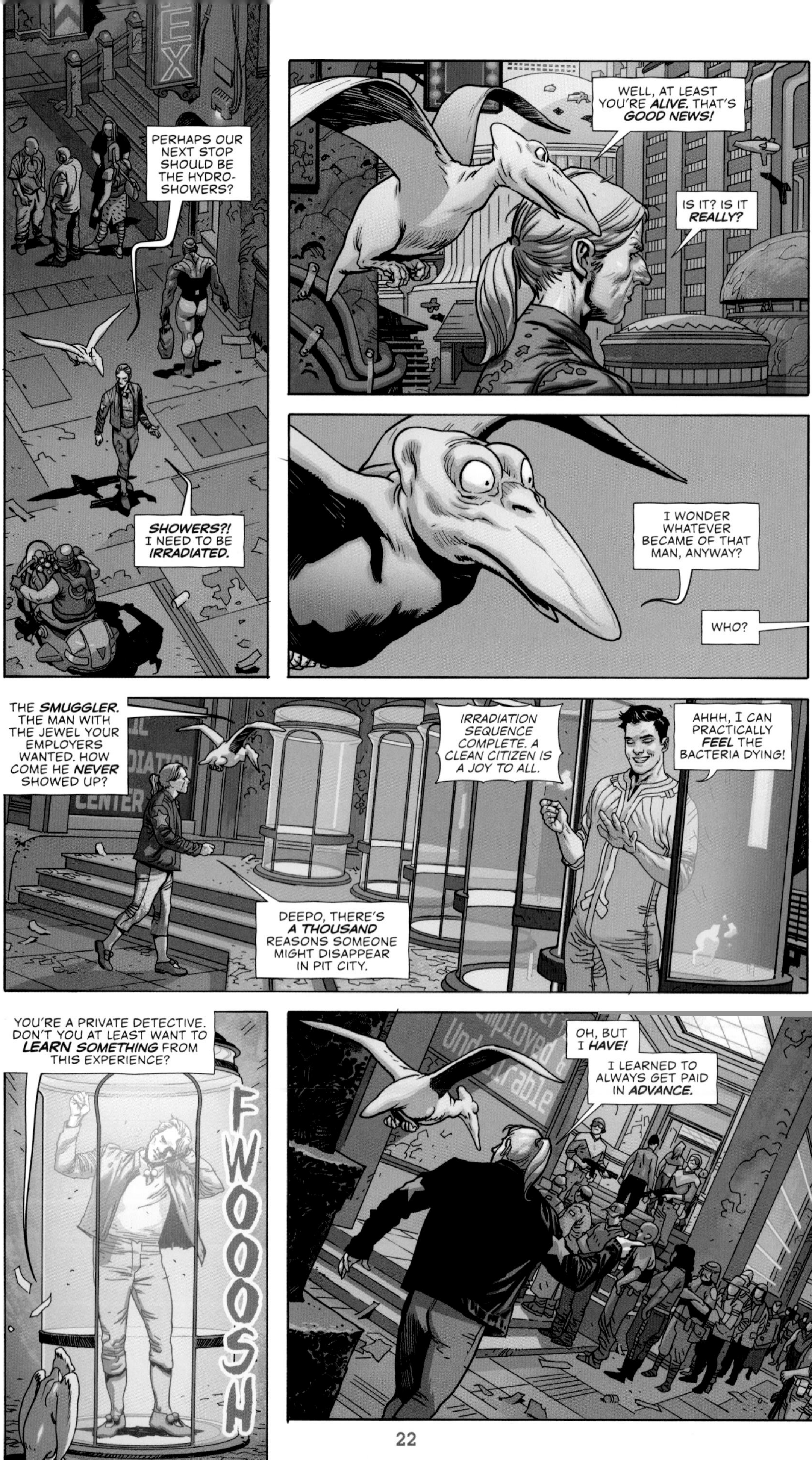
PERHAPS OUR NEXT STOP SHOULD BE THE HYDRO-SHOWERS?
SHOWERS?! I NEED TO BE IRRADIATED.
WELL, AT LEAST YOU'RE ALIVE. THAT'S GOOD NEWS!
IS IT? IS IT REALLY?
I WONDER WHATEVER BECAME OF THAT MAN, ANYWAY?
WHO?
THE SMUGGLER. THE MAN WITH THE JEWEL YOUR EMPLOYERS WANTED. HOW COME HE NEVER SHOWED UP?
DEEPO, THERE'S A THOUSAND REASONS SOMEONE MIGHT DISAPPEAR IN PIT CITY.
IRRADIATION SEQUENCE COMPLETE. A CLEAN CITIZEN IS A JOY TO ALL.
AHHH, I CAN PRACTICALLY FEEL THE BACTERIA DYING!
YOU'RE A PRIVATE DETECTIVE. DON'T YOU AT LEAST WANT TO LEARN SOMETHING FROM THIS EXPERIENCE?
FWOOOOSH
OH, BUT I HAVE!
I LEARNED TO ALWAYS GET PAID IN ADVANCE.

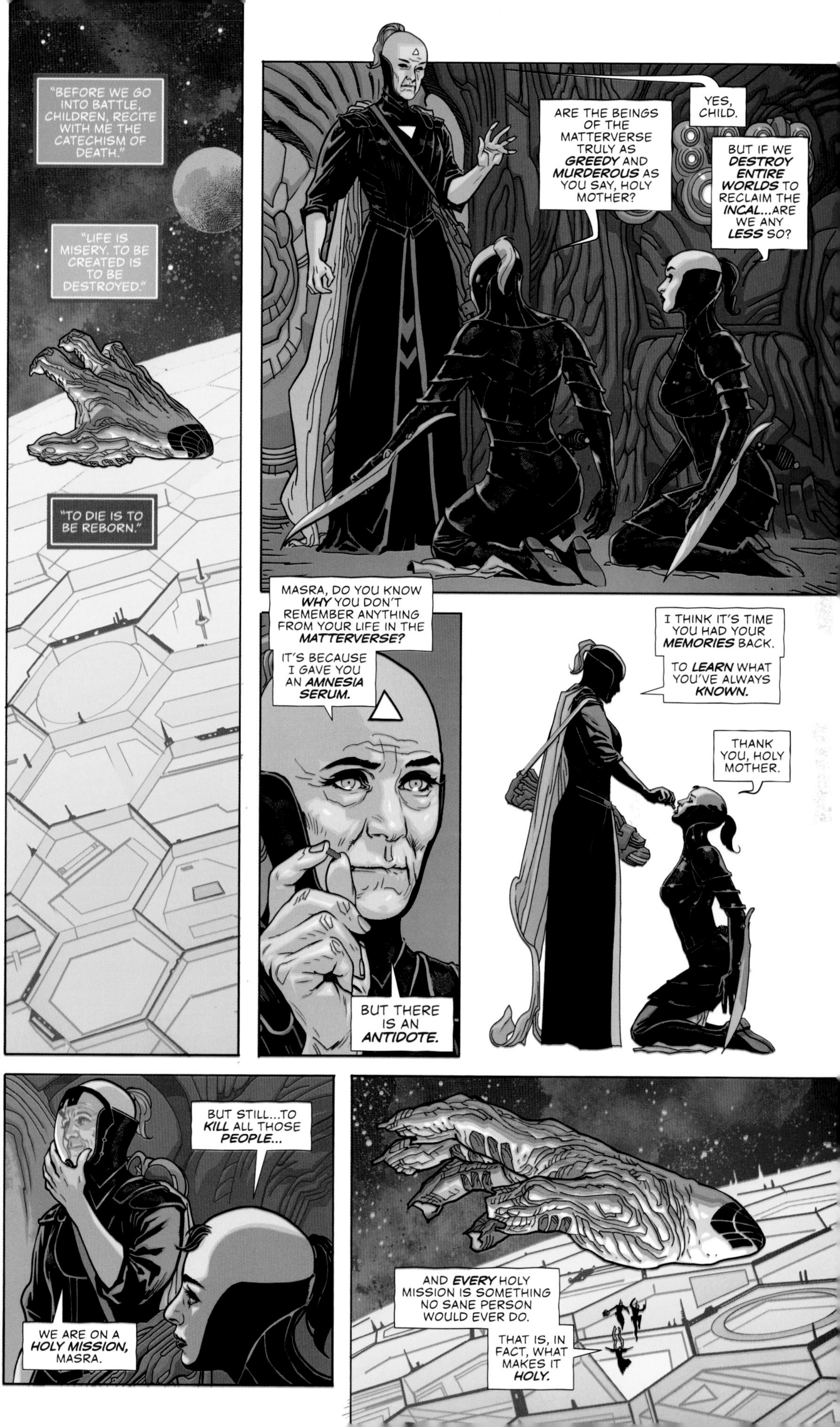
"BEFORE WE GO INTO BATTLE, CHILDREN, RECITE WITH ME THE CATECHISM OF DEATH."
"LIFE IS MISERY. TO BE CREATED IS TO BE DESTROYED."
"TO DIE IS TO BE REBORN."
ARE THE BEINGS OF THE MATTERVERSE TRULY AS GREEDY AND MURDEROUS AS YOU SAY, HOLY MOTHER?
YES, CHILD.
BUT IF WE DESTROY ENTIRE WORLDS TO RECLAIM THE INCAL...ARE WE ANY LESS SO?
MASRA, DO YOU KNOW WHY YOU DON'T REMEMBER ANYTHING FROM YOUR LIFE IN THE MATTERVERSE?
IT'S BECAUSE I GAVE YOU AN AMNESIA SERUM.
BUT THERE IS AN ANTIDOTE.
I THINK IT'S TIME YOU HAD YOUR MEMORIES BACK.
TO LEARN WHAT YOU'VE ALWAYS KNOWN.
THANK YOU, HOLY MOTHER.
BUT STILL...TO KILL ALL THOSE PEOPLE...
WE ARE ON A HOLY MISSION, MASRA.
AND EVERY HOLY MISSION IS SOMETHING NO SANE PERSON WOULD EVER DO.
THAT IS, IN FACT, WHAT MAKES IT HOLY.

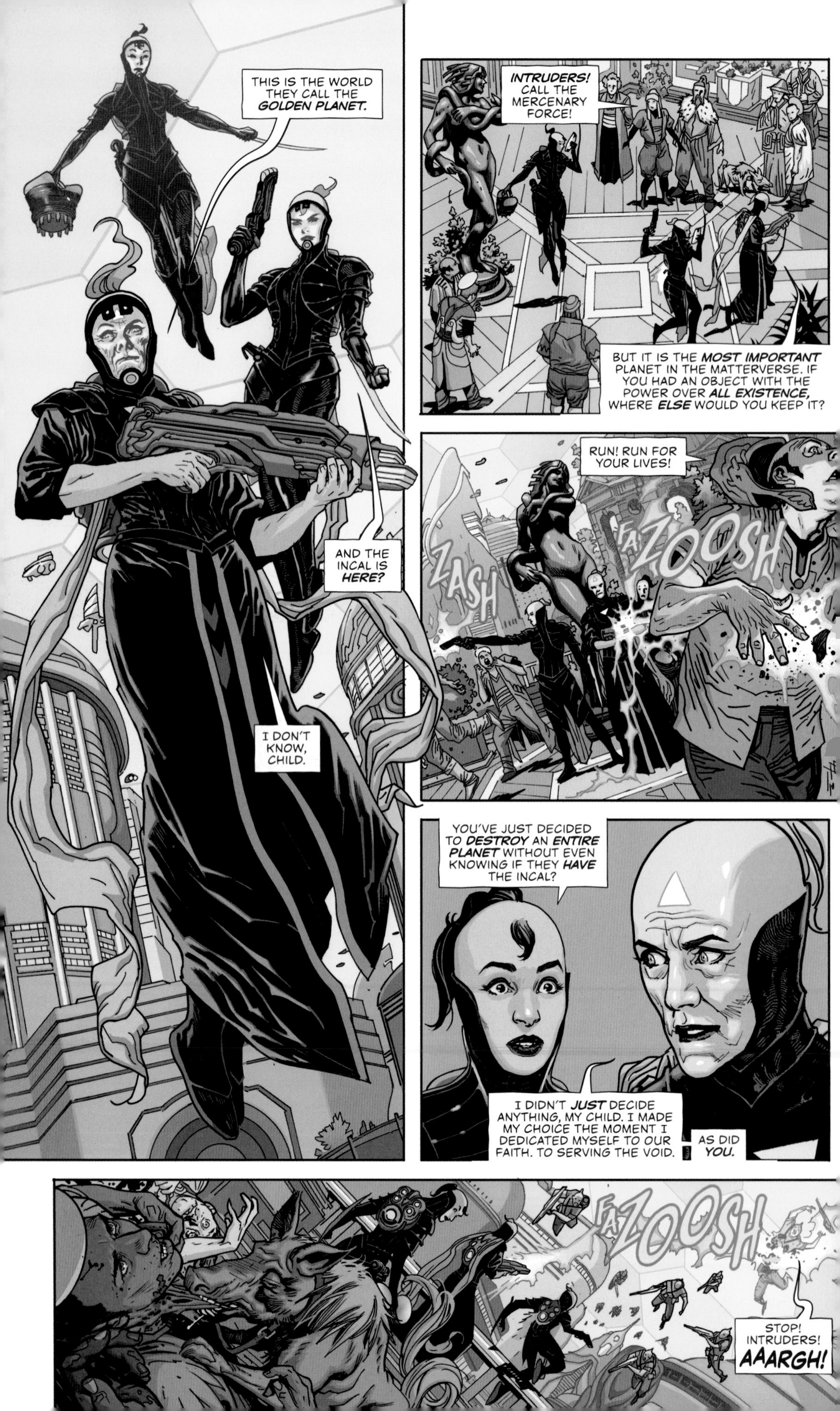
THIS IS THE WORLD THEY CALL THE GOLDEN PLANET.
AND THE INCAL IS HERE?
I DON'T KNOW, CHILD.
INTRUDERS! CALL THE MERCENARY FORCE!
BUT IT IS THE MOST IMPORTANT PLANET IN THE MATTERVERSE. IF YOU HAD AN OBJECT WITH THE POWER OVER ALL EXISTENCE, WHERE ELSE WOULD YOU KEEP IT?
RUN! RUN FOR YOUR LIVES!
ZASH
FAZOOSH
YOU'VE JUST DECIDED TO DESTROY AN ENTIRE PLANET WITHOUT EVEN KNOWING IF THEY HAVE THE INCAL?
I DIDN'T JUST DECIDE ANYTHING, MY CHILD. I MADE MY CHOICE THE MOMENT I DEDICATED MYSELF TO OUR FAITH. TO SERVING THE VOID.
AS DID YOU.
FAZOOSH
STOP! INTRUDERS! AAARGH!

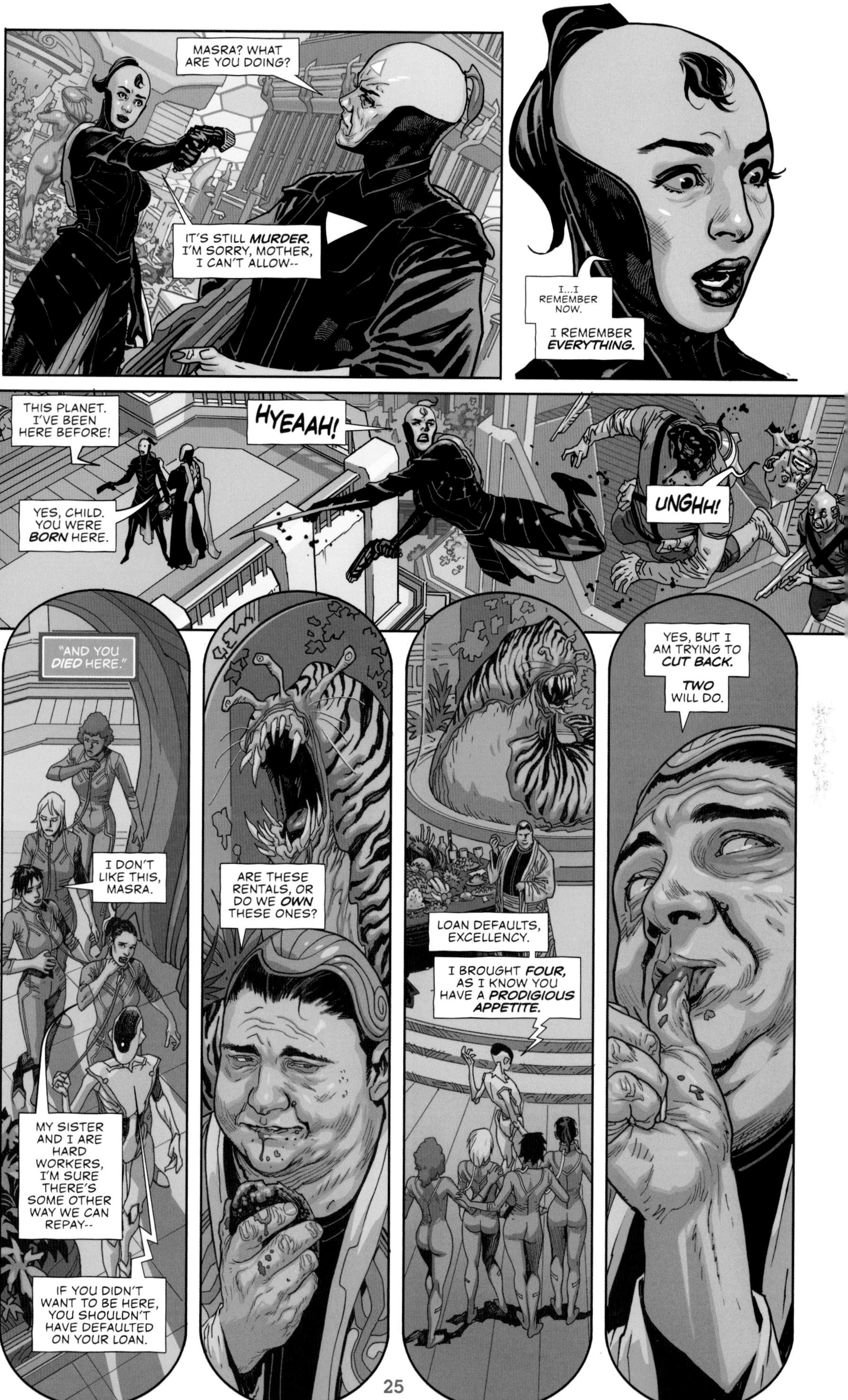

MASRA? WHAT ARE YOU DOING?
IT'S STILL MURDER. I'M SORRY, MOTHER, I CAN'T ALLOW--
I...I REMEMBER NOW.
I REMEMBER EVERYTHING.
THIS PLANET. I'VE BEEN HERE BEFORE!
YES, CHILD. YOU WERE BORN HERE.
HYEAAH!
UNGHH!
"AND YOU DIED HERE."
I DON'T LIKE THIS, MASRA.
MY SISTER AND I ARE HARD WORKERS, I'M SURE THERE'S SOME OTHER WAY WE CAN REPAY--
IF YOU DIDN'T WANT TO BE HERE, YOU SHOULDN'T HAVE DEFAULTED ON YOUR LOAN.
ARE THESE RENTALS, OR DO WE OWN THESE ONES?
LOAN DEFAULTS, EXCELLENCY.
I BROUGHT FOUR, AS I KNOW YOU HAVE A PRODIGIOUS APPETITE.
YES, BUT I AM TRYING TO CUT BACK.
TWO WILL DO.

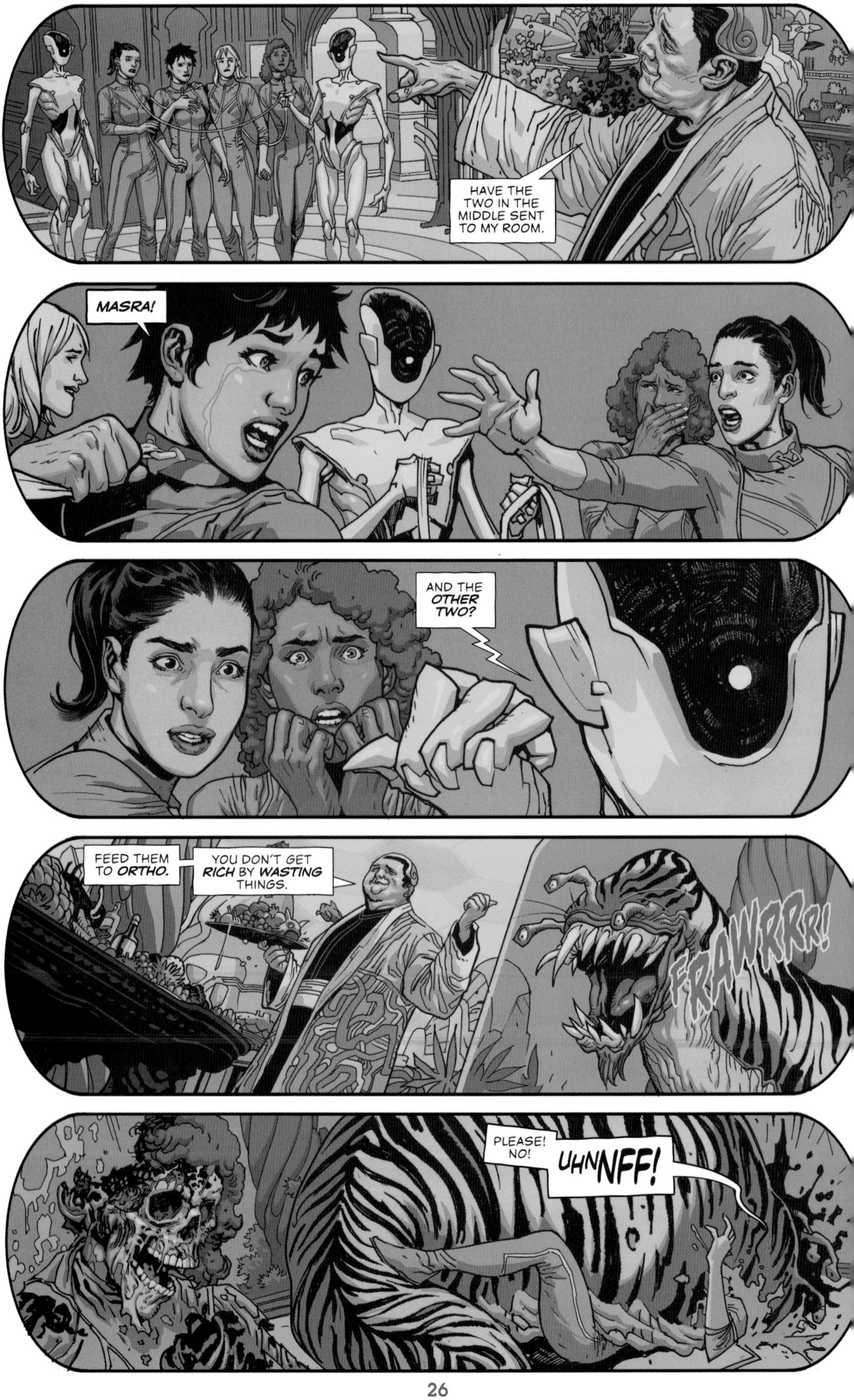
HAVE THE TWO IN THE MIDDLE SENT TO MY ROOM.
MASRA!
AND THE OTHER TWO?
FEED THEM TO ORTHO.
YOU DON'T GET RICH BY WASTING THINGS.
FRAWRRR!
PLEASE! NO!
UHNNFF!

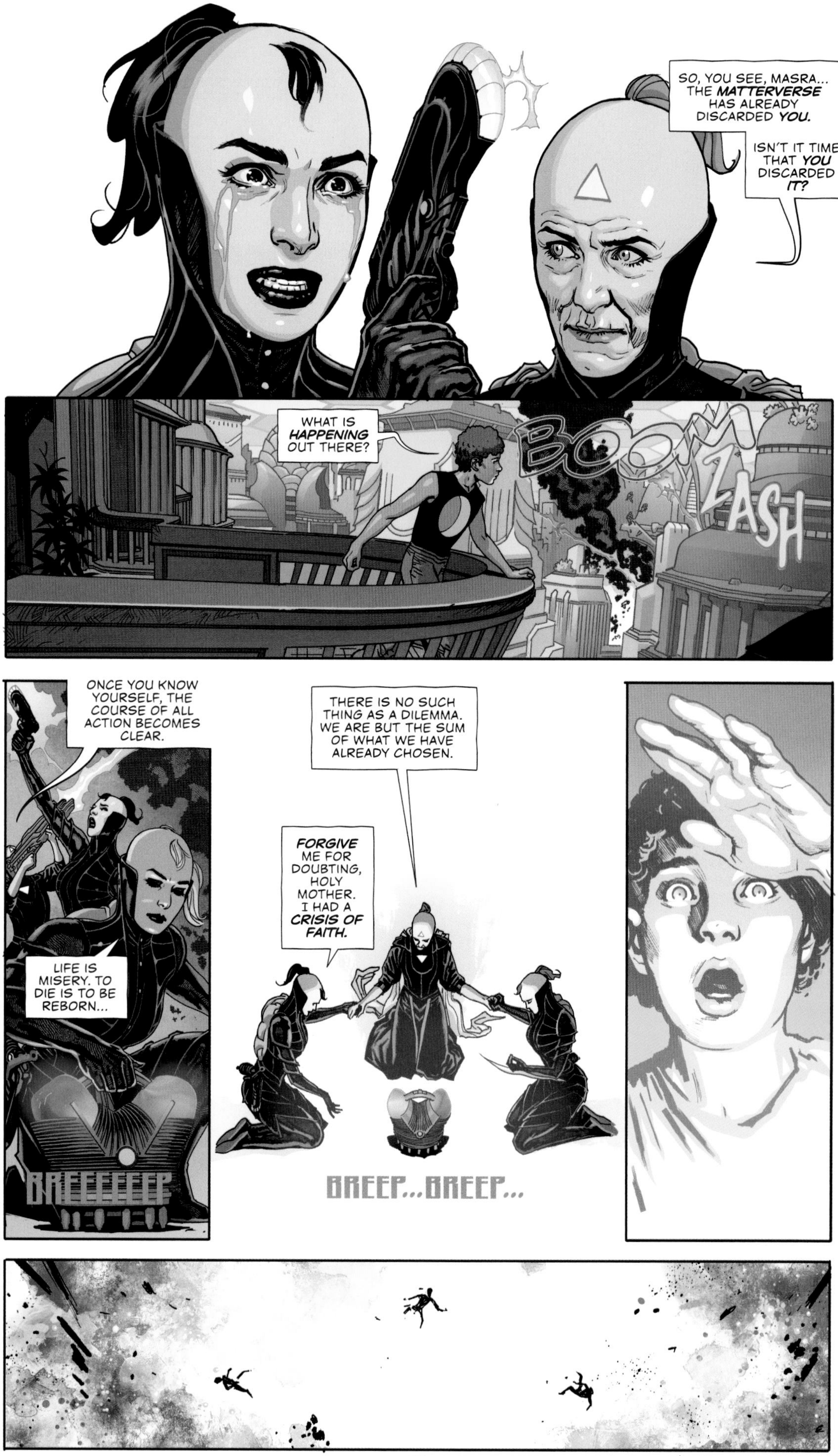
SO, YOU SEE, MASRA... THE ***MATTERVERSE*** HAS ALREADY DISCARDED ***YOU.***
ISN'T IT TIME THAT ***YOU*** DISCARDED ***IT?***
WHAT IS ***HAPPENING*** OUT THERE?
BOOM
ZASH
ONCE YOU KNOW YOURSELF, THE COURSE OF ALL ACTION BECOMES CLEAR.
LIFE IS MISERY. TO DIE IS TO BE REBORN...
BREEEEEEP
THERE IS NO SUCH THING AS A DILEMMA. WE ARE BUT THE SUM OF WHAT WE HAVE ALREADY CHOSEN.
FORGIVE ME FOR DOUBTING, HOLY MOTHER. I HAD A ***CRISIS OF FAITH.***
BREEP...BREEP...

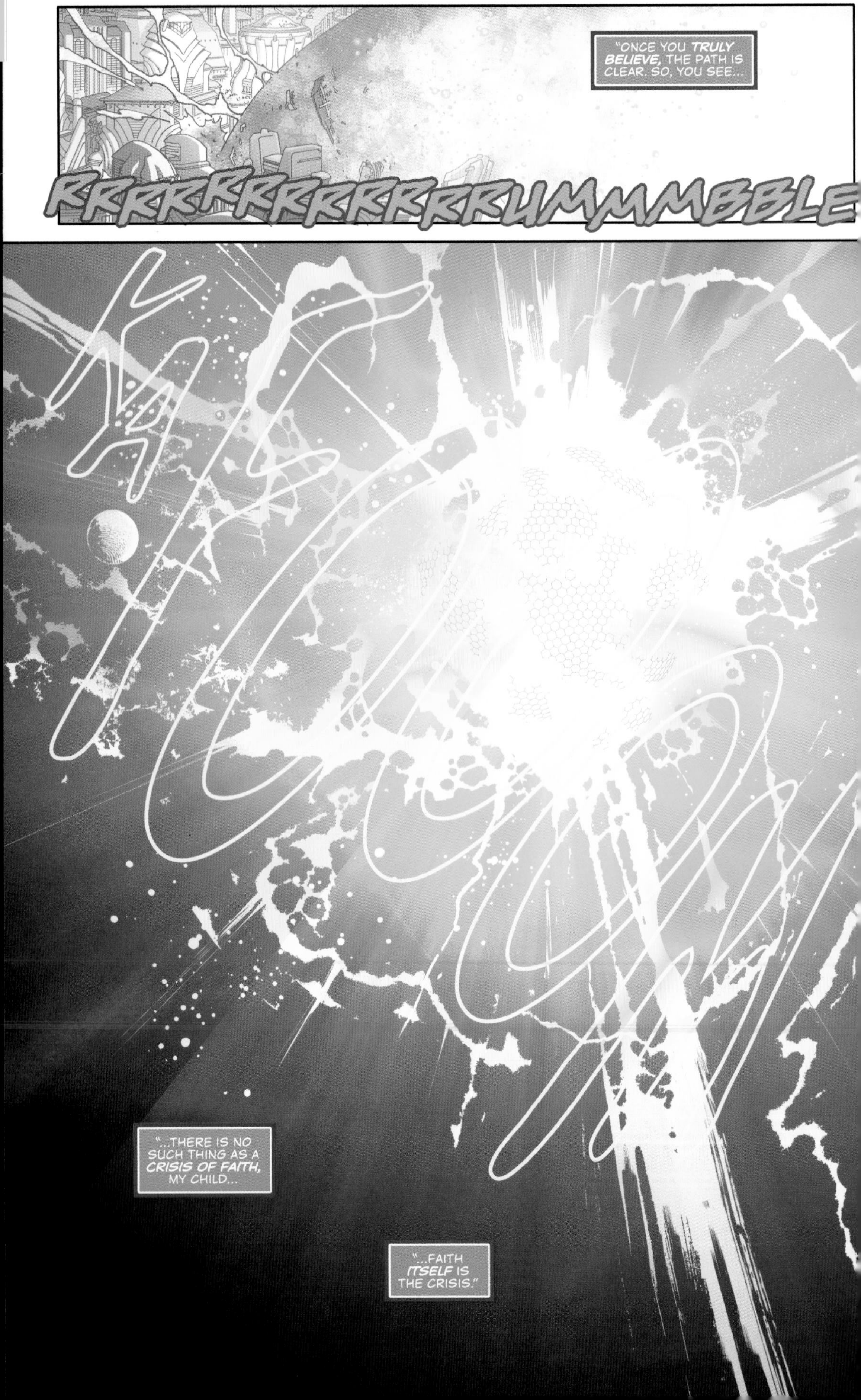
"ONCE YOU **TRULY BELIEVE,** THE PATH IS CLEAR. SO, YOU SEE...
RRRRRRRRRRRRRUMMMMBBLE
"...THERE IS NO SUCH THING AS A ***CRISIS OF FAITH,*** MY CHILD...
"...FAITH ***ITSELF*** IS THE CRISIS."

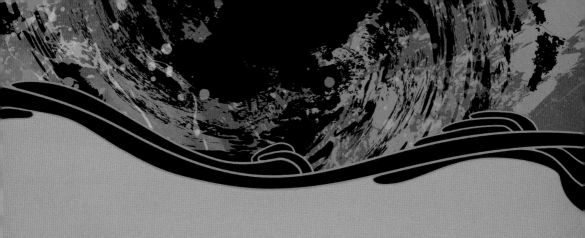

CHAPTER 2

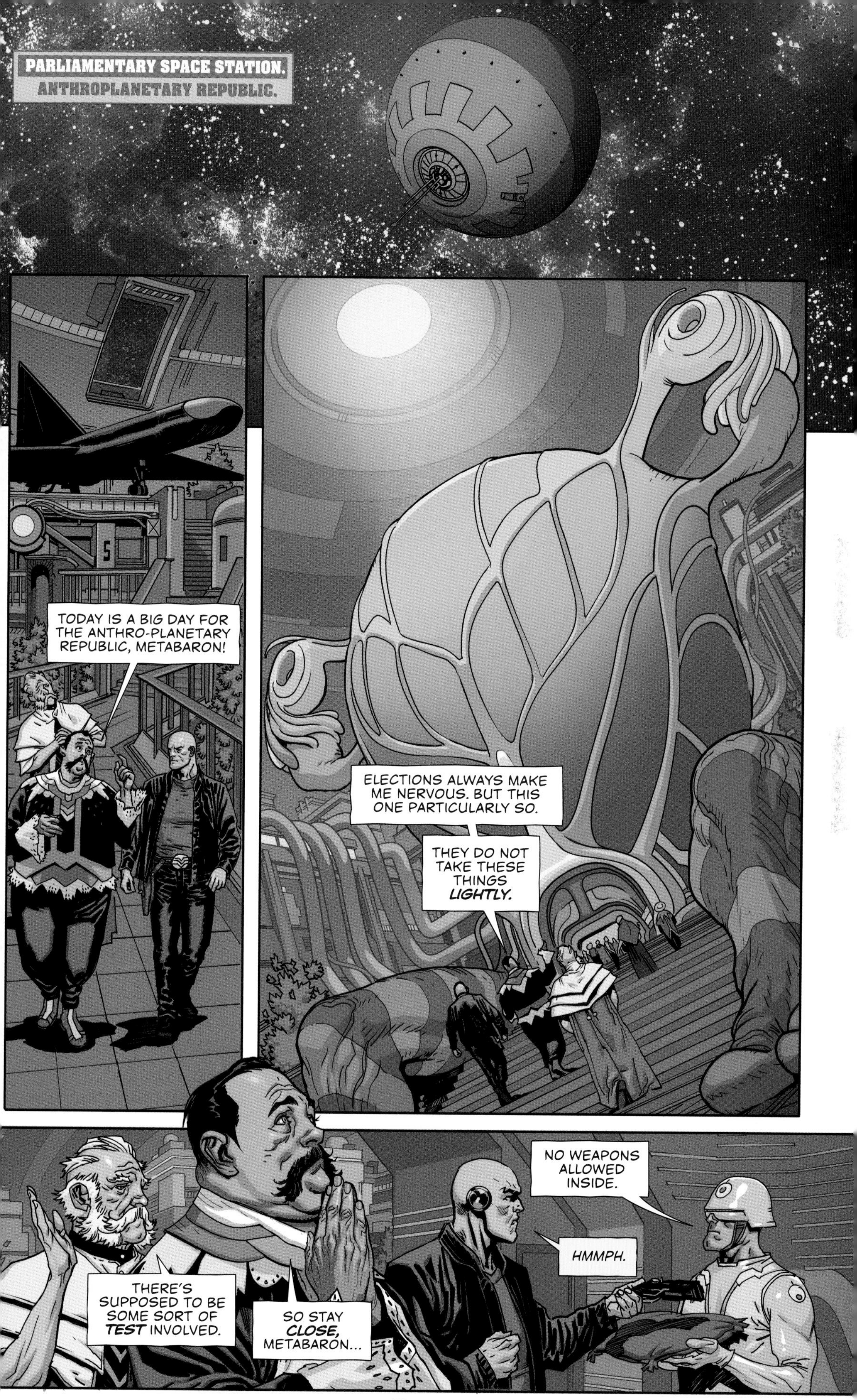
PARLIAMENTARY SPACE STATION.
ANTHROPLANETARY REPUBLIC.
TODAY IS A BIG DAY FOR THE ANTHRO-PLANETARY REPUBLIC, METABARON!
ELECTIONS ALWAYS MAKE ME NERVOUS. BUT THIS ONE PARTICULARLY SO.
THEY DO NOT TAKE THESE THINGS *LIGHTLY.*
THERE'S SUPPOSED TO BE SOME SORT OF *TEST* INVOLVED.
SO STAY *CLOSE,* METABARON...
NO WEAPONS ALLOWED INSIDE.
HMMPH.

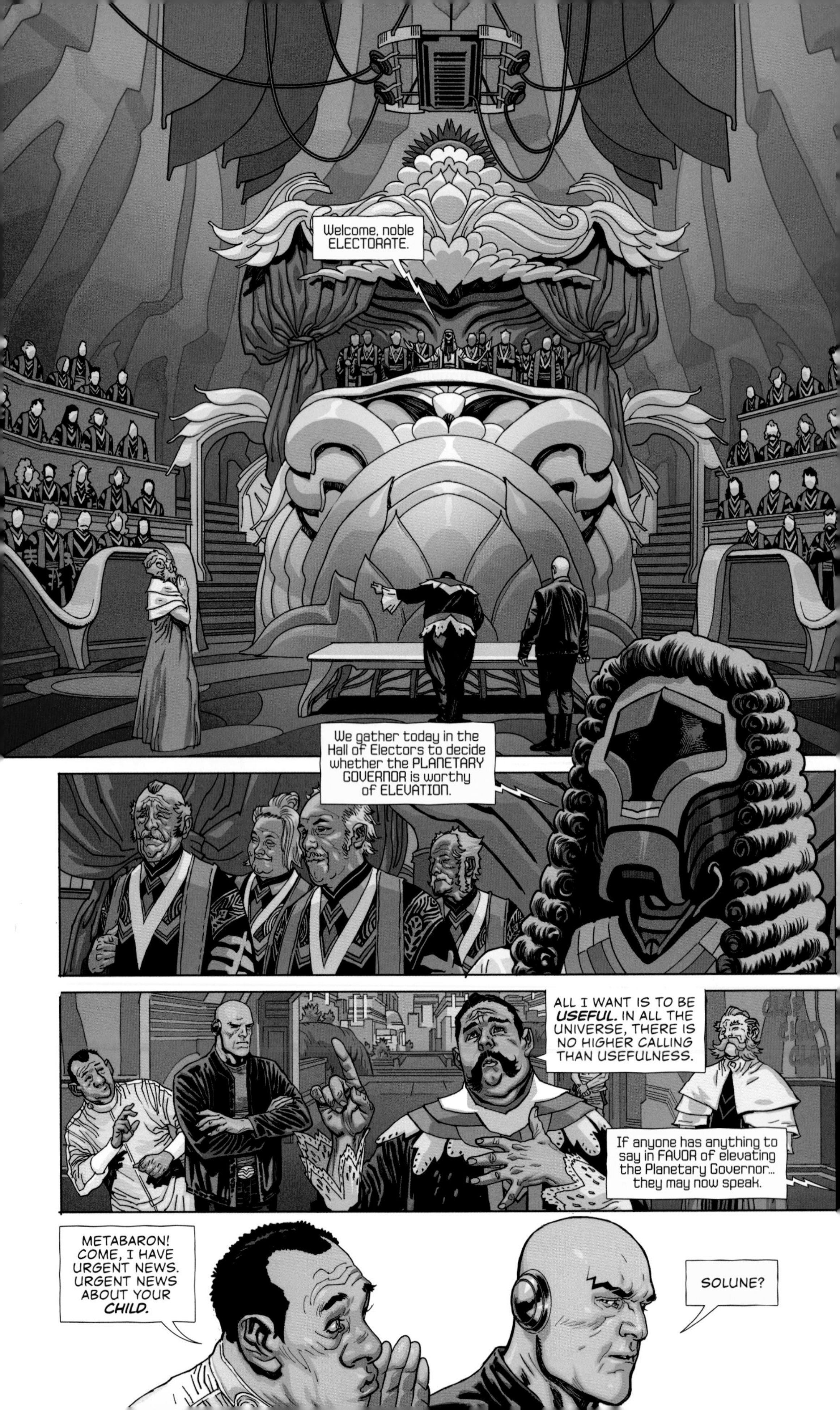
Welcome, noble ELECTORATE.
We gather today in the Hall of Electors to decide whether the PLANETARY GOVERNOR is worthy of ELEVATION.
ALL I WANT IS TO BE USEFUL. IN ALL THE UNIVERSE, THERE IS NO HIGHER CALLING THAN USEFULNESS.
CLAP CLAP CLAP
If anyone has anything to say in FAVOR of elevating the Planetary Governor... they may now speak.
METABARON! COME, I HAVE URGENT NEWS. URGENT NEWS ABOUT YOUR CHILD.
SOLUNE?

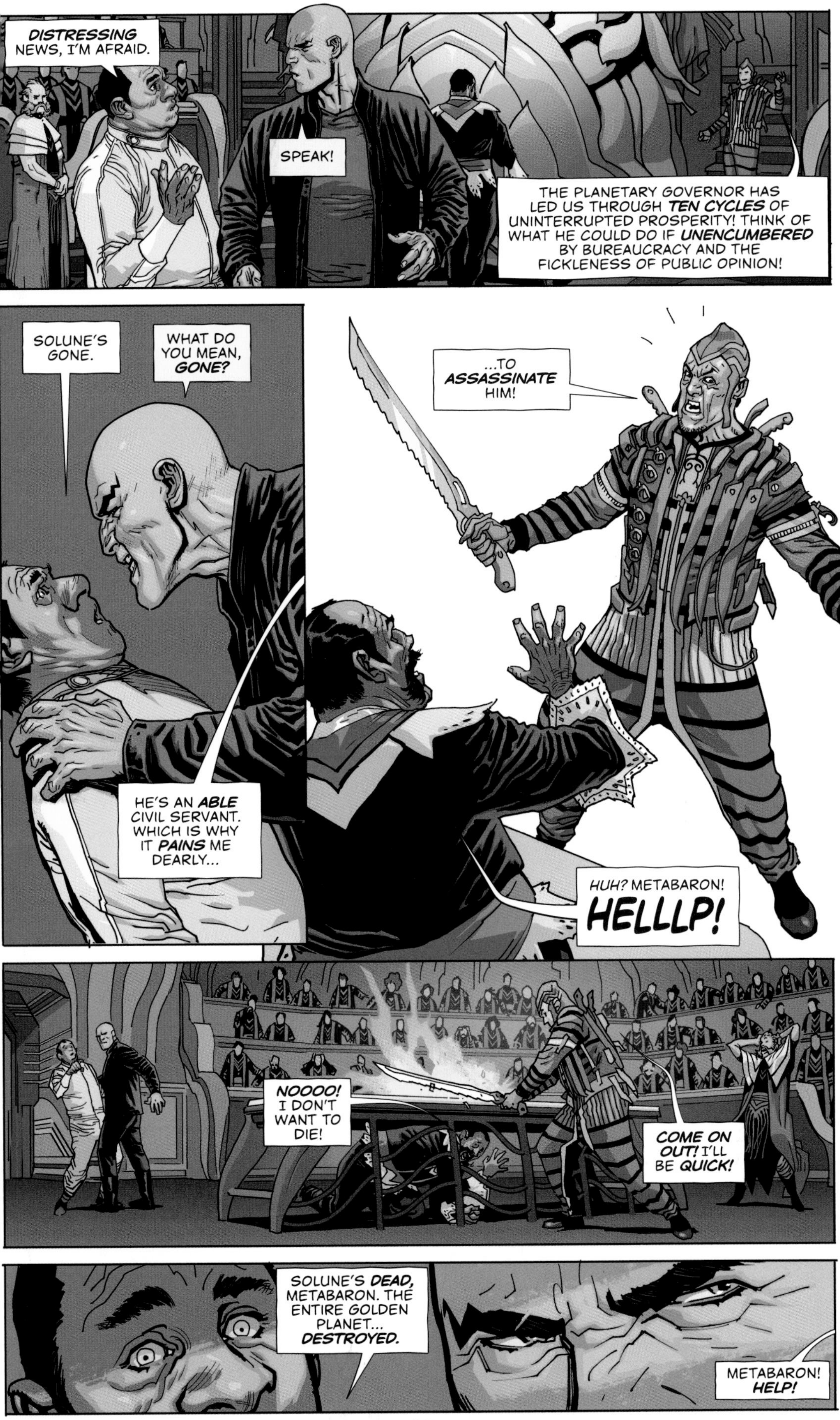
DISTRESSING NEWS, I'M AFRAID.
SPEAK!
THE PLANETARY GOVERNOR HAS LED US THROUGH *TEN CYCLES* OF UNINTERRUPTED PROSPERITY! THINK OF WHAT HE COULD DO IF *UNENCUMBERED* BY BUREAUCRACY AND THE FICKLENESS OF PUBLIC OPINION!
SOLUNE'S GONE.
WHAT DO YOU MEAN, *GONE?*
...TO *ASSASSINATE* HIM!
HE'S AN *ABLE* CIVIL SERVANT. WHICH IS WHY IT *PAINS* ME DEARLY...
HUH? METABARON! HELLLP!
NOOOO! I DON'T WANT TO DIE!
COME ON OUT! I'LL BE *QUICK!*
SOLUNE'S *DEAD,* METABARON. THE ENTIRE GOLDEN PLANET... *DESTROYED.*
METABARON! *HELP!*

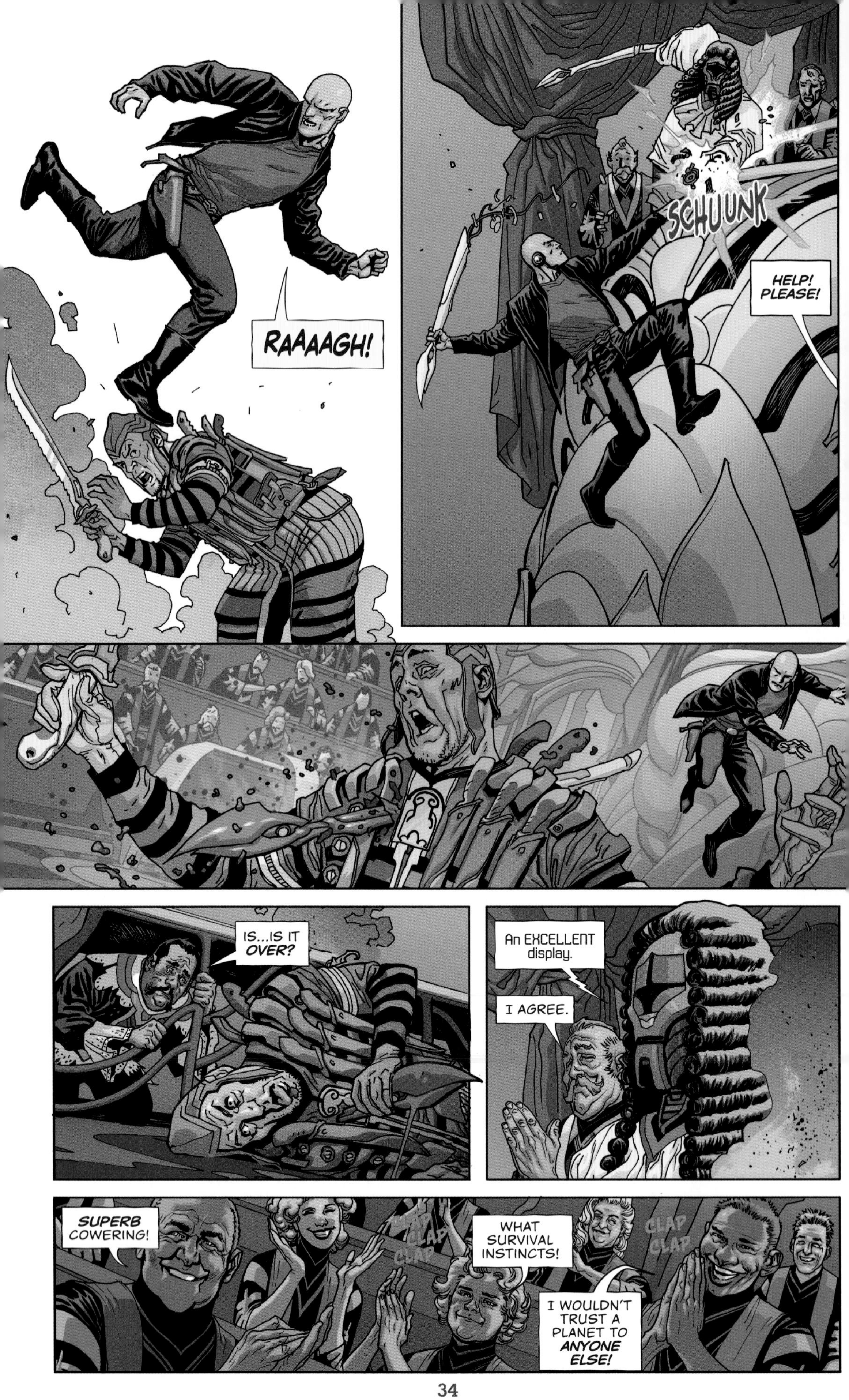
RAAAAGH!
SCHUUNK
HELP! PLEASE!
IS...IS IT OVER?
An EXCELLENT display.
I AGREE.
SUPERB COWERING!
CLAP CLAP CLAP
WHAT SURVIVAL INSTINCTS!
CLAP CLAP
I WOULDN'T TRUST A PLANET TO ANYONE ELSE!

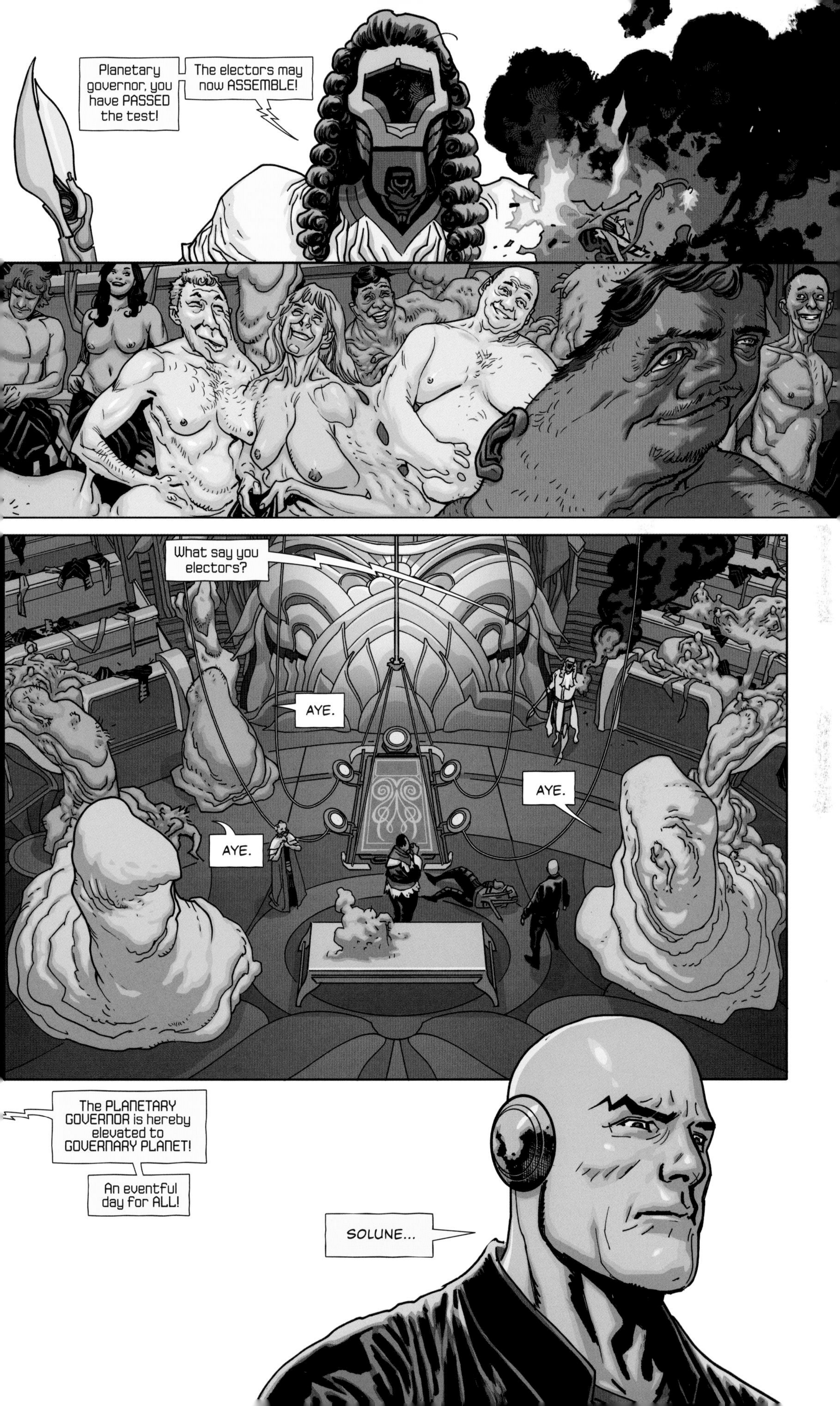

Planetary governor, you have PASSED the test!
The electors may now ASSEMBLE!
What say you electors?
AYE.
AYE.
AYE.
The PLANETARY GOVERNOR is hereby elevated to GOVERNARY PLANET!
An eventful day for ALL!
SOLUNE...

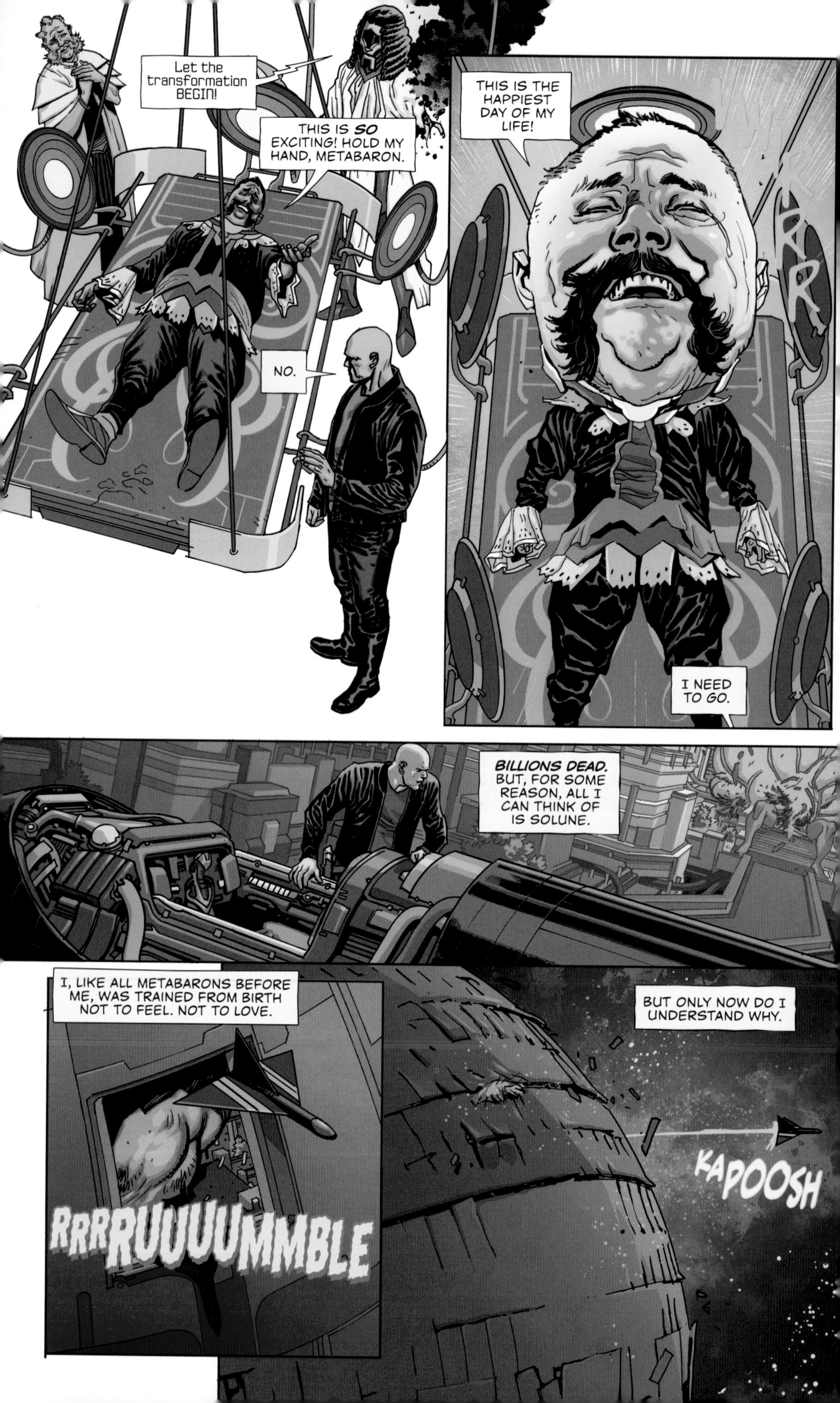
Let the transformation BEGIN!
THIS IS SO EXCITING! HOLD MY HAND, METABARON.
NO.
THIS IS THE HAPPIEST DAY OF MY LIFE!
I NEED TO GO.
BILLIONS DEAD. BUT, FOR SOME REASON, ALL I CAN THINK OF IS SOLUNE.
I, LIKE ALL METABARONS BEFORE ME, WAS TRAINED FROM BIRTH NOT TO FEEL. NOT TO LOVE.
RRRRUUUUMMBLE
BUT ONLY NOW DO I UNDERSTAND WHY.
KAPOOSH

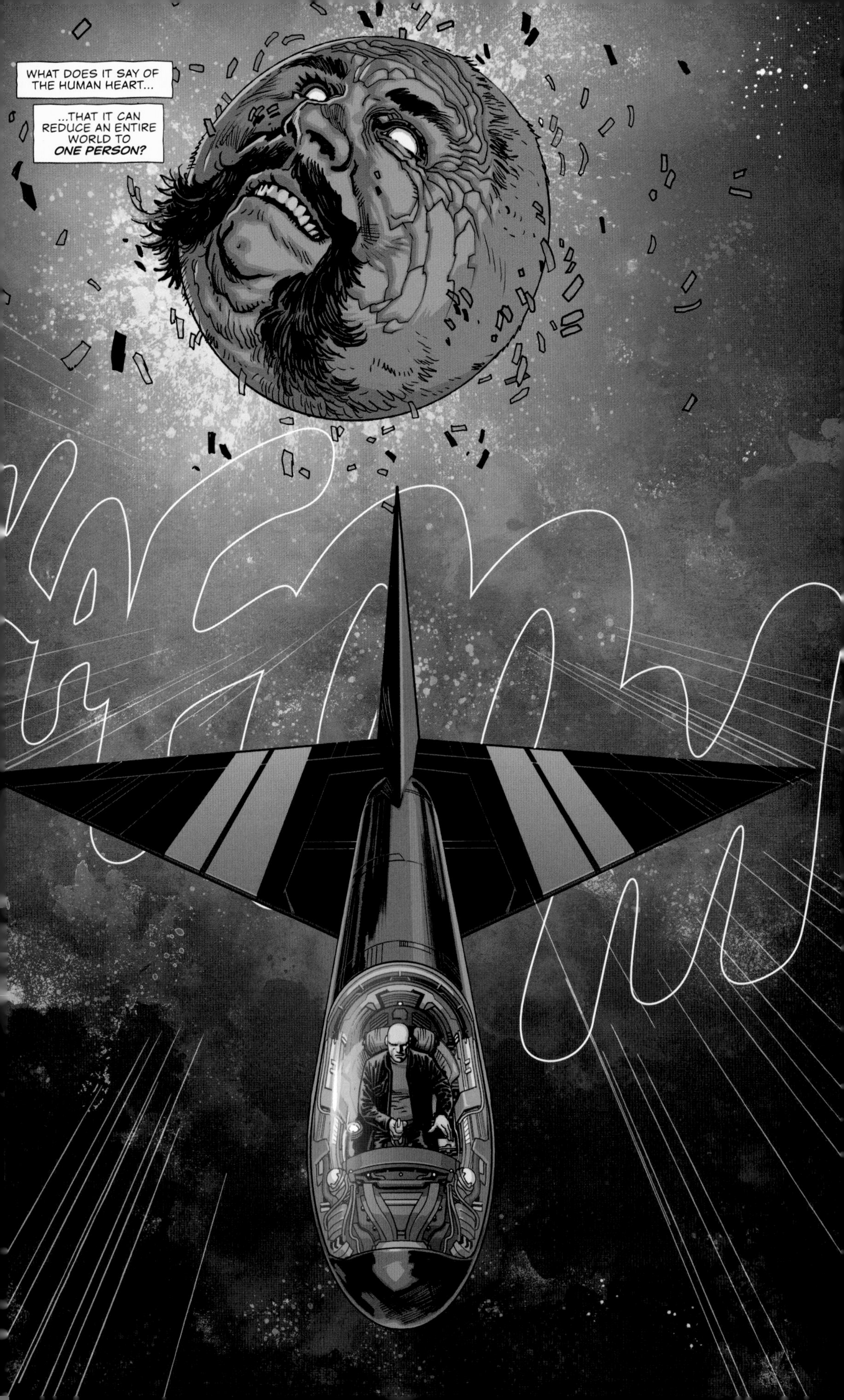
WHAT DOES IT SAY OF THE HUMAN HEART...
...THAT IT CAN REDUCE AN ENTIRE WORLD TO ONE PERSON?

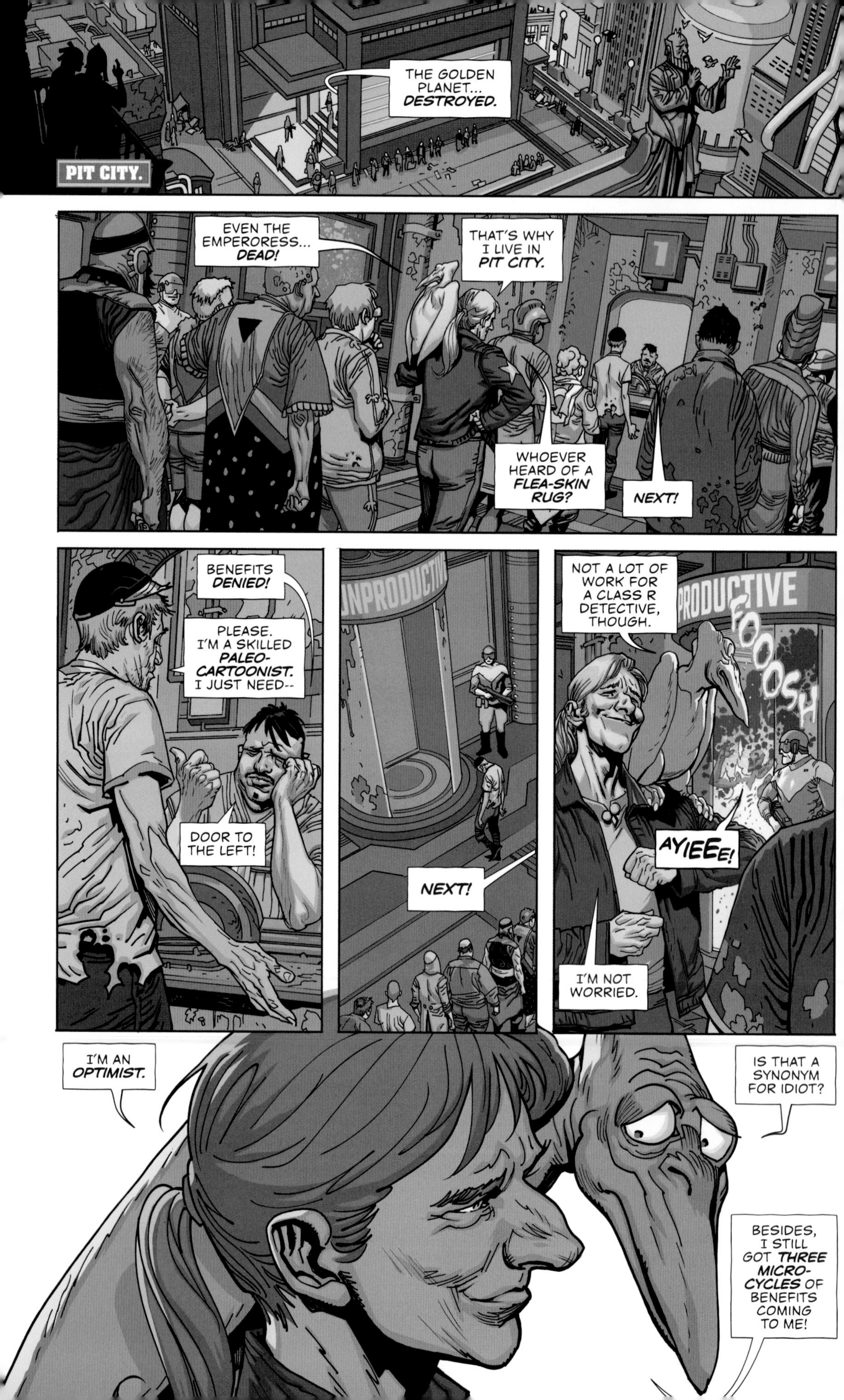
THE GOLDEN PLANET... DESTROYED.
PIT CITY.
EVEN THE EMPERORESS... DEAD!
THAT'S WHY I LIVE IN PIT CITY.
WHOEVER HEARD OF A FLEA-SKIN RUG?
NEXT!
BENEFITS DENIED!
PLEASE. I'M A SKILLED PALEO-CARTOONIST. I JUST NEED--
DOOR TO THE LEFT!
UNPRODUCTIVE
NEXT!
NOT A LOT OF WORK FOR A CLASS R DETECTIVE, THOUGH.
PRODUCTIVE
FOOOSH
AYIEEEE!
I'M NOT WORRIED.
I'M AN OPTIMIST.
IS THAT A SYNONYM FOR IDIOT?
BESIDES, I STILL GOT THREE MICRO-CYCLES OF BENEFITS COMING TO ME!

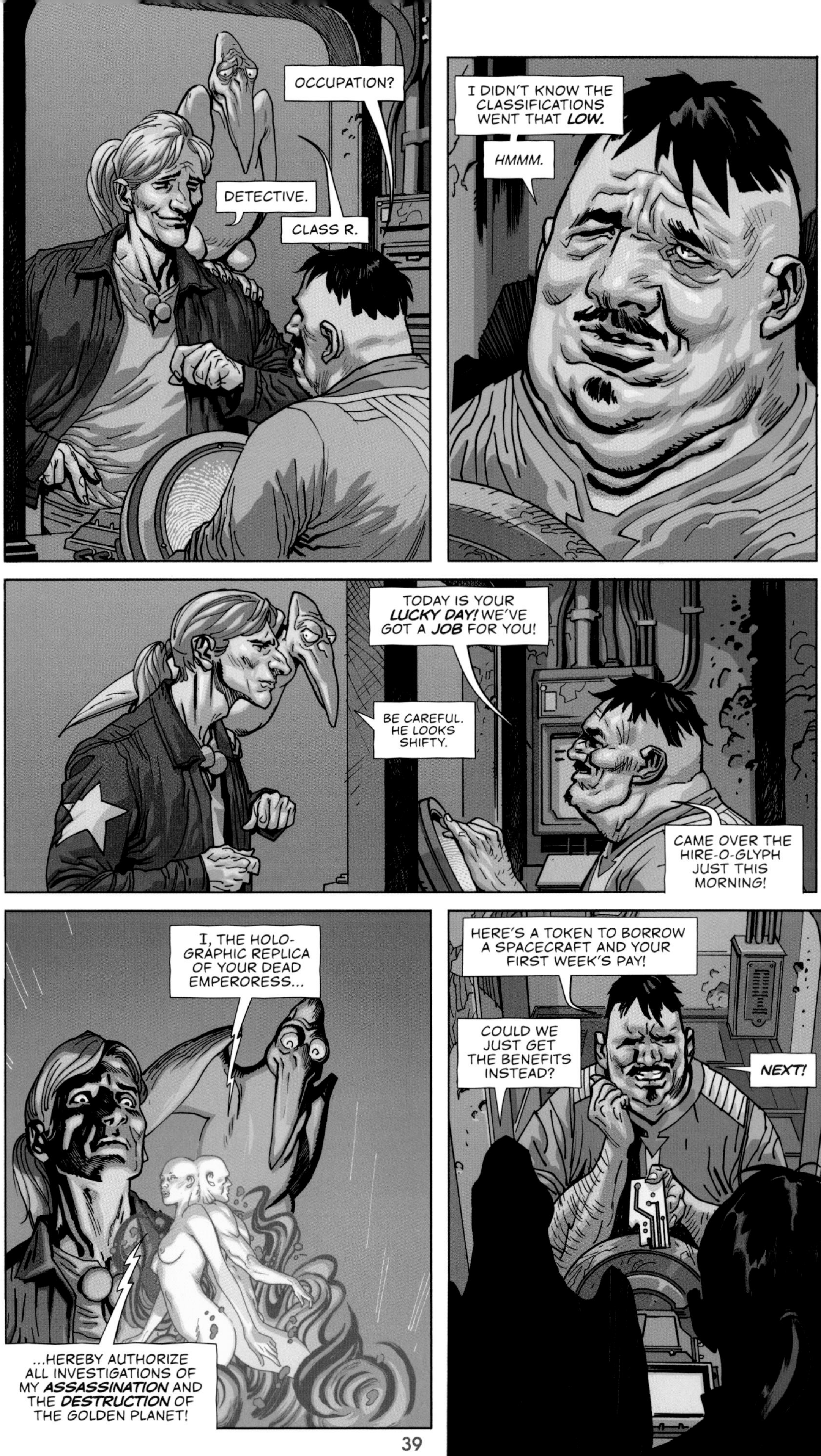
OCCUPATION?
DETECTIVE.
CLASS R.
I DIDN'T KNOW THE CLASSIFICATIONS WENT THAT LOW.
HMMM.
TODAY IS YOUR LUCKY DAY! WE'VE GOT A JOB FOR YOU!
BE CAREFUL. HE LOOKS SHIFTY.
CAME OVER THE HIRE-O-GLYPH JUST THIS MORNING!
I, THE HOLO-GRAPHIC REPLICA OF YOUR DEAD EMPERORESS...
...HEREBY AUTHORIZE ALL INVESTIGATIONS OF MY ASSASSINATION AND THE DESTRUCTION OF THE GOLDEN PLANET!
HERE'S A TOKEN TO BORROW A SPACECRAFT AND YOUR FIRST WEEK'S PAY!
COULD WE JUST GET THE BENEFITS INSTEAD?
NEXT!

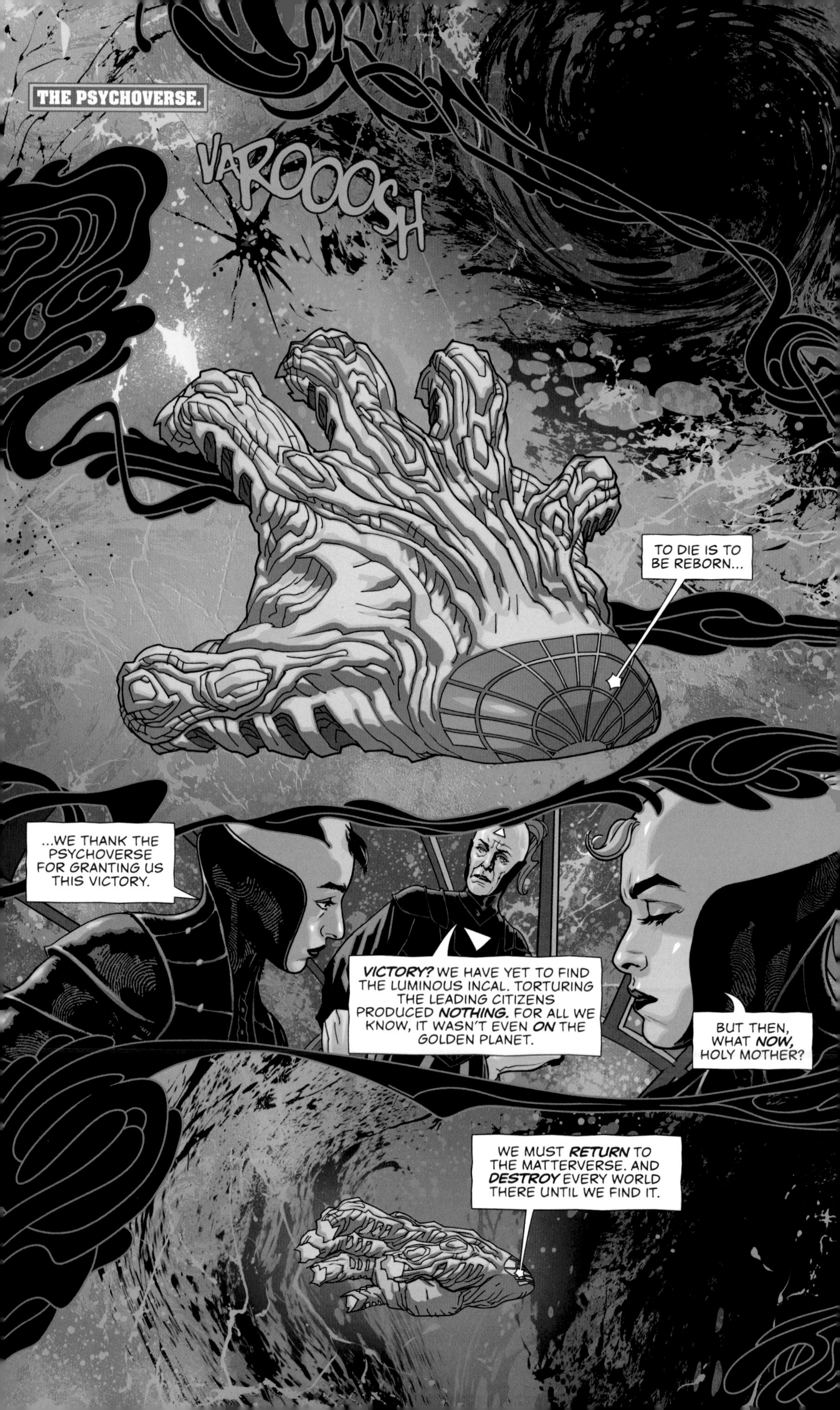
THE PSYCHOVERSE.
VAROOOSH
TO DIE IS TO BE REBORN...
...WE THANK THE PSYCHOVERSE FOR GRANTING US THIS VICTORY.
VICTORY? WE HAVE YET TO FIND THE LUMINOUS INCAL. TORTURING THE LEADING CITIZENS PRODUCED NOTHING. FOR ALL WE KNOW, IT WASN'T EVEN ON THE GOLDEN PLANET.
BUT THEN, WHAT NOW, HOLY MOTHER?
WE MUST RETURN TO THE MATTERVERSE. AND DESTROY EVERY WORLD THERE UNTIL WE FIND IT.

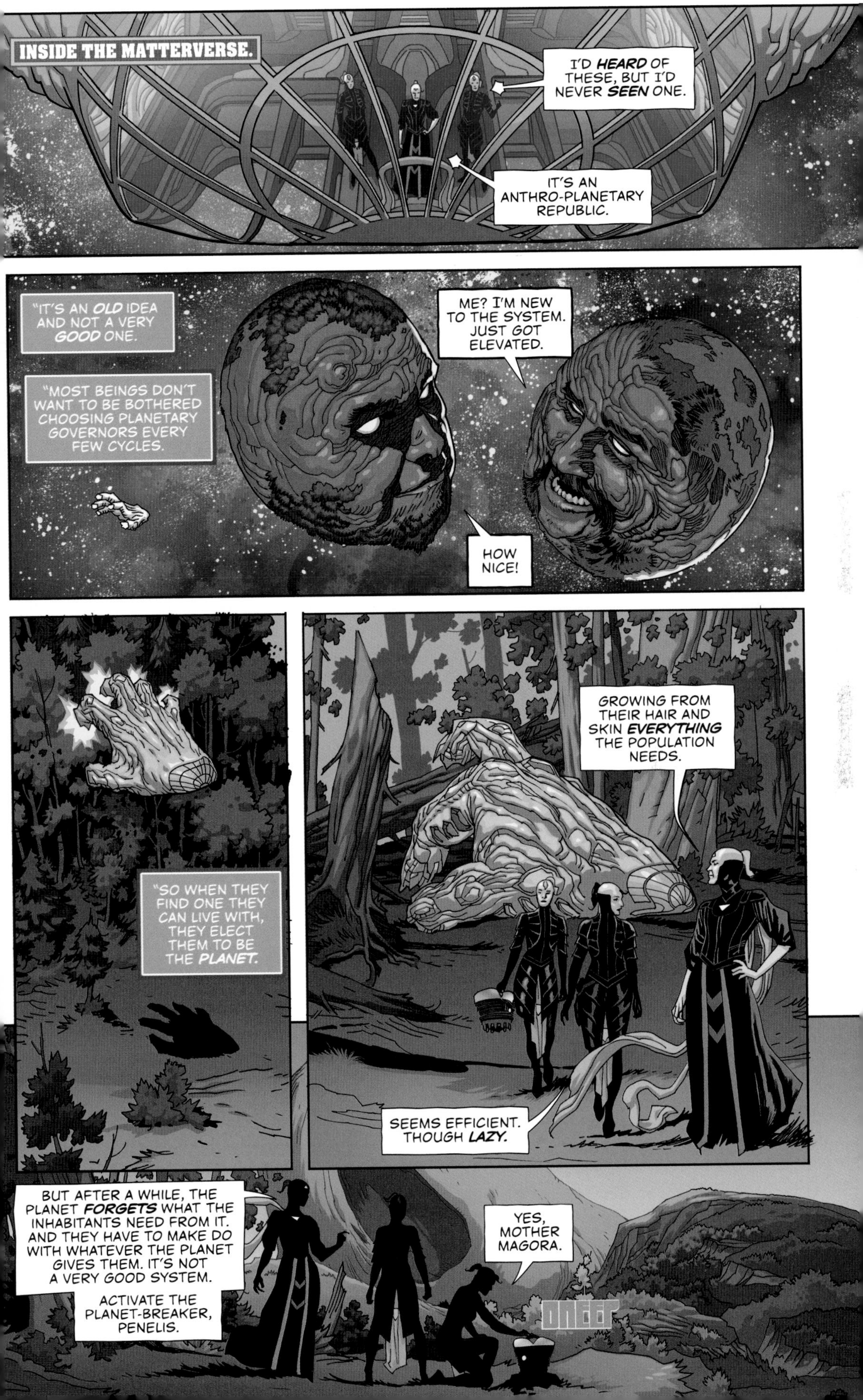
INSIDE THE MATTERVERSE.
I'D HEARD OF THESE, BUT I'D NEVER SEEN ONE.
IT'S AN ANTHRO-PLANETARY REPUBLIC.
"IT'S AN OLD IDEA AND NOT A VERY GOOD ONE.
"MOST BEINGS DON'T WANT TO BE BOTHERED CHOOSING PLANETARY GOVERNORS EVERY FEW CYCLES.
ME? I'M NEW TO THE SYSTEM. JUST GOT ELEVATED.
HOW NICE!
"SO WHEN THEY FIND ONE THEY CAN LIVE WITH, THEY ELECT THEM TO BE THE PLANET.
GROWING FROM THEIR HAIR AND SKIN EVERYTHING THE POPULATION NEEDS.
SEEMS EFFICIENT. THOUGH LAZY.
BUT AFTER A WHILE, THE PLANET FORGETS WHAT THE INHABITANTS NEED FROM IT. AND THEY HAVE TO MAKE DO WITH WHATEVER THE PLANET GIVES THEM. IT'S NOT A VERY GOOD SYSTEM.
ACTIVATE THE PLANET-BREAKER, PENELIS.
YES, MOTHER MAGORA.
DNEEP

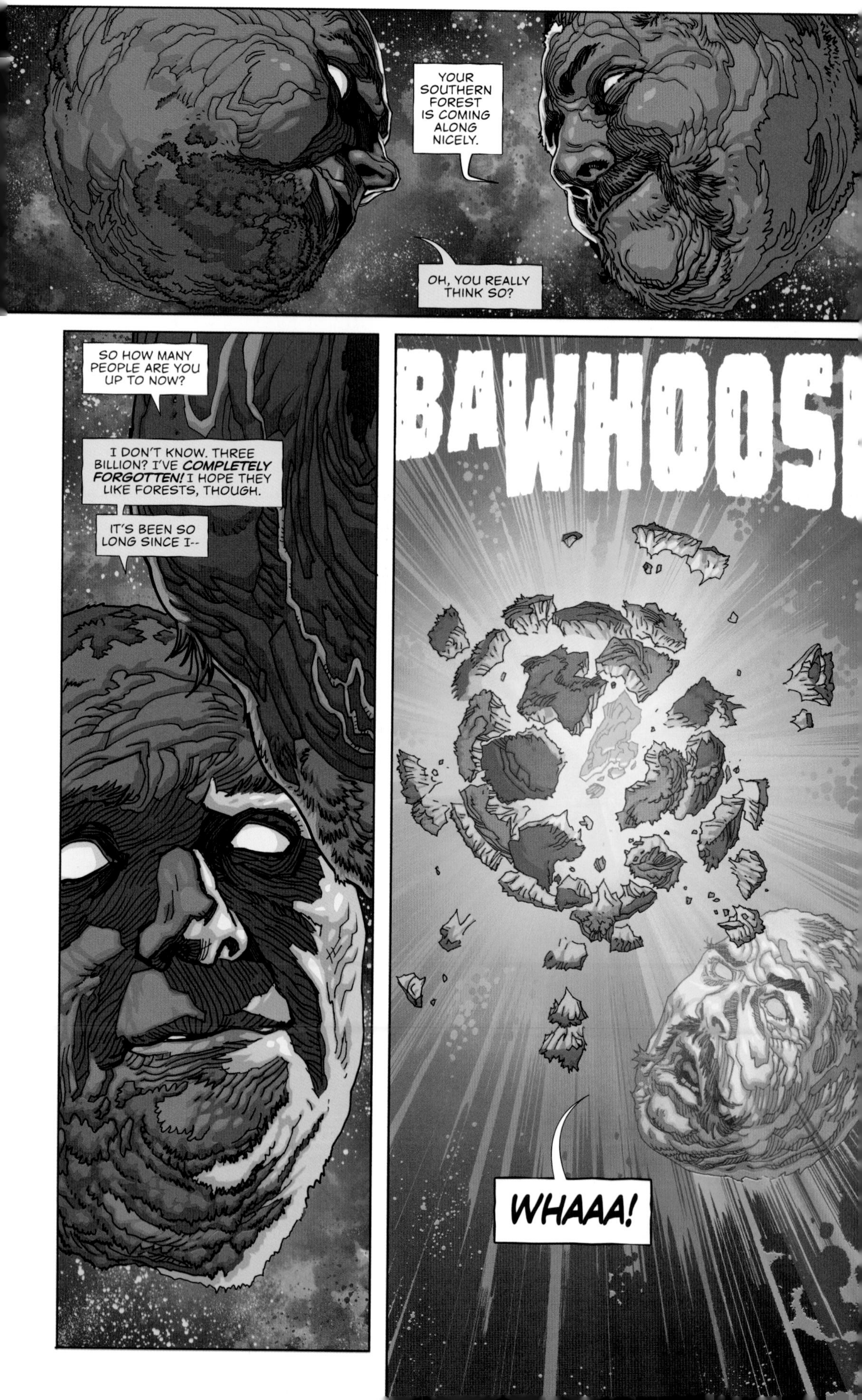
YOUR SOUTHERN FOREST IS COMING ALONG NICELY.
OH, YOU REALLY THINK SO?
SO HOW MANY PEOPLE ARE YOU UP TO NOW?
I DON'T KNOW. THREE BILLION? I'VE *COMPLETELY FORGOTTEN!* I HOPE THEY LIKE FORESTS, THOUGH.
IT'S BEEN SO LONG SINCE I--
BAWHOOSH
WHAAA!

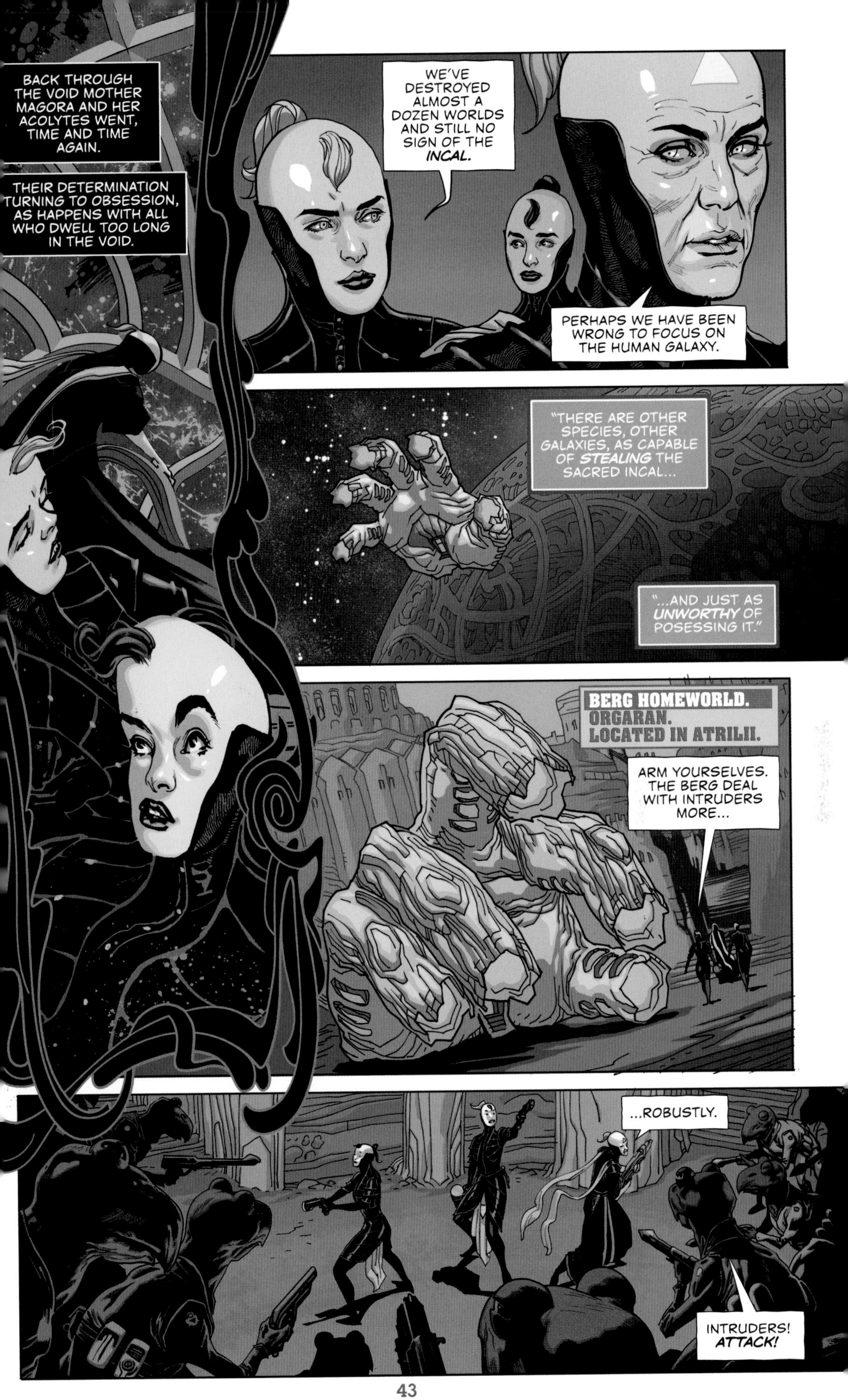

BACK THROUGH THE VOID MOTHER MAGORA AND HER ACOLYTES WENT, TIME AND TIME AGAIN.
THEIR DETERMINATION TURNING TO OBSESSION, AS HAPPENS WITH ALL WHO DWELL TOO LONG IN THE VOID.
WE'VE DESTROYED ALMOST A DOZEN WORLDS AND STILL NO SIGN OF THE *INCAL.*
PERHAPS WE HAVE BEEN WRONG TO FOCUS ON THE HUMAN GALAXY.
"THERE ARE OTHER SPECIES, OTHER GALAXIES, AS CAPABLE OF *STEALING* THE SACRED INCAL...
"...AND JUST AS *UNWORTHY* OF POSESSING IT."
BERG HOMEWORLD. ORGARAN. LOCATED IN ATRILII.
ARM YOURSELVES. THE BERG DEAL WITH INTRUDERS MORE...
...ROBUSTLY.
INTRUDERS! *ATTACK!*

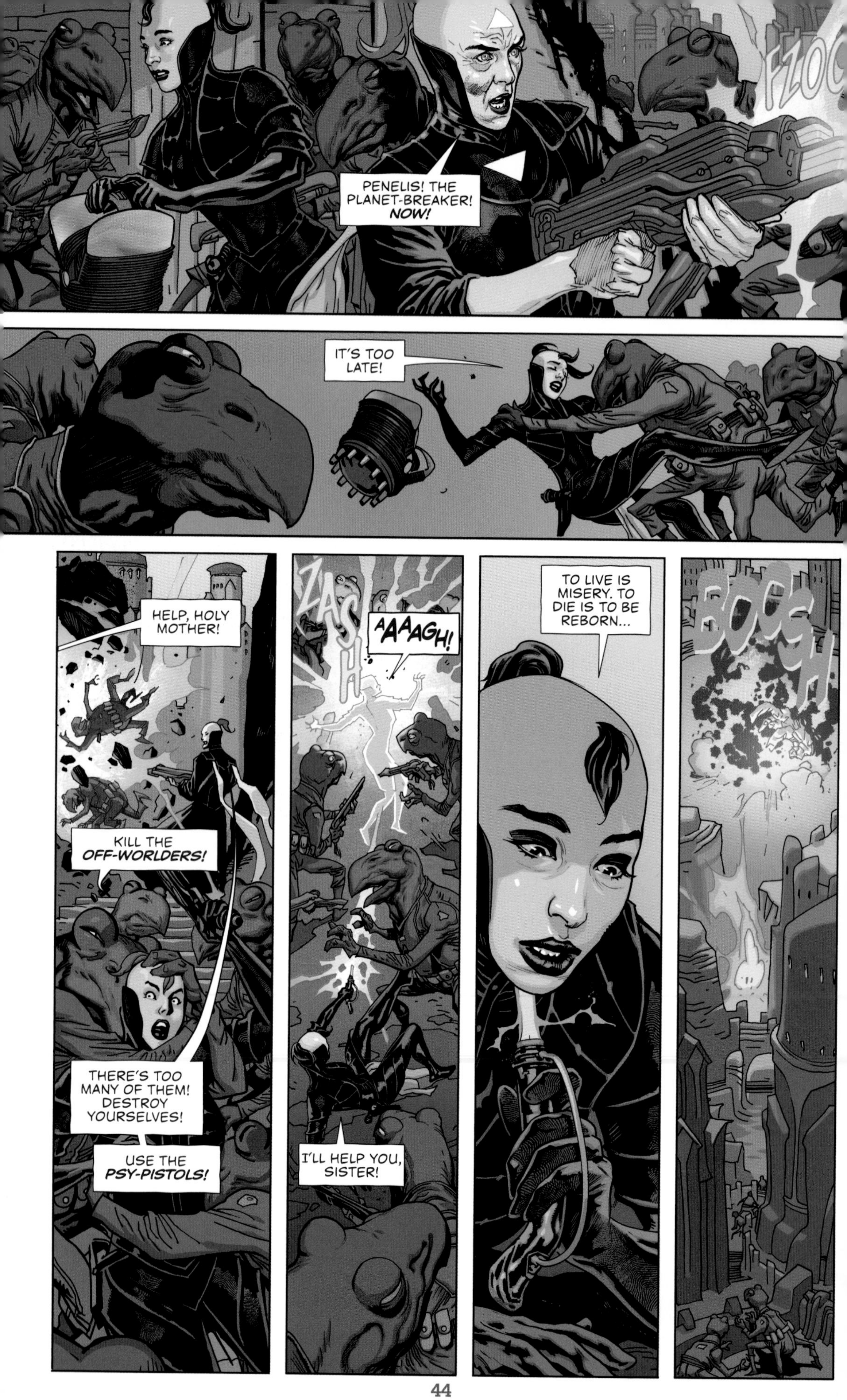
FZOO
PENELIS! THE PLANET-BREAKER! NOW!
IT'S TOO LATE!
HELP, HOLY MOTHER!
KILL THE OFF-WORLDERS!
THERE'S TOO MANY OF THEM! DESTROY YOURSELVES!
USE THE PSY-PISTOLS!
ZASH
AAAAGH!
I'LL HELP YOU, SISTER!
TO LIVE IS MISERY. TO DIE IS TO BE REBORN...
BOOSH

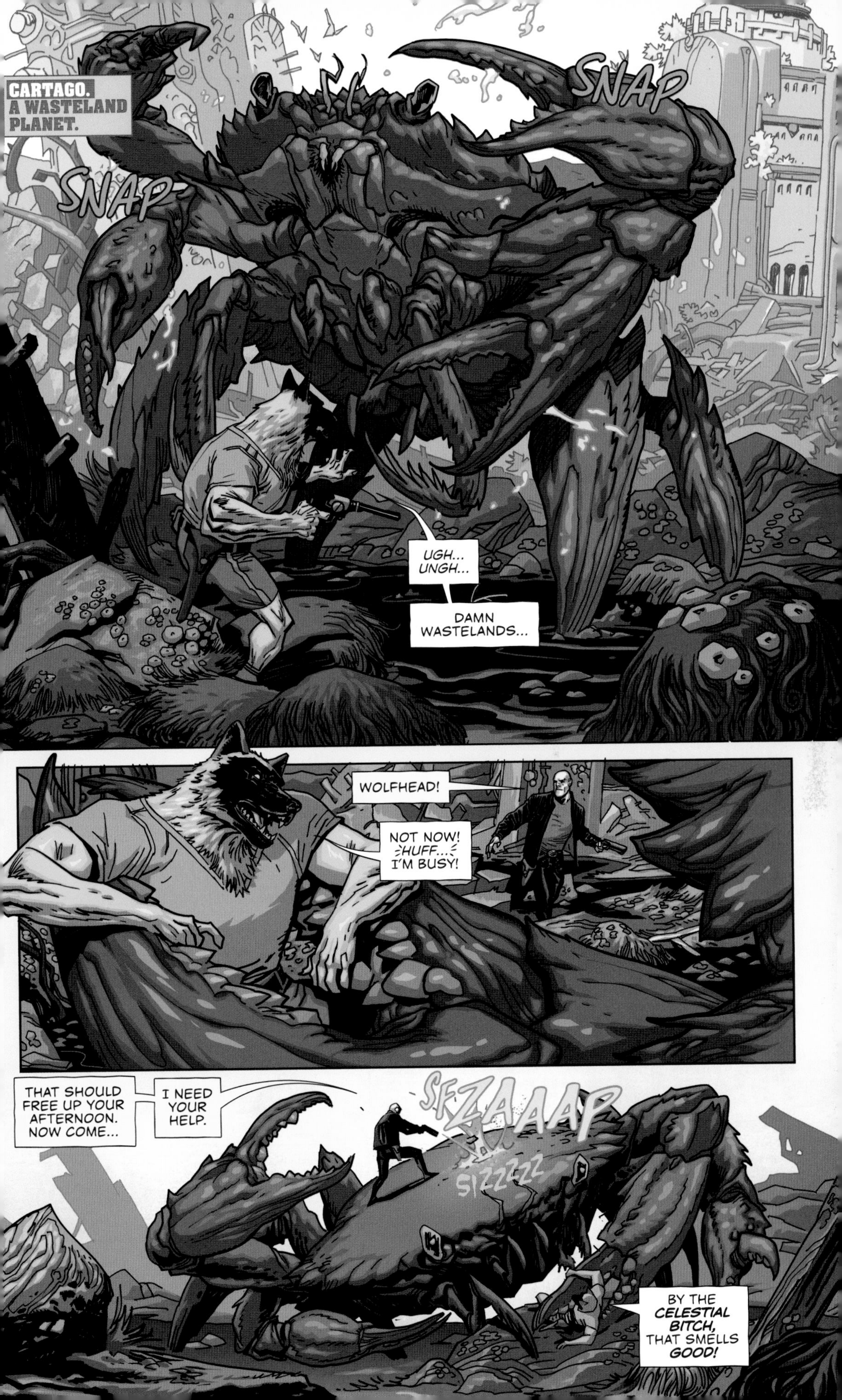
CARTAGO. A WASTELAND PLANET.
SNAP
SNAP
UGH... UNGH...
DAMN WASTELANDS...
WOLFHEAD!
NOT NOW! HUFF... I'M BUSY!
I NEED YOUR HELP.
THAT SHOULD FREE UP YOUR AFTERNOON. NOW COME...
SFZAAAP
SIZZZZZ
BY THE CELESTIAL BITCH, THAT SMELLS GOOD!

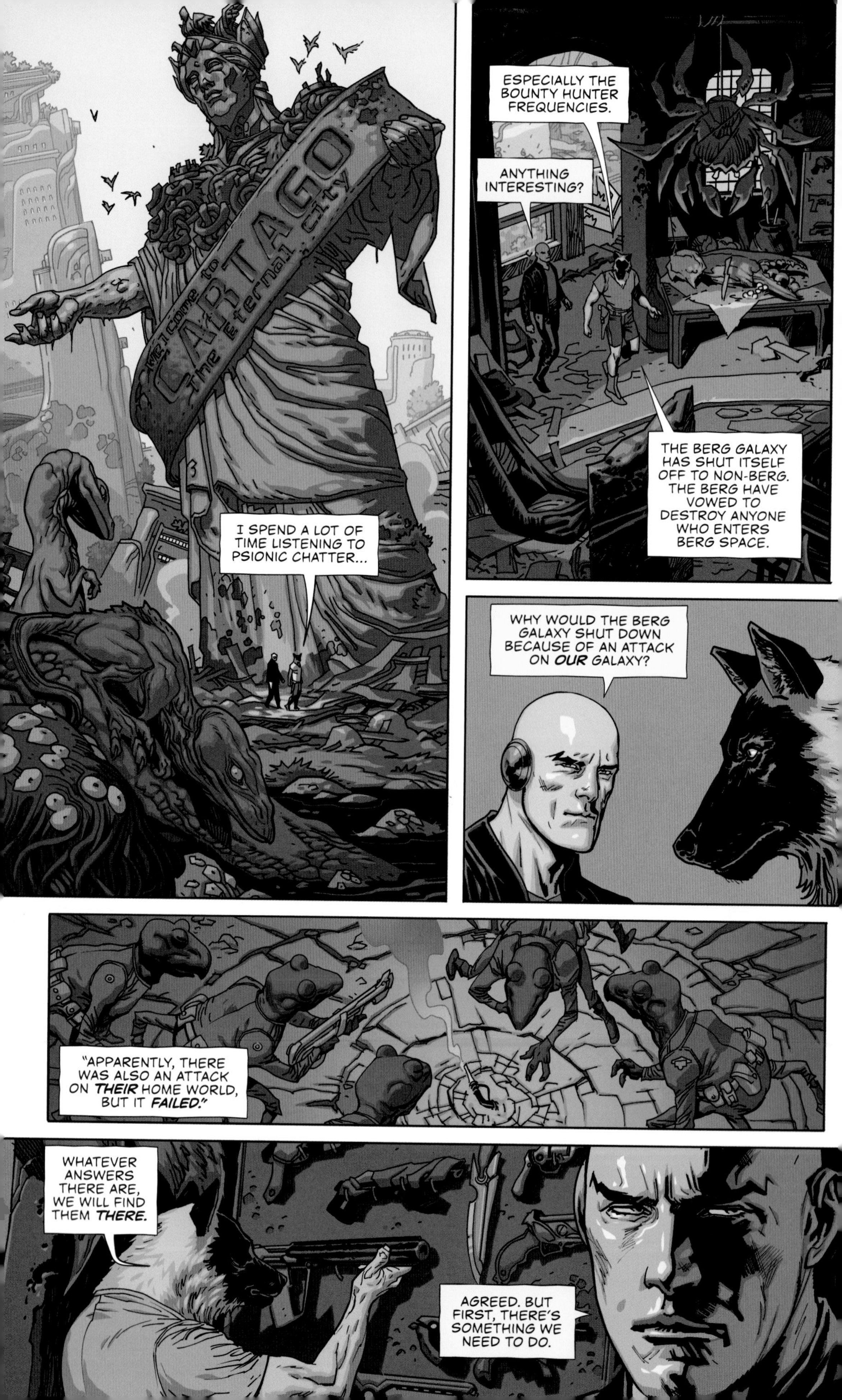
Welcome to CARTAGO The Eternal City
I SPEND A LOT OF TIME LISTENING TO PSIONIC CHATTER...
ESPECIALLY THE BOUNTY HUNTER FREQUENCIES.
ANYTHING INTERESTING?
THE BERG GALAXY HAS SHUT ITSELF OFF TO NON-BERG. THE BERG HAVE VOWED TO DESTROY ANYONE WHO ENTERS BERG SPACE.
WHY WOULD THE BERG GALAXY SHUT DOWN BECAUSE OF AN ATTACK ON OUR GALAXY?
"APPARENTLY, THERE WAS ALSO AN ATTACK ON THEIR HOME WORLD, BUT IT FAILED."
WHATEVER ANSWERS THERE ARE, WE WILL FIND THEM THERE.
AGREED. BUT FIRST, THERE'S SOMETHING WE NEED TO DO.

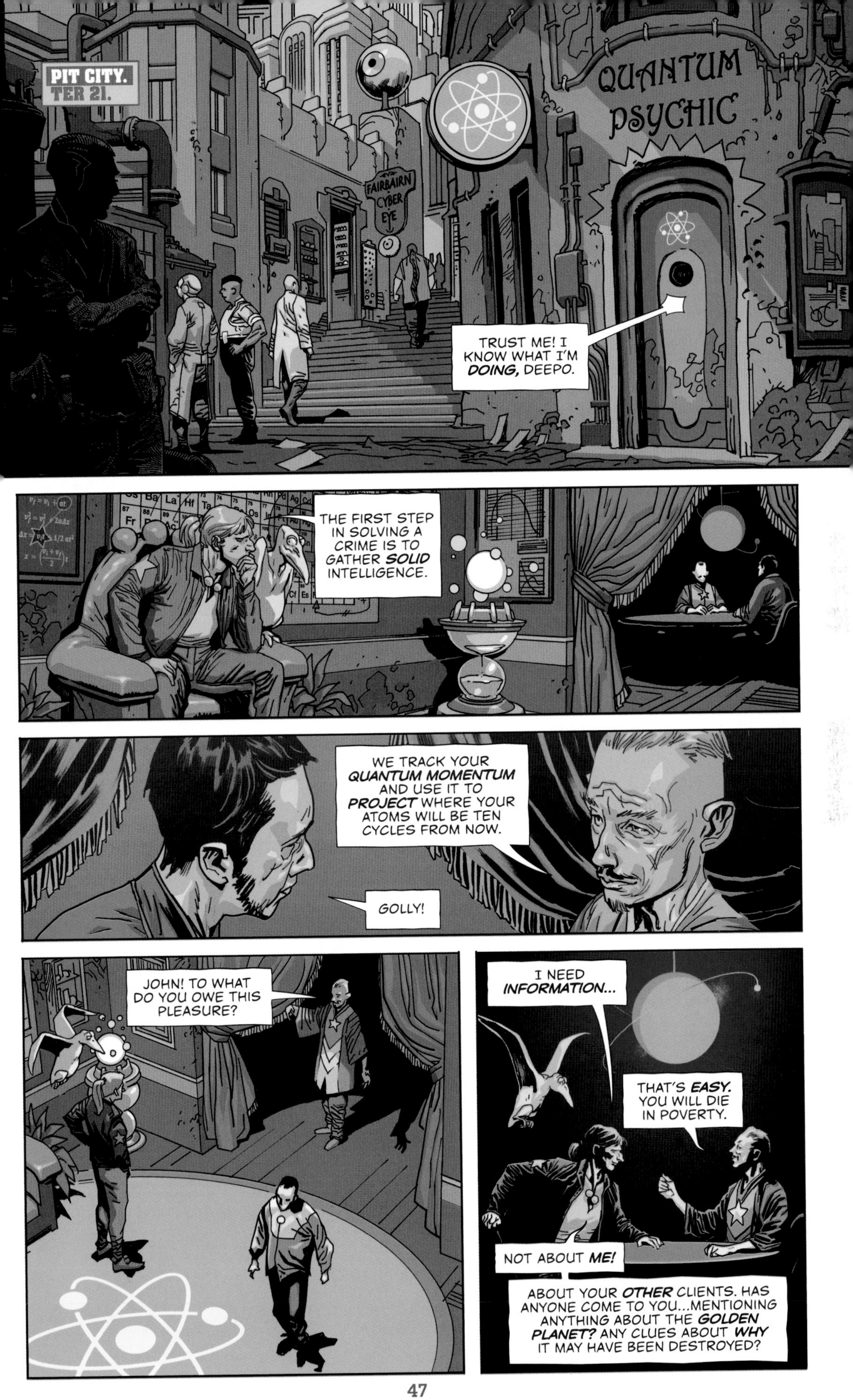
PIT CITY. TER 21.
QUANTUM PSYCHIC
FAIRBAIRN CYBER EYE
TRUST ME! I KNOW WHAT I'M DOING, DEEPO.
THE FIRST STEP IN SOLVING A CRIME IS TO GATHER SOLID INTELLIGENCE.
WE TRACK YOUR QUANTUM MOMENTUM AND USE IT TO PROJECT WHERE YOUR ATOMS WILL BE TEN CYCLES FROM NOW.
GOLLY!
JOHN! TO WHAT DO YOU OWE THIS PLEASURE?
I NEED INFORMATION...
THAT'S EASY. YOU WILL DIE IN POVERTY.
NOT ABOUT ME!
ABOUT YOUR OTHER CLIENTS. HAS ANYONE COME TO YOU...MENTIONING ANYTHING ABOUT THE GOLDEN PLANET? ANY CLUES ABOUT WHY IT MAY HAVE BEEN DESTROYED?

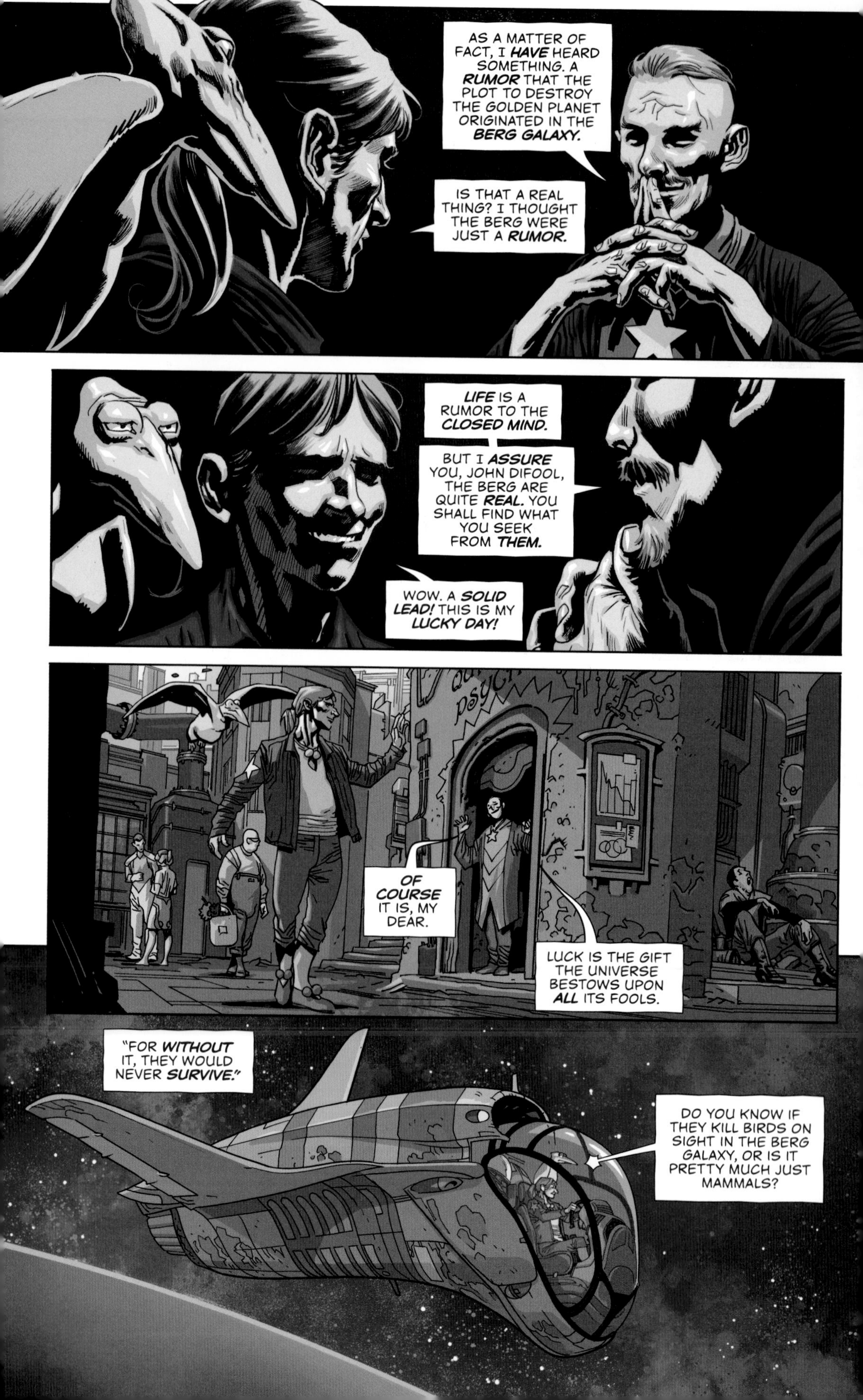
AS A MATTER OF FACT, I **HAVE** HEARD SOMETHING. A **RUMOR** THAT THE PLOT TO DESTROY THE GOLDEN PLANET ORIGINATED IN THE **BERG GALAXY.**
IS THAT A REAL THING? I THOUGHT THE BERG WERE JUST A **RUMOR.**
LIFE IS A RUMOR TO THE **CLOSED MIND.**
BUT I **ASSURE** YOU, JOHN DIFOOL, THE BERG ARE QUITE **REAL.** YOU SHALL FIND WHAT YOU SEEK FROM **THEM.**
WOW. A **SOLID LEAD!** THIS IS MY **LUCKY DAY!**
OF COURSE IT IS, MY DEAR.
LUCK IS THE GIFT THE UNIVERSE BESTOWS UPON **ALL** ITS FOOLS.
"FOR **WITHOUT** IT, THEY WOULD NEVER **SURVIVE.**"
DO YOU KNOW IF THEY KILL BIRDS ON SIGHT IN THE BERG GALAXY, OR IS IT PRETTY MUCH JUST MAMMALS?

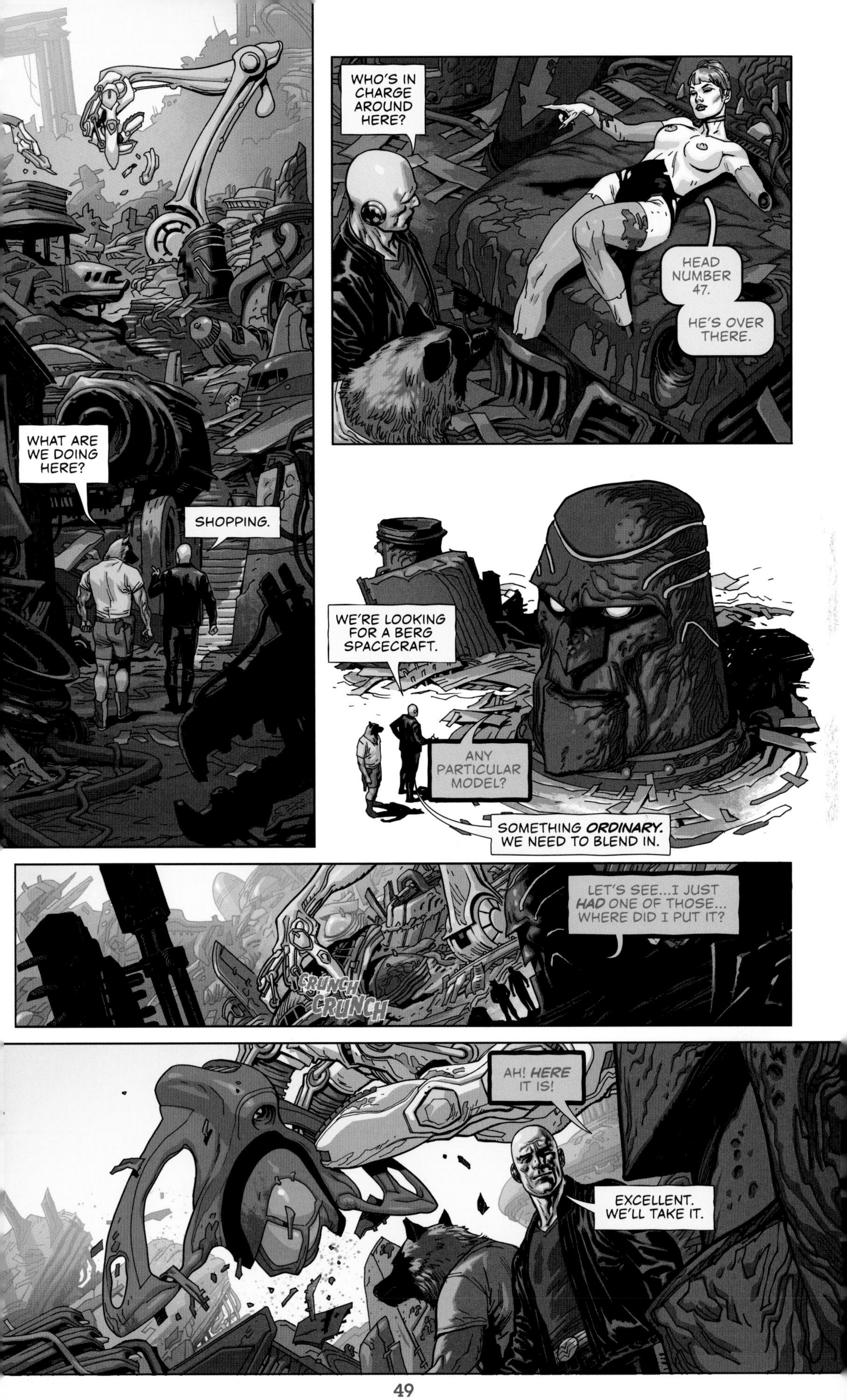
WHAT ARE WE DOING HERE?
SHOPPING.
WHO'S IN CHARGE AROUND HERE?
HEAD NUMBER 47.
HE'S OVER THERE.
WE'RE LOOKING FOR A BERG SPACECRAFT.
ANY PARTICULAR MODEL?
SOMETHING ORDINARY. WE NEED TO BLEND IN.
LET'S SEE...I JUST HAD ONE OF THOSE... WHERE DID I PUT IT?
CRUNCH
CRUNCH
AH! HERE IT IS!
EXCELLENT. WE'LL TAKE IT.

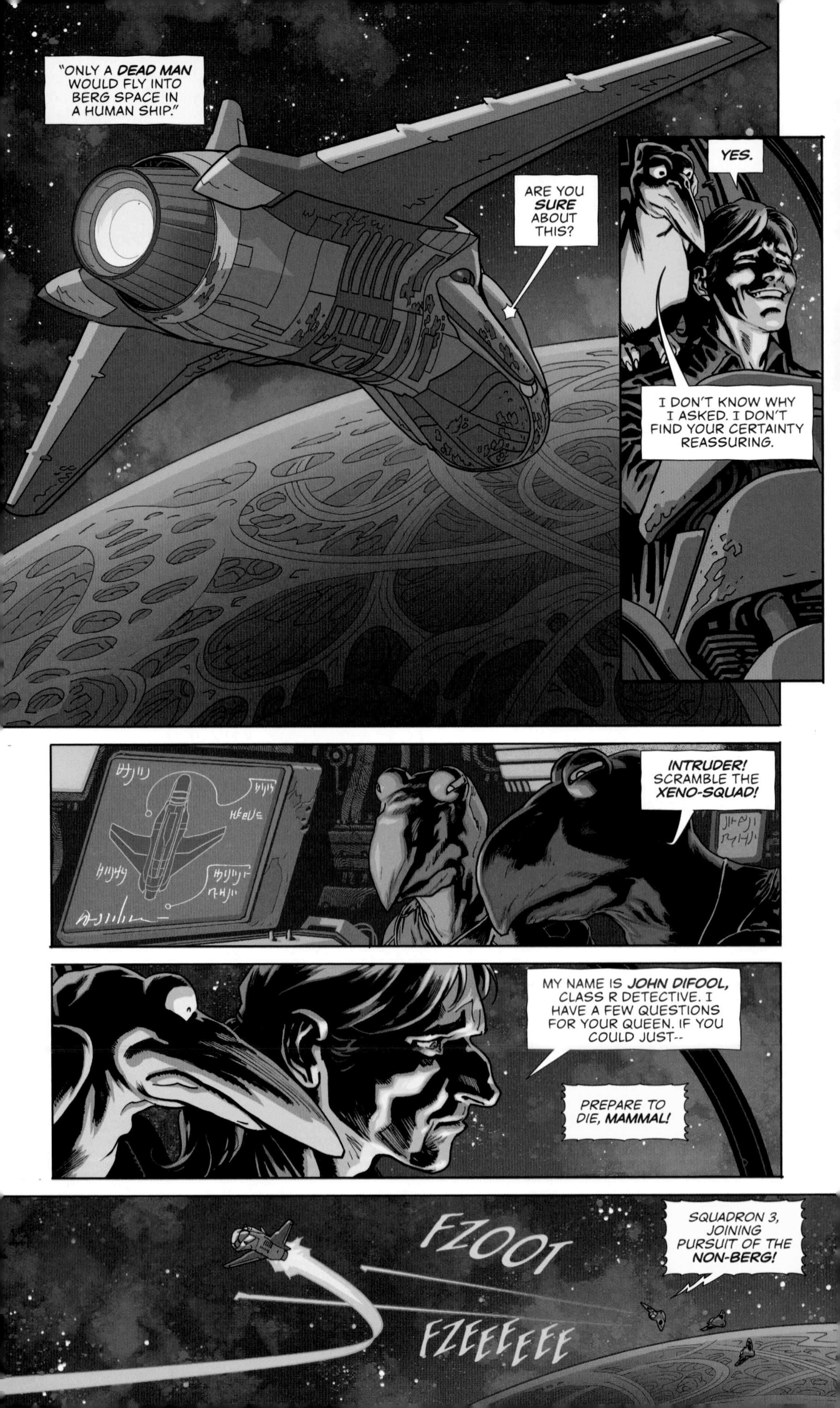
"ONLY A **DEAD MAN** WOULD FLY INTO BERG SPACE IN A HUMAN SHIP."
ARE YOU **SURE** ABOUT THIS?
YES.
I DON'T KNOW WHY I ASKED. I DON'T FIND YOUR CERTAINTY REASSURING.
INTRUDER! SCRAMBLE THE **XENO-SQUAD!**
MY NAME IS **JOHN DIFOOL**, CLASS R DETECTIVE. I HAVE A FEW QUESTIONS FOR YOUR QUEEN. IF YOU COULD JUST--
PREPARE TO DIE, **MAMMAL!**
FZOOT
FZEEEEEE
SQUADRON 3, JOINING PURSUIT OF THE **NON-BERG!**

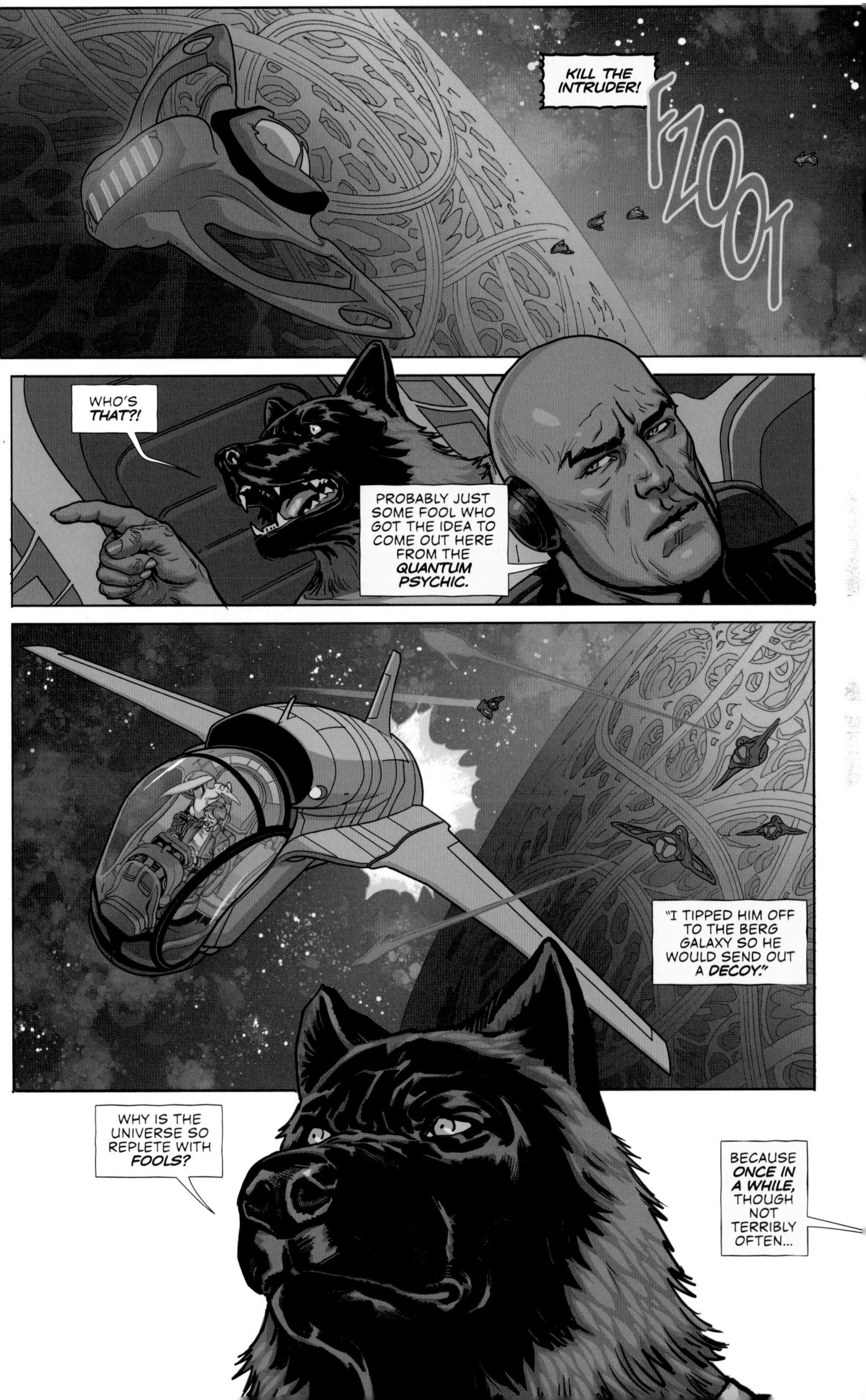

KILL THE INTRUDER!
FZOOT
WHO'S THAT?!
PROBABLY JUST SOME FOOL WHO GOT THE IDEA TO COME OUT HERE FROM THE QUANTUM PSYCHIC.
"I TIPPED HIM OFF TO THE BERG GALAXY SO HE WOULD SEND OUT A DECOY."
WHY IS THE UNIVERSE SO REPLETE WITH FOOLS?
BECAUSE ONCE IN A WHILE, THOUGH NOT TERRIBLY OFTEN...

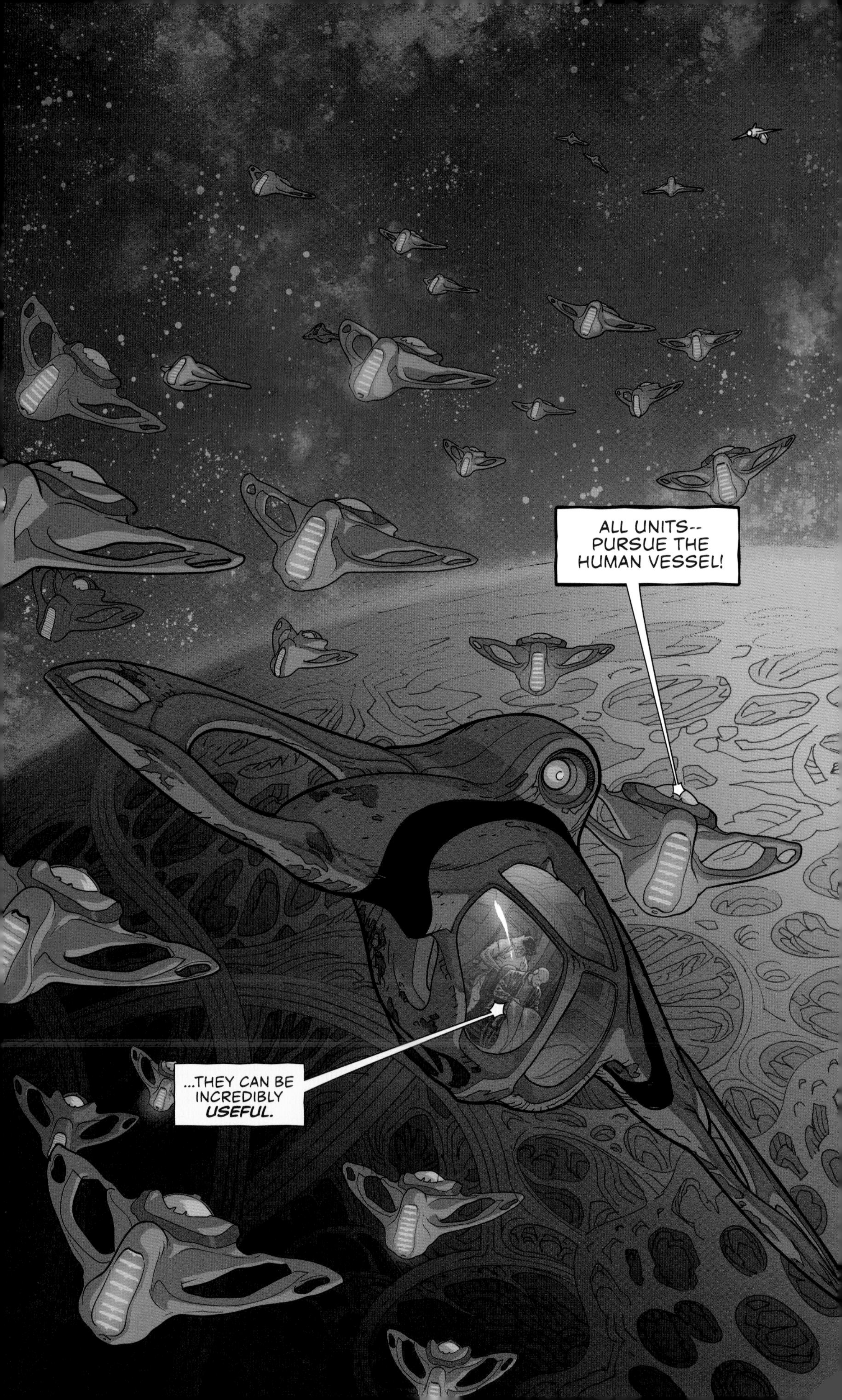
ALL UNITS--
PURSUE THE
HUMAN VESSEL!
...THEY CAN BE
INCREDIBLY
USEFUL.

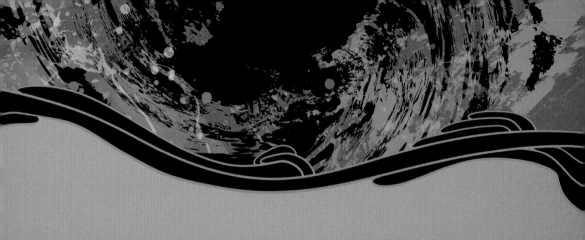

CHAPTER 3

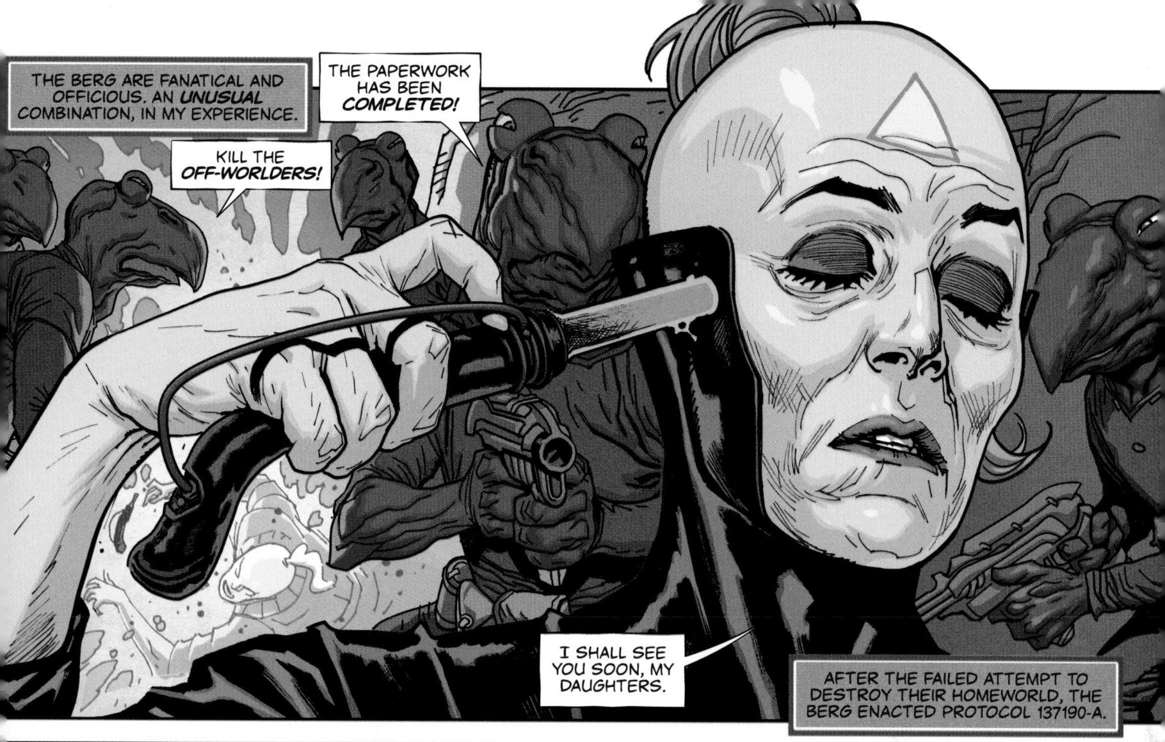
THE BERG ARE FANATICAL AND OFFICIOUS. AN *UNUSUAL* COMBINATION, IN MY EXPERIENCE.
THE PAPERWORK HAS BEEN *COMPLETED!*
KILL THE *OFF-WORLDERS!*
I SHALL SEE YOU SOON, MY DAUGHTERS.
AFTER THE FAILED ATTEMPT TO DESTROY THEIR HOMEWORLD, THE BERG ENACTED PROTOCOL 137190-A.

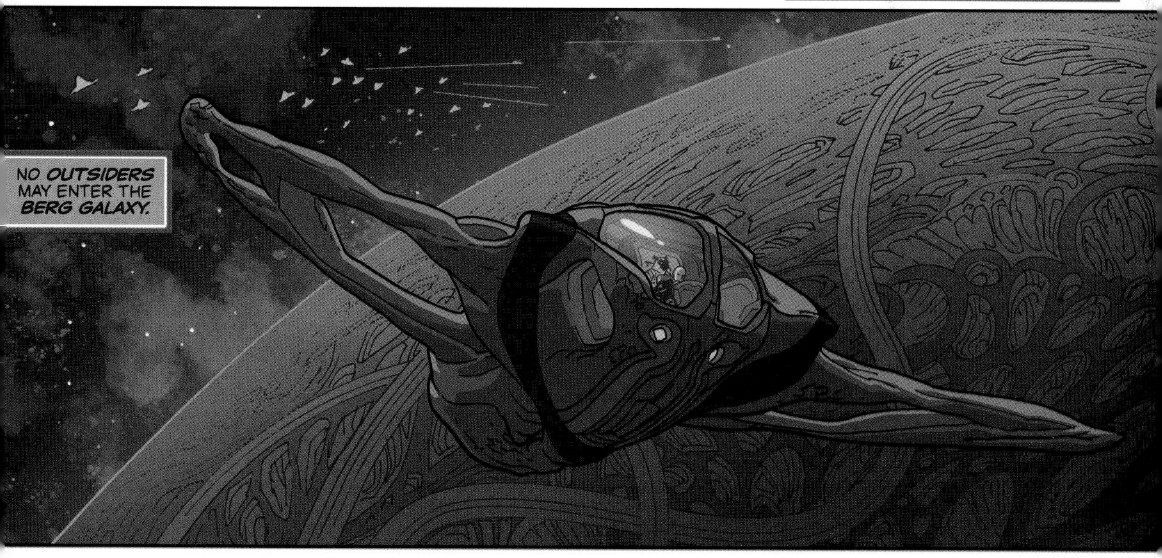
NO *OUTSIDERS* MAY ENTER THE *BERG GALAXY.*

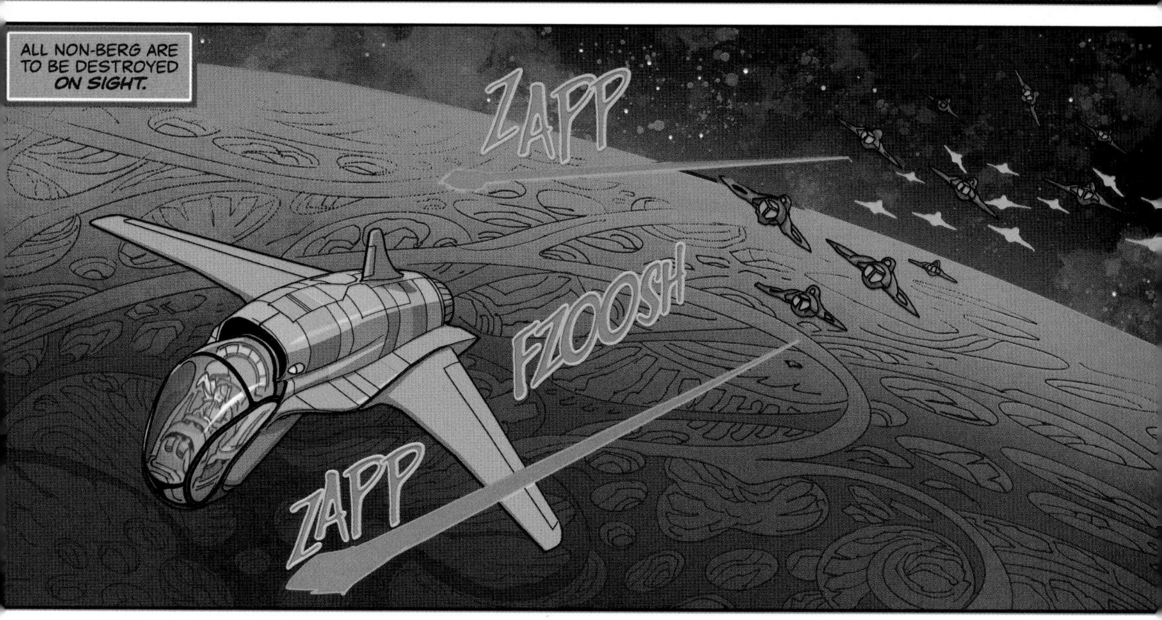
ALL NON-BERG ARE TO BE DESTROYED *ON SIGHT.*
ZAPP
FZOOSH
ZAPP

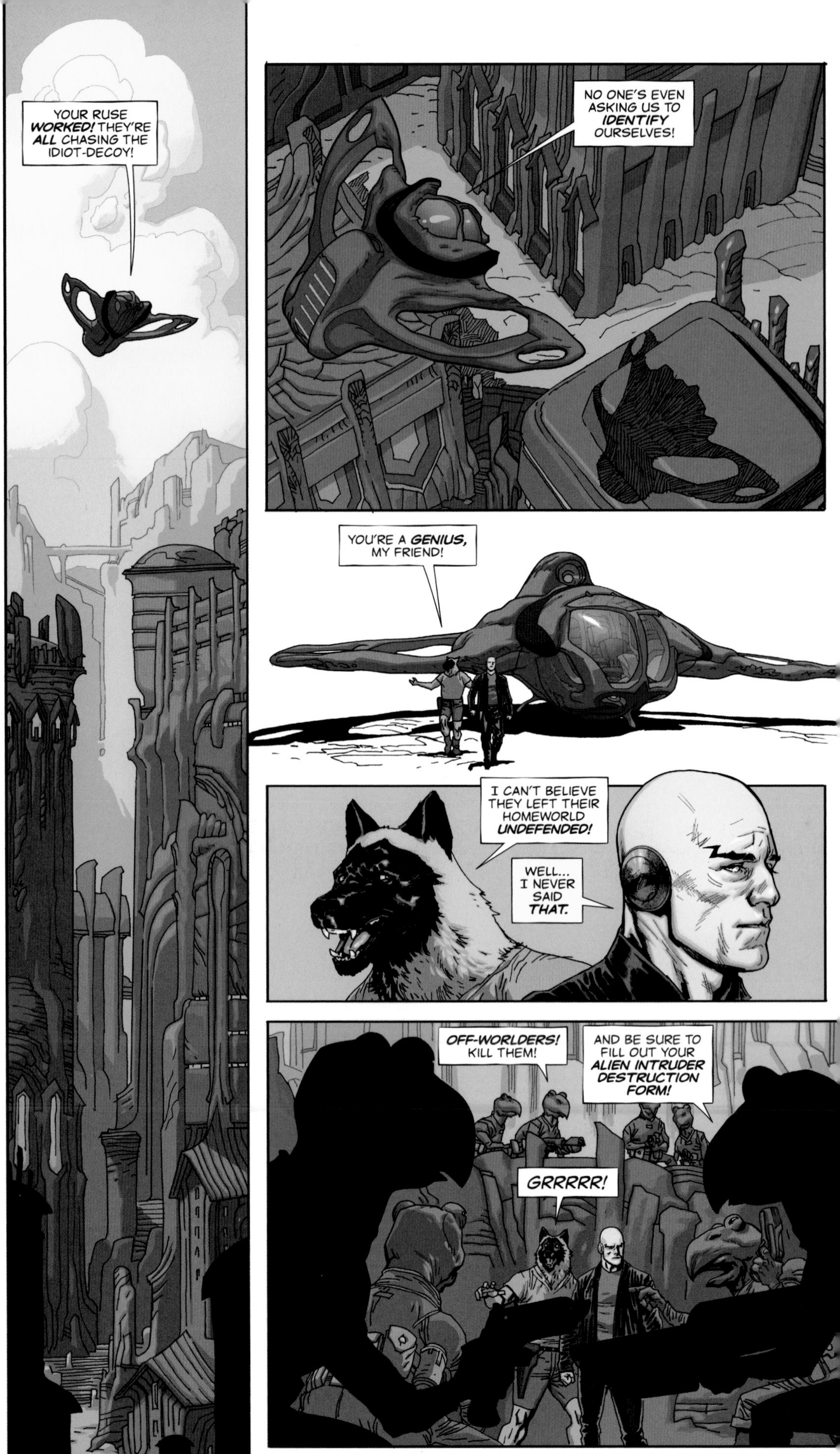
YOUR RUSE WORKED! THEY'RE ALL CHASING THE IDIOT-DECOY!
NO ONE'S EVEN ASKING US TO IDENTIFY OURSELVES!
YOU'RE A GENIUS, MY FRIEND!
I CAN'T BELIEVE THEY LEFT THEIR HOMEWORLD UNDEFENDED!
WELL... I NEVER SAID THAT.
OFF-WORLDERS! KILL THEM!
AND BE SURE TO FILL OUT YOUR ALIEN INTRUDER DESTRUCTION FORM!
GRRRRR!

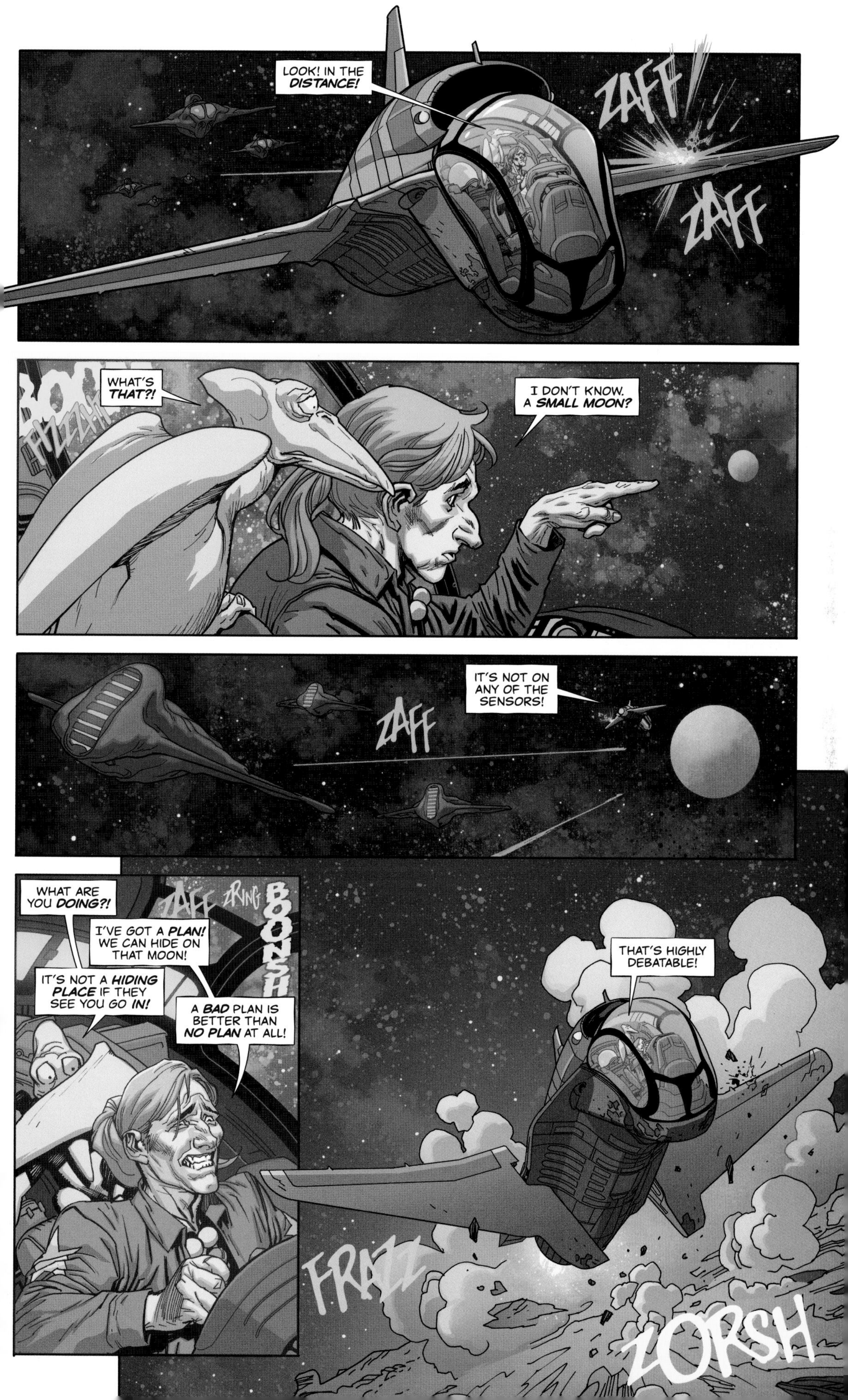

LOOK! IN THE DISTANCE!
ZAFF
ZAFF
WHAT'S THAT?!
I DON'T KNOW. A SMALL MOON?
IT'S NOT ON ANY OF THE SENSORS!
ZAFF
WHAT ARE YOU DOING?!
ZAFF
ZRING
BOONSH
I'VE GOT A PLAN! WE CAN HIDE ON THAT MOON!
IT'S NOT A HIDING PLACE IF THEY SEE YOU GO IN!
A BAD PLAN IS BETTER THAN NO PLAN AT ALL!
THAT'S HIGHLY DEBATABLE!
FRAZZ
ZORSH

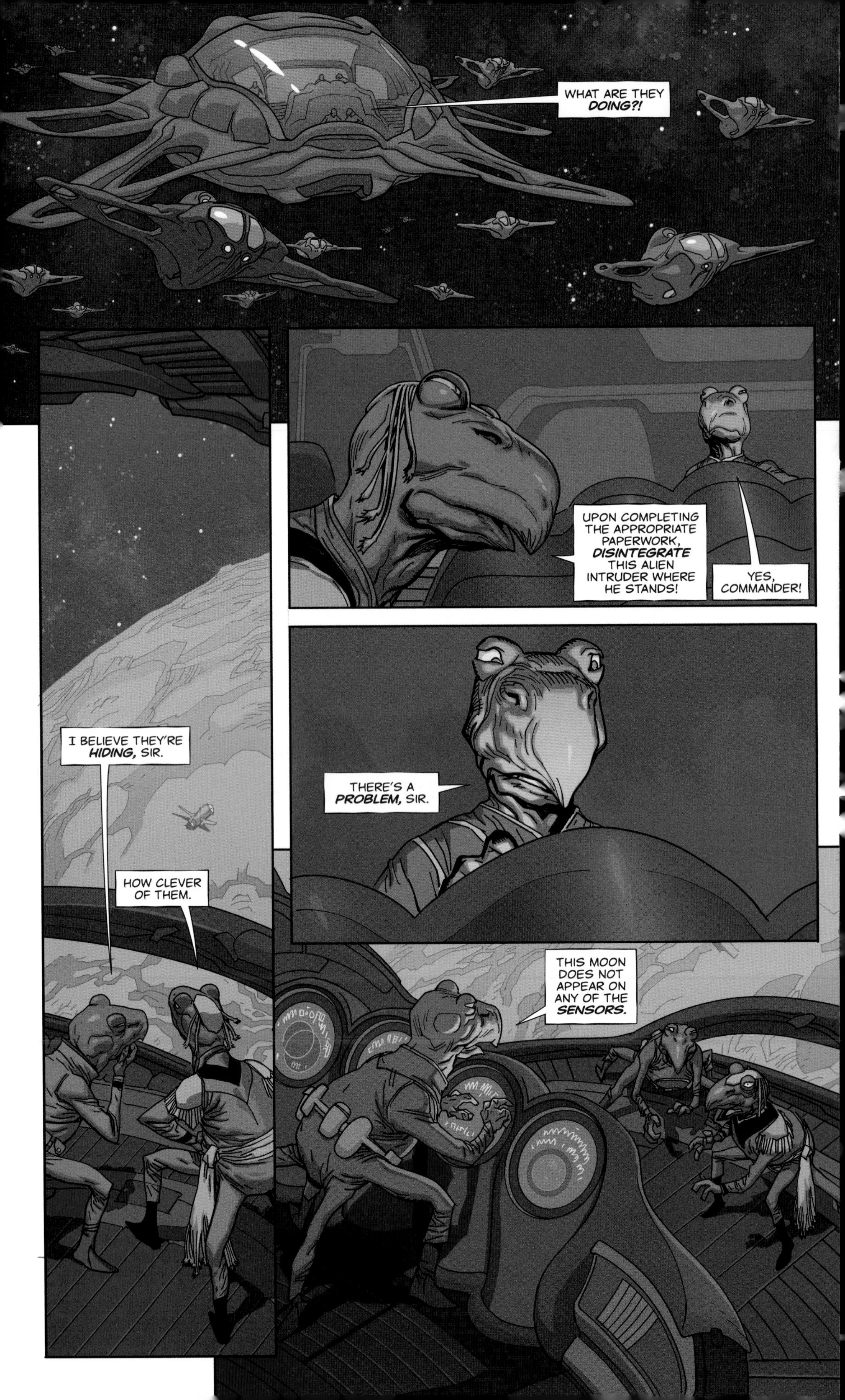
WHAT ARE THEY DOING?!
I BELIEVE THEY'RE HIDING, SIR.
HOW CLEVER OF THEM.
UPON COMPLETING THE APPROPRIATE PAPERWORK, DISINTEGRATE THIS ALIEN INTRUDER WHERE HE STANDS!
YES, COMMANDER!
THERE'S A PROBLEM, SIR.
THIS MOON DOES NOT APPEAR ON ANY OF THE SENSORS.

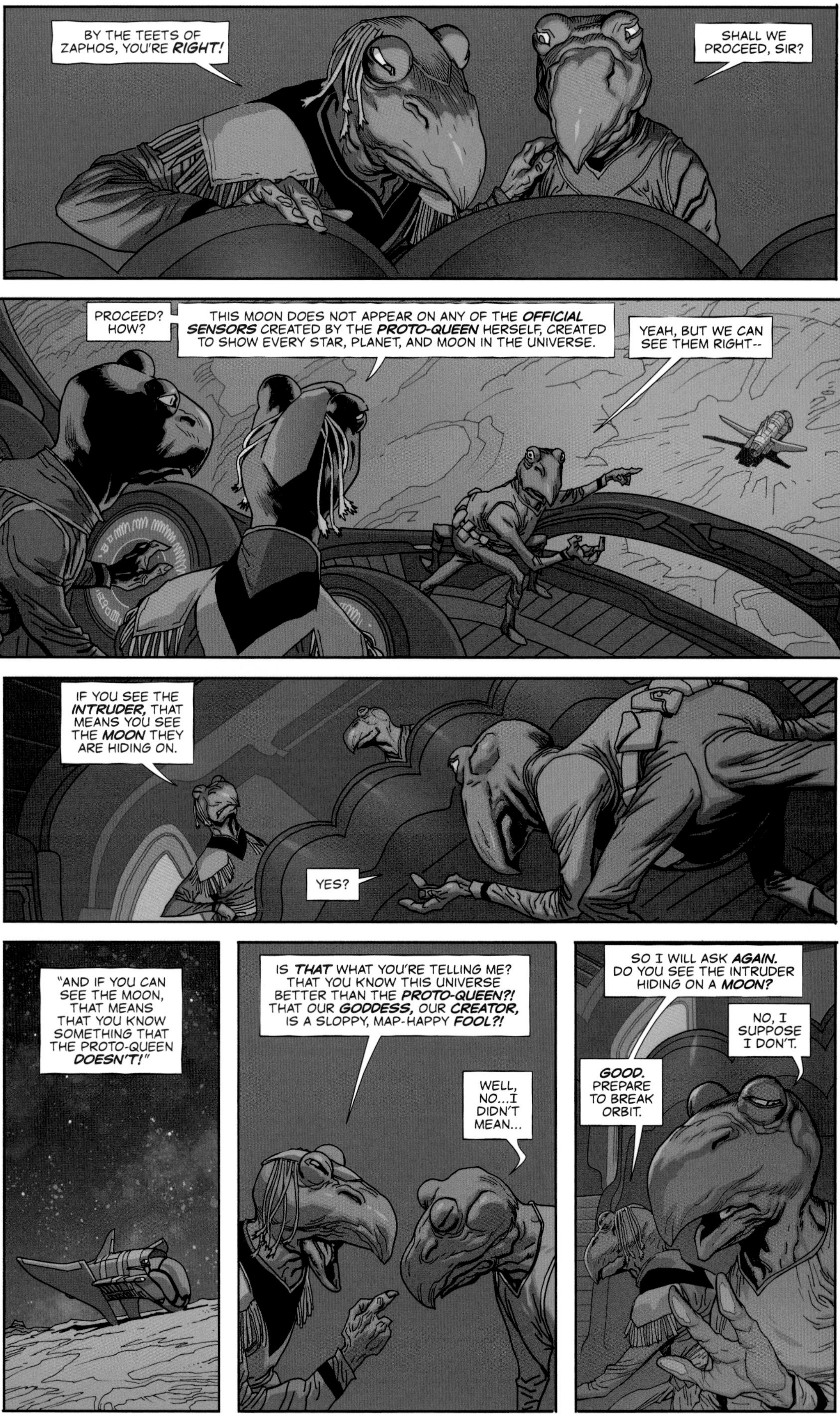
BY THE TEETS OF ZAPHOS, YOU'RE RIGHT!
SHALL WE PROCEED, SIR?
PROCEED? HOW?
THIS MOON DOES NOT APPEAR ON ANY OF THE OFFICIAL SENSORS CREATED BY THE PROTO-QUEEN HERSELF, CREATED TO SHOW EVERY STAR, PLANET, AND MOON IN THE UNIVERSE.
YEAH, BUT WE CAN SEE THEM RIGHT--
IF YOU SEE THE INTRUDER, THAT MEANS YOU SEE THE MOON THEY ARE HIDING ON.
YES?
"AND IF YOU CAN SEE THE MOON, THAT MEANS THAT YOU KNOW SOMETHING THAT THE PROTO-QUEEN DOESN'T!"
IS THAT WHAT YOU'RE TELLING ME? THAT YOU KNOW THIS UNIVERSE BETTER THAN THE PROTO-QUEEN?! THAT OUR GODDESS, OUR CREATOR, IS A SLOPPY, MAP-HAPPY FOOL?!
WELL, NO...I DIDN'T MEAN...
SO I WILL ASK AGAIN. DO YOU SEE THE INTRUDER HIDING ON A MOON?
NO, I SUPPOSE I DON'T.
GOOD. PREPARE TO BREAK ORBIT.

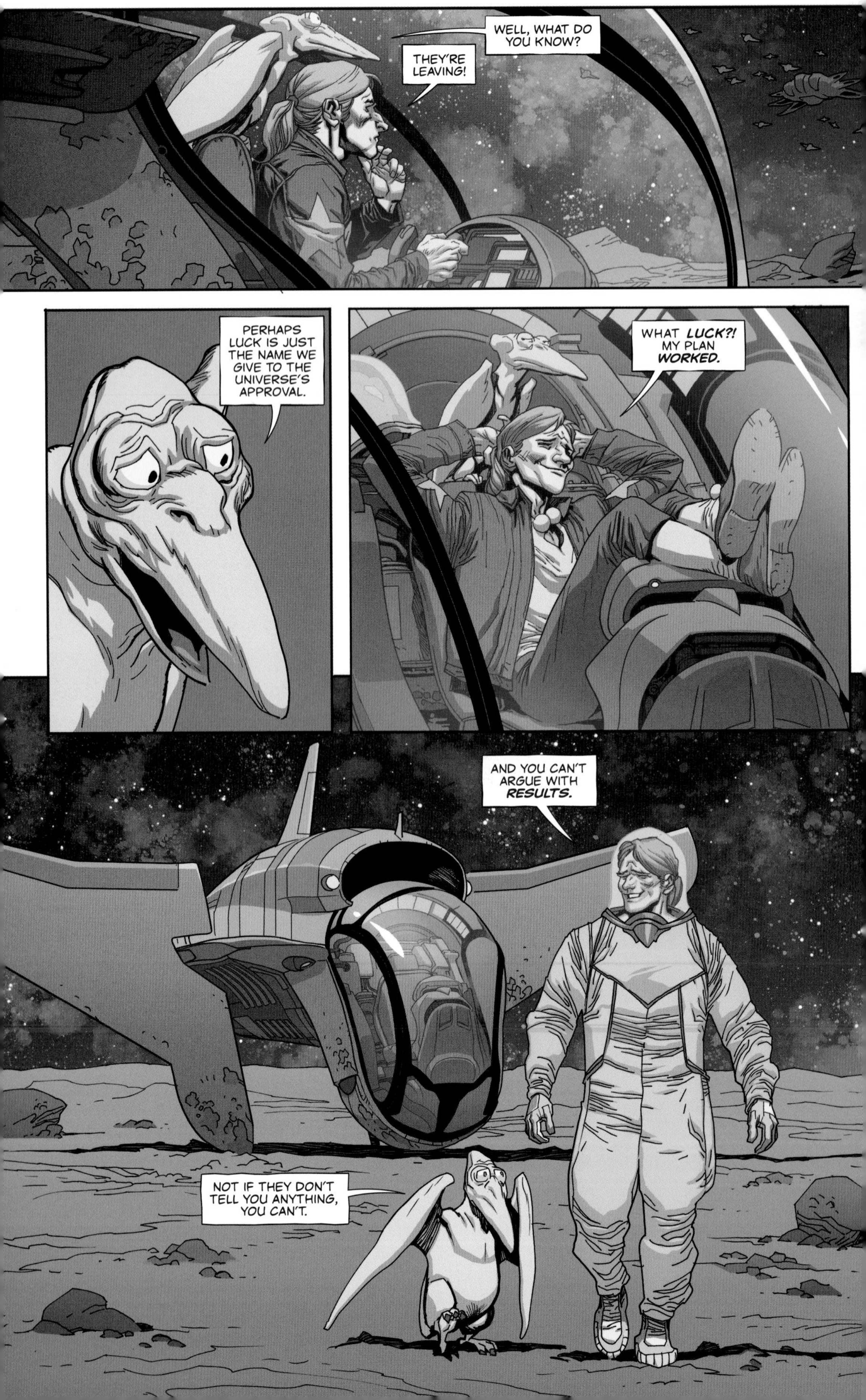
WELL, WHAT DO YOU KNOW?
THEY'RE LEAVING!
PERHAPS LUCK IS JUST THE NAME WE GIVE TO THE UNIVERSE'S APPROVAL.
WHAT *LUCK?!* MY PLAN *WORKED.*
AND YOU CAN'T ARGUE WITH *RESULTS.*
NOT IF THEY DON'T TELL YOU ANYTHING, YOU CAN'T.

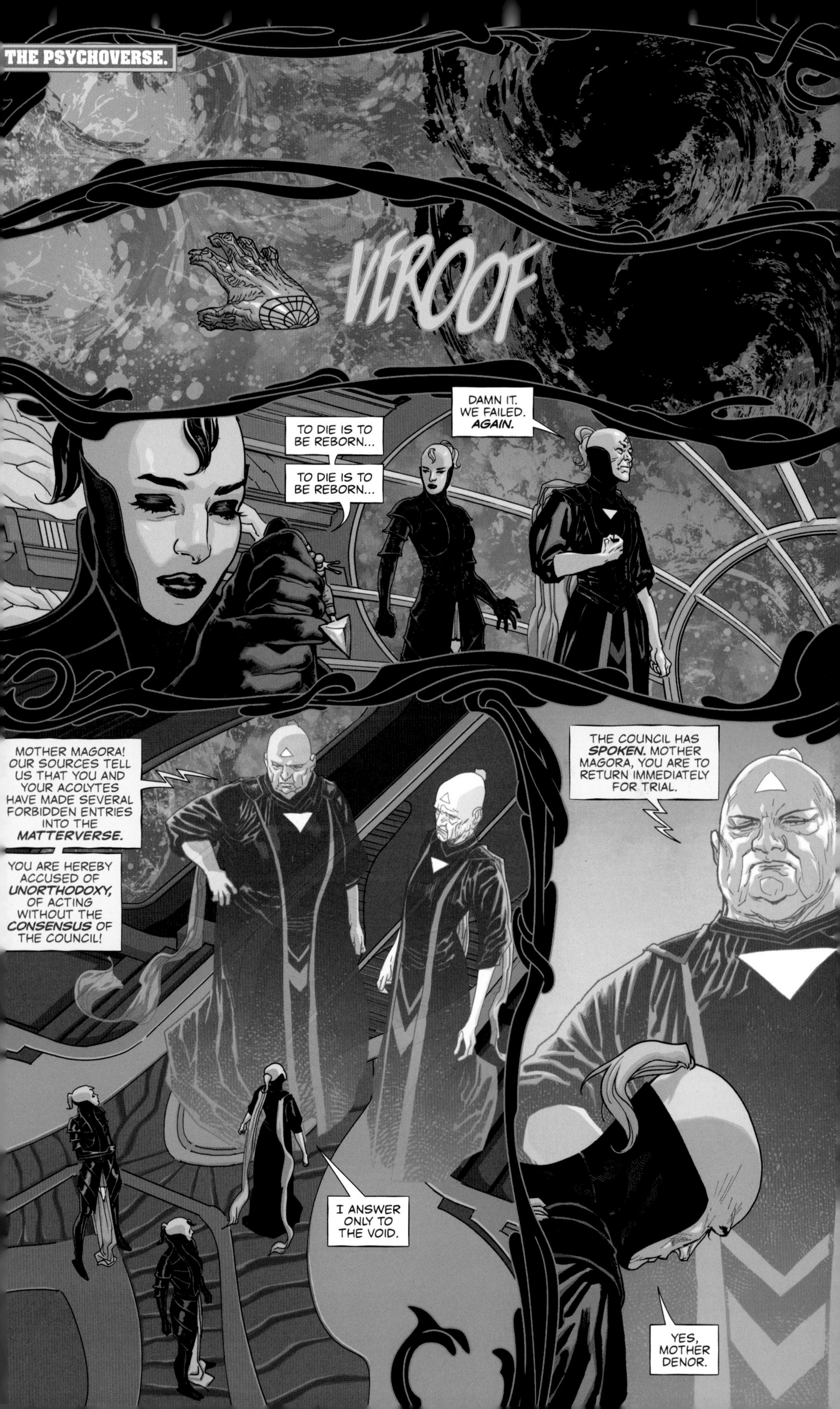
THE PSYCHOVERSE.
VLROOF
TO DIE IS TO BE REBORN...
TO DIE IS TO BE REBORN...
DAMN IT. WE FAILED. AGAIN.
MOTHER MAGORA! OUR SOURCES TELL US THAT YOU AND YOUR ACOLYTES HAVE MADE SEVERAL FORBIDDEN ENTRIES INTO THE MATTERVERSE.
YOU ARE HEREBY ACCUSED OF UNORTHODOXY, OF ACTING WITHOUT THE CONSENSUS OF THE COUNCIL!
THE COUNCIL HAS SPOKEN. MOTHER MAGORA, YOU ARE TO RETURN IMMEDIATELY FOR TRIAL.
I ANSWER ONLY TO THE VOID.
YES, MOTHER DENOR.

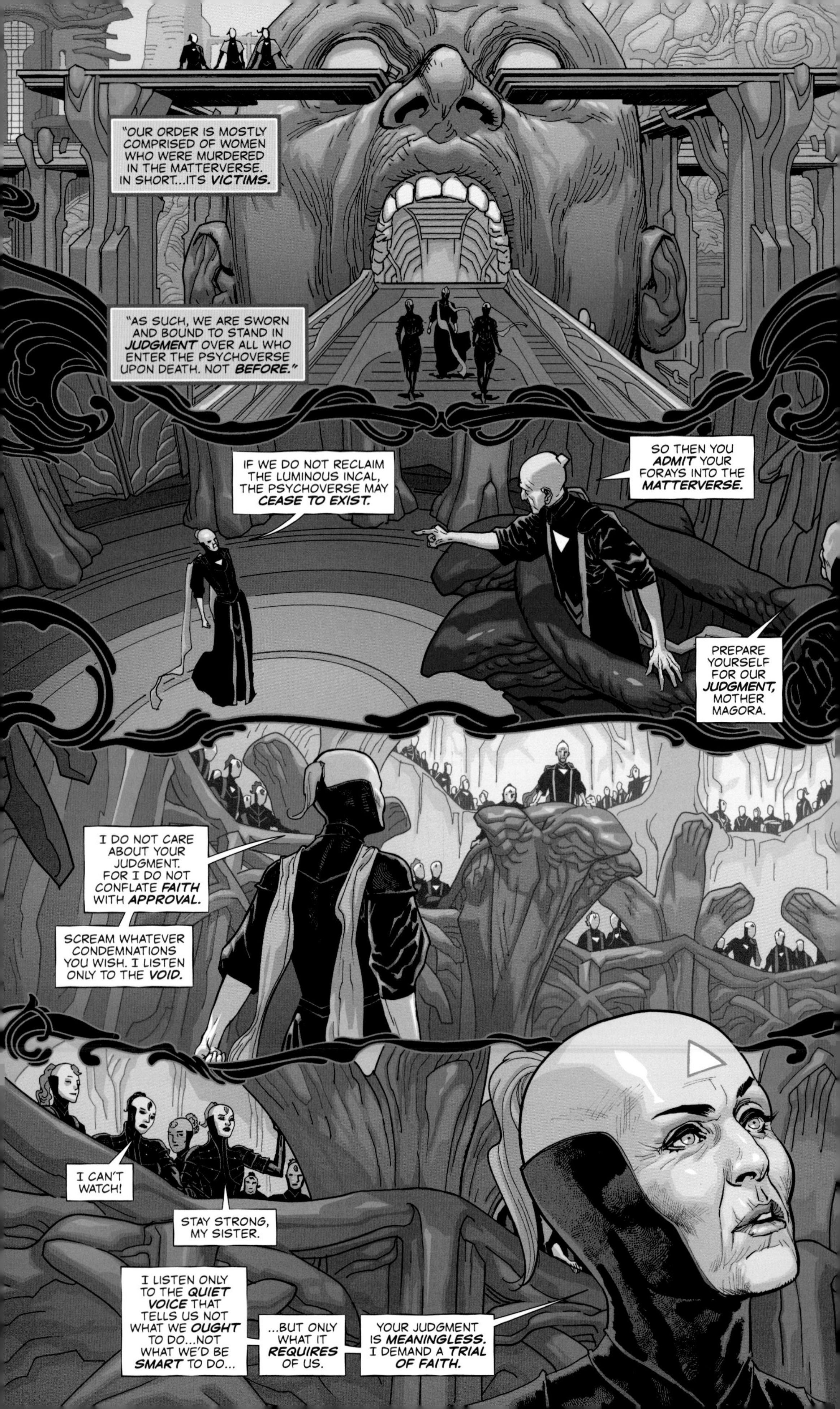
"OUR ORDER IS MOSTLY COMPRISED OF WOMEN WHO WERE MURDERED IN THE MATTERVERSE. IN SHORT...ITS *VICTIMS.*
"AS SUCH, WE ARE SWORN AND BOUND TO STAND IN *JUDGMENT* OVER ALL WHO ENTER THE PSYCHOVERSE UPON DEATH. NOT *BEFORE.*"
IF WE DO NOT RECLAIM THE LUMINOUS INCAL, THE PSYCHOVERSE MAY *CEASE TO EXIST.*
SO THEN YOU *ADMIT* YOUR FORAYS INTO THE *MATTERVERSE.*
PREPARE YOURSELF FOR OUR *JUDGMENT,* MOTHER MAGORA.
I DO NOT CARE ABOUT YOUR JUDGMENT. FOR I DO NOT CONFLATE *FAITH* WITH *APPROVAL.*
SCREAM WHATEVER CONDEMNATIONS YOU WISH. I LISTEN ONLY TO THE *VOID.*
I CAN'T WATCH!
STAY STRONG, MY SISTER.
I LISTEN ONLY TO THE *QUIET VOICE* THAT TELLS US NOT WHAT WE *OUGHT* TO DO...NOT WHAT WE'D BE *SMART* TO DO...
...BUT ONLY WHAT IT *REQUIRES* OF US.
YOUR JUDGMENT IS *MEANINGLESS.* I DEMAND A *TRIAL OF FAITH.*

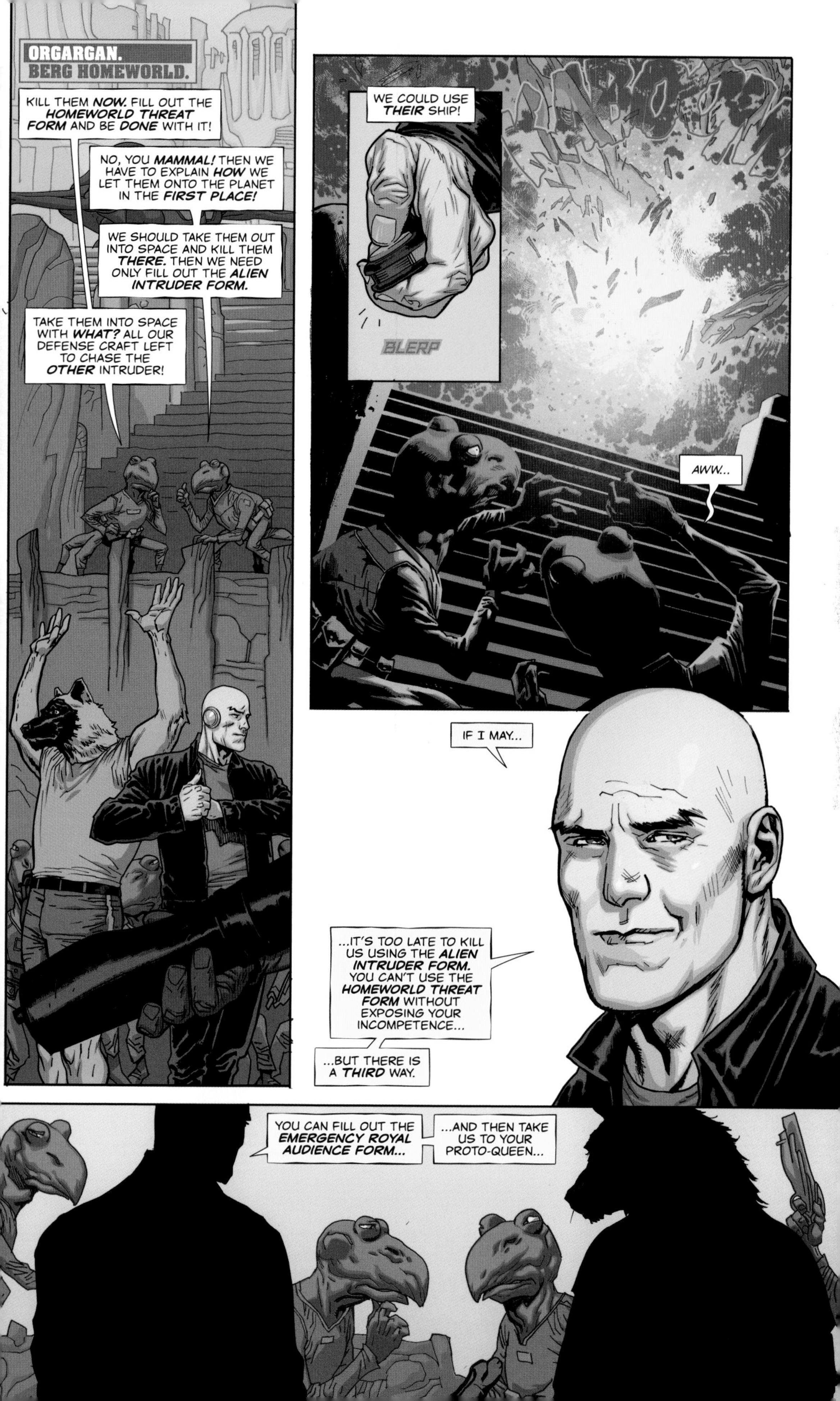
ORGARGAN.
BERG HOMEWORLD.
KILL THEM NOW. FILL OUT THE HOMEWORLD THREAT FORM AND BE DONE WITH IT!
NO, YOU MAMMAL! THEN WE HAVE TO EXPLAIN HOW WE LET THEM ONTO THE PLANET IN THE FIRST PLACE!
WE SHOULD TAKE THEM OUT INTO SPACE AND KILL THEM THERE. THEN WE NEED ONLY FILL OUT THE ALIEN INTRUDER FORM.
TAKE THEM INTO SPACE WITH WHAT? ALL OUR DEFENSE CRAFT LEFT TO CHASE THE OTHER INTRUDER!
WE COULD USE THEIR SHIP!
BLERP
AWW...
IF I MAY...
...IT'S TOO LATE TO KILL US USING THE ALIEN INTRUDER FORM. YOU CAN'T USE THE HOMEWORLD THREAT FORM WITHOUT EXPOSING YOUR INCOMPETENCE...
...BUT THERE IS A THIRD WAY.
YOU CAN FILL OUT THE EMERGENCY ROYAL AUDIENCE FORM...
...AND THEN TAKE US TO YOUR PROTO-QUEEN...

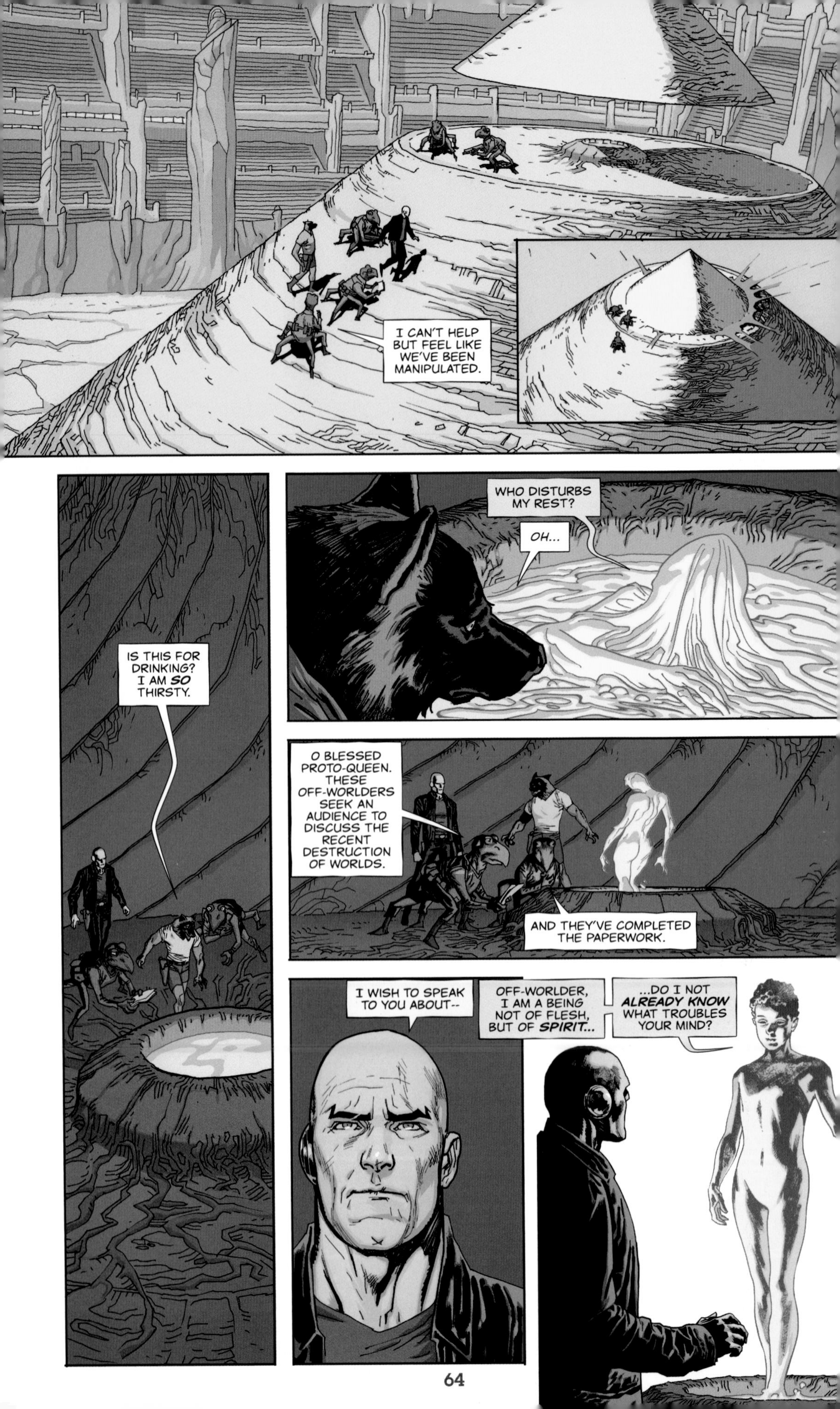

I CAN'T HELP BUT FEEL LIKE WE'VE BEEN MANIPULATED.
WHO DISTURBS MY REST?
OH...
IS THIS FOR DRINKING? I AM SO THIRSTY.
O BLESSED PROTO-QUEEN. THESE OFF-WORLDERS SEEK AN AUDIENCE TO DISCUSS THE RECENT DESTRUCTION OF WORLDS.
AND THEY'VE COMPLETED THE PAPERWORK.
I WISH TO SPEAK TO YOU ABOUT--
OFF-WORLDER, I AM A BEING NOT OF FLESH, BUT OF SPIRIT...
...DO I NOT ALREADY KNOW WHAT TROUBLES YOUR MIND?

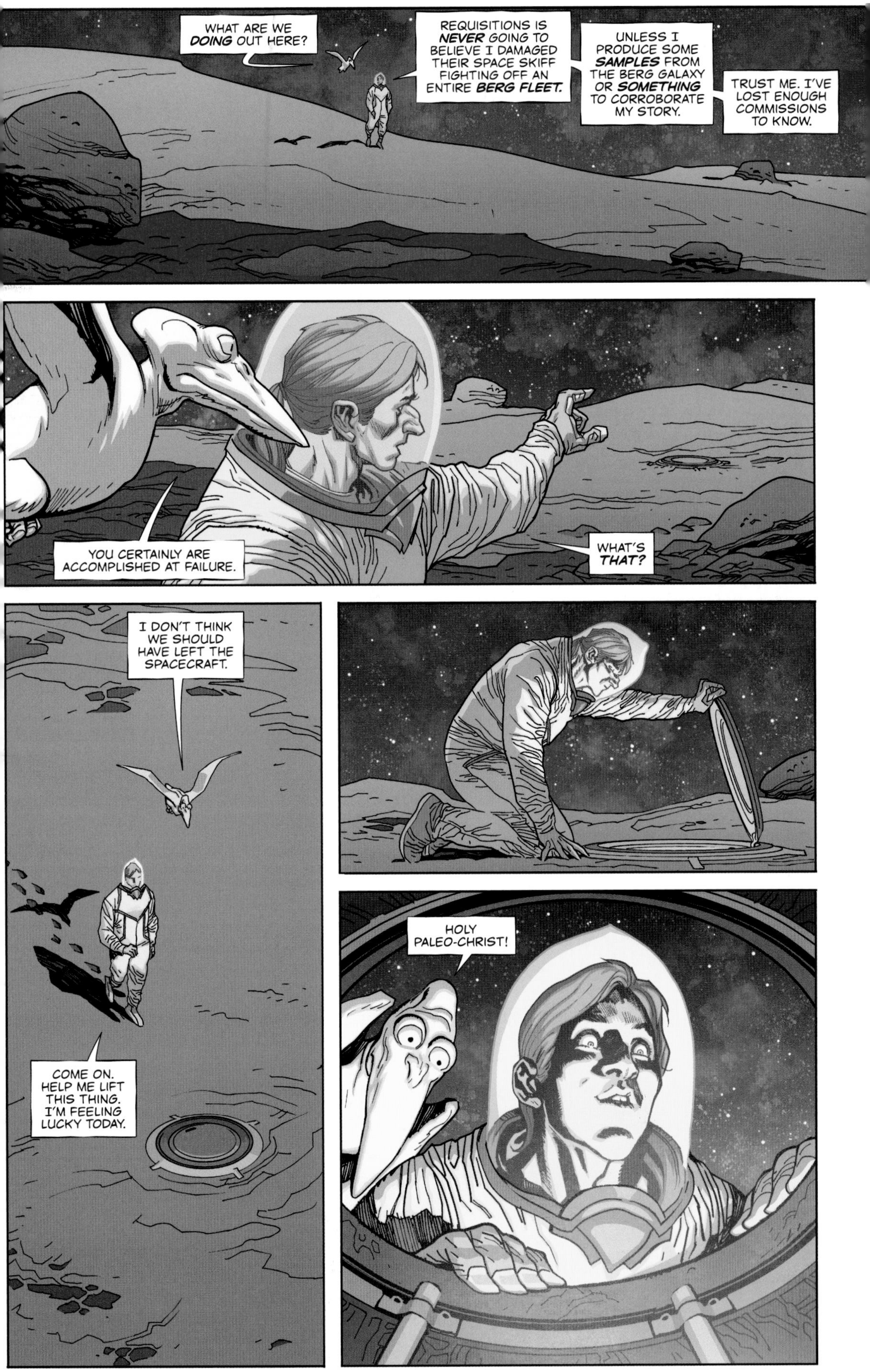
WHAT ARE WE DOING OUT HERE?
REQUISITIONS IS NEVER GOING TO BELIEVE I DAMAGED THEIR SPACE SKIFF FIGHTING OFF AN ENTIRE BERG FLEET.
UNLESS I PRODUCE SOME SAMPLES FROM THE BERG GALAXY OR SOMETHING TO CORROBORATE MY STORY.
TRUST ME. I'VE LOST ENOUGH COMMISSIONS TO KNOW.
YOU CERTAINLY ARE ACCOMPLISHED AT FAILURE.
WHAT'S THAT?
I DON'T THINK WE SHOULD HAVE LEFT THE SPACECRAFT.
COME ON. HELP ME LIFT THIS THING. I'M FEELING LUCKY TODAY.
HOLY PALEO-CHRIST!

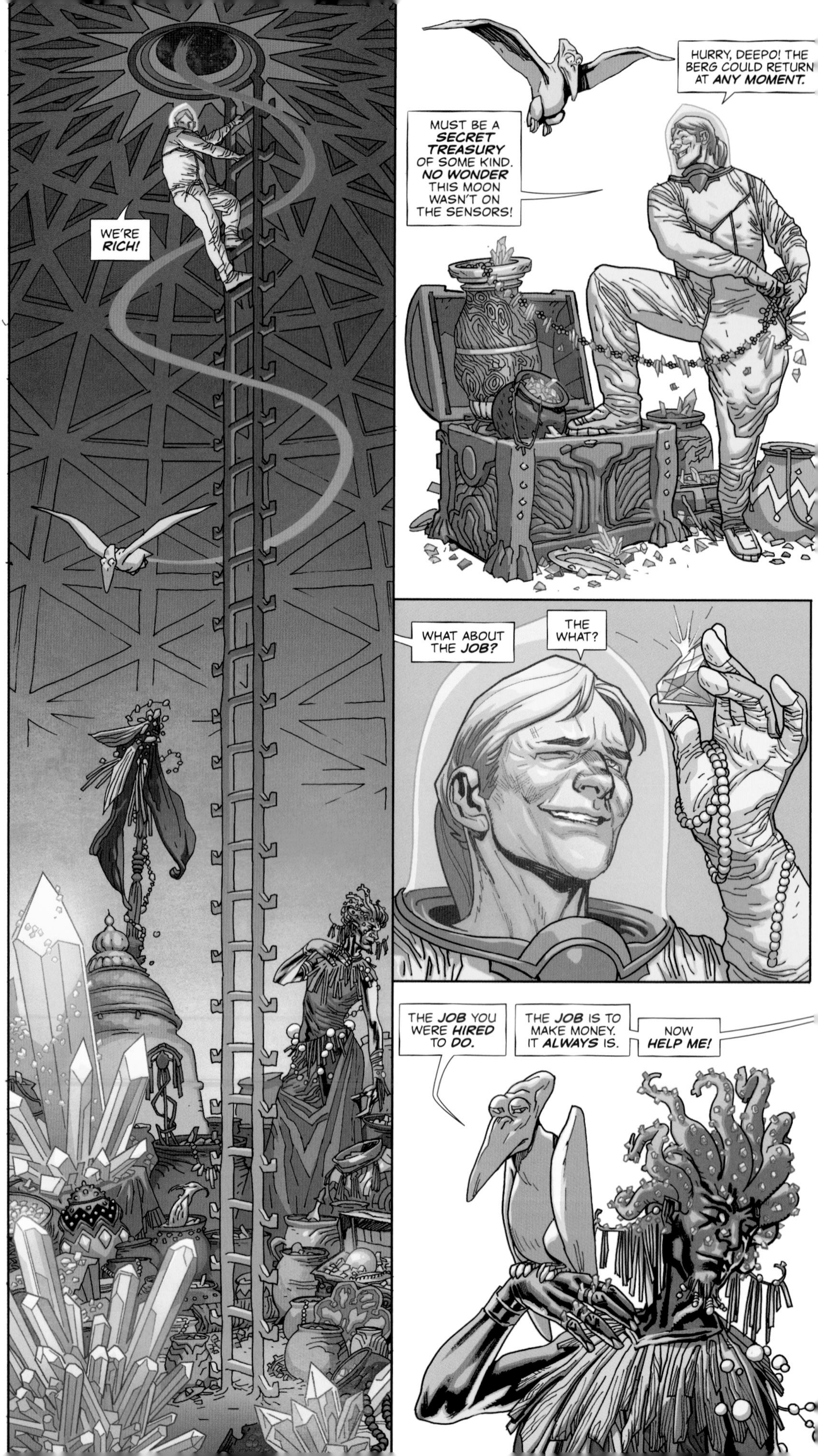
WE'RE *RICH!*
HURRY, DEEPO! THE BERG COULD RETURN AT *ANY MOMENT.*
MUST BE A ***SECRET TREASURY*** OF SOME KIND. ***NO WONDER*** THIS MOON WASN'T ON THE SENSORS!
WHAT ABOUT THE *JOB?*
THE WHAT?
THE *JOB* YOU WERE *HIRED* TO *DO.*
THE *JOB* IS TO MAKE MONEY. IT *ALWAYS* IS.
NOW *HELP ME!*

WE'RE GOING TO EAT THE *BEST* FOOD, LIVE IN THE *BIGGEST* CON-APT, SLEEP WITH THE MOST *EXPENSIVE* HOMEO-WHORES...

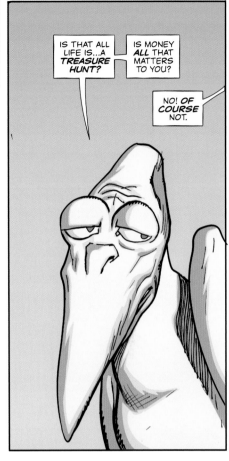

IS THAT ALL LIFE IS...A *TREASURE HUNT?*

IS MONEY *ALL* THAT MATTERS TO YOU?

NO! *OF COURSE* NOT.

BUT THIS *MONEY* WILL ALLOW ME TO PURSUE A MORE *SPIRITUAL EXISTENCE.*

I'LL HAVE THE *BEST* SPIRITUAL ADVISORS! THE *BIGGEST* TEMPLE! GO TO THE MOST *EXPENSIVE* SPIRITUAL RETREATS...

I THINK I SEE A SLIGHT PROBLEM WITH YOUR PLAN.

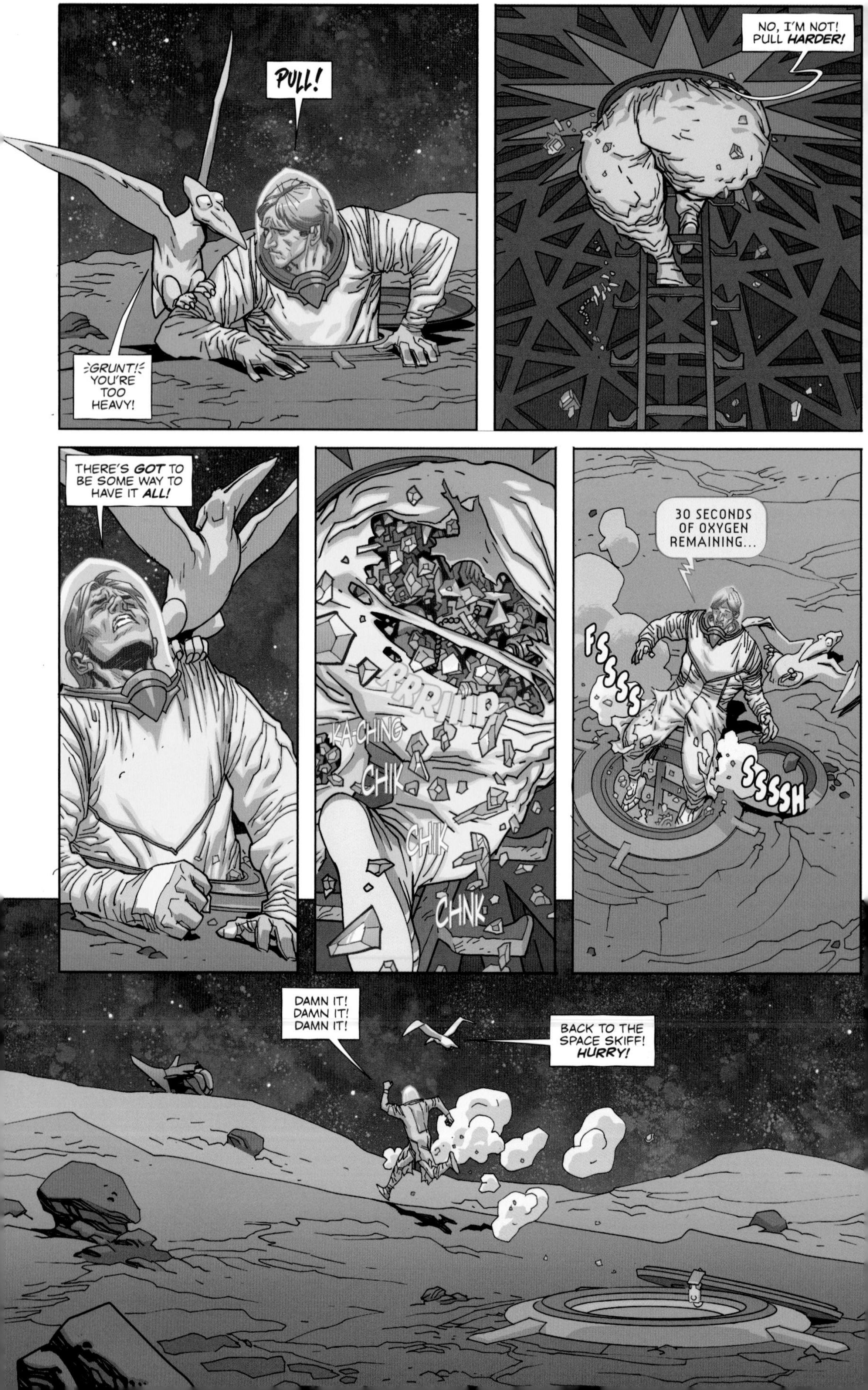
PULL!
:GRUNT!: YOU'RE TOO HEAVY!
NO, I'M NOT! PULL HARDER!
THERE'S GOT TO BE SOME WAY TO HAVE IT ALL!
RRRIIIP
KA-CHING
CHIK
CHIK
CHNK
30 SECONDS OF OXYGEN REMAINING...
FSSSS
SSSSH
DAMN IT! DAMN IT! DAMN IT!
BACK TO THE SPACE SKIFF! HURRY!

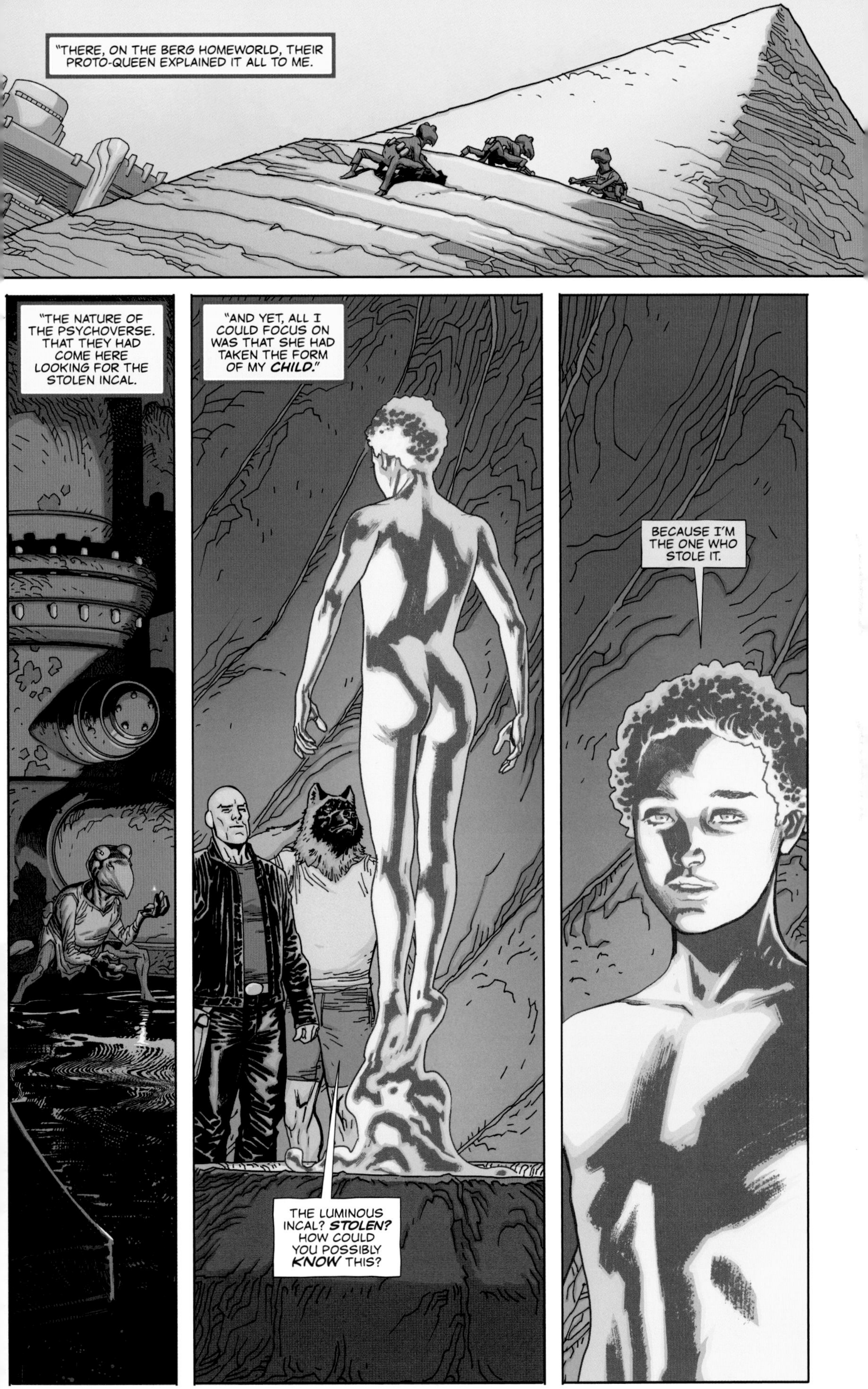
"THERE, ON THE BERG HOMEWORLD, THEIR PROTO-QUEEN EXPLAINED IT ALL TO ME.
"THE NATURE OF THE PSYCHOVERSE. THAT THEY HAD COME HERE LOOKING FOR THE STOLEN INCAL.
"AND YET, ALL I COULD FOCUS ON WAS THAT SHE HAD TAKEN THE FORM OF MY CHILD."
THE LUMINOUS INCAL? STOLEN? HOW COULD YOU POSSIBLY KNOW THIS?
BECAUSE I'M THE ONE WHO STOLE IT.

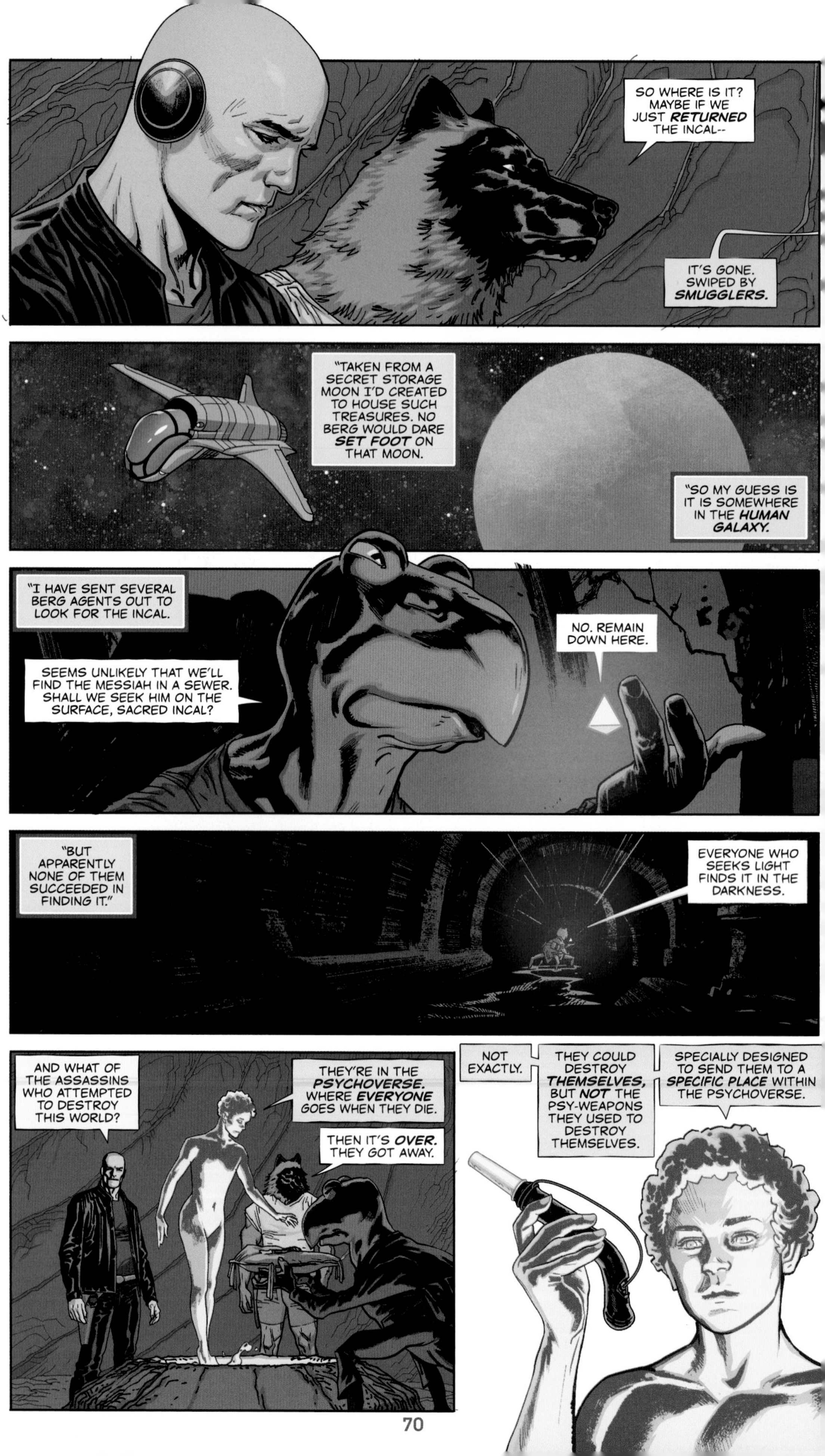
SO WHERE IS IT? MAYBE IF WE JUST RETURNED THE INCAL--
IT'S GONE. SWIPED BY SMUGGLERS.
"TAKEN FROM A SECRET STORAGE MOON I'D CREATED TO HOUSE SUCH TREASURES. NO BERG WOULD DARE SET FOOT ON THAT MOON.
"SO MY GUESS IS IT IS SOMEWHERE IN THE HUMAN GALAXY.
"I HAVE SENT SEVERAL BERG AGENTS OUT TO LOOK FOR THE INCAL.
SEEMS UNLIKELY THAT WE'LL FIND THE MESSIAH IN A SEWER. SHALL WE SEEK HIM ON THE SURFACE, SACRED INCAL?
NO. REMAIN DOWN HERE.
"BUT APPARENTLY NONE OF THEM SUCCEEDED IN FINDING IT."
EVERYONE WHO SEEKS LIGHT FINDS IT IN THE DARKNESS.
AND WHAT OF THE ASSASSINS WHO ATTEMPTED TO DESTROY THIS WORLD?
THEY'RE IN THE PSYCHOVERSE. WHERE EVERYONE GOES WHEN THEY DIE.
THEN IT'S OVER. THEY GOT AWAY.
NOT EXACTLY.
THEY COULD DESTROY THEMSELVES, BUT NOT THE PSY-WEAPONS THEY USED TO DESTROY THEMSELVES.
SPECIALLY DESIGNED TO SEND THEM TO A SPECIFIC PLACE WITHIN THE PSYCHOVERSE.

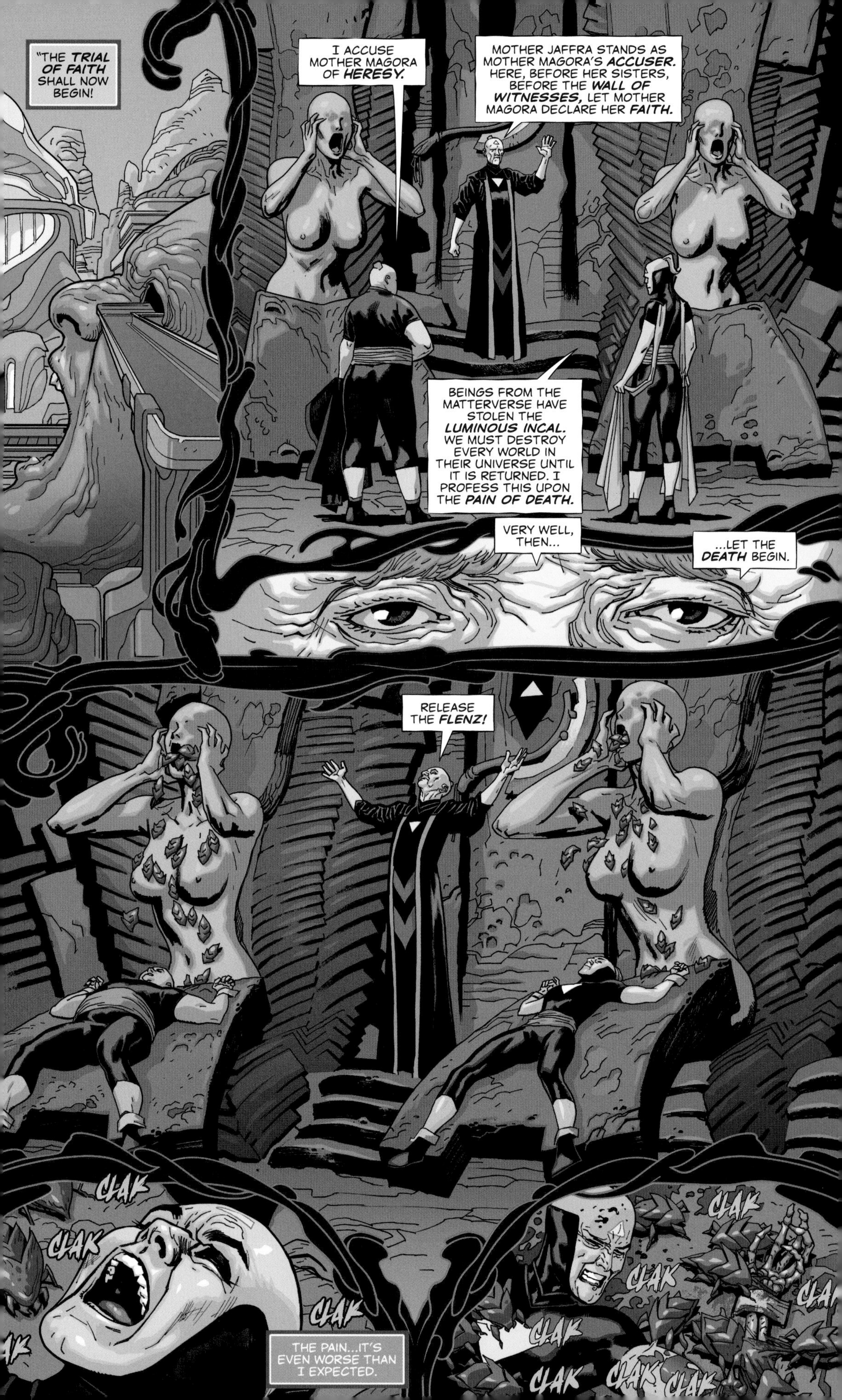
"THE TRIAL OF FAITH SHALL NOW BEGIN!
I ACCUSE MOTHER MAGORA OF HERESY.
MOTHER JAFFRA STANDS AS MOTHER MAGORA'S ACCUSER. HERE, BEFORE HER SISTERS, BEFORE THE WALL OF WITNESSES, LET MOTHER MAGORA DECLARE HER FAITH.
BEINGS FROM THE MATTERVERSE HAVE STOLEN THE LUMINOUS INCAL. WE MUST DESTROY EVERY WORLD IN THEIR UNIVERSE UNTIL IT IS RETURNED. I PROFESS THIS UPON THE PAIN OF DEATH.
VERY WELL, THEN...
...LET THE DEATH BEGIN.
RELEASE THE FLENZ!
CLAK
CLAK
CLAK
CLAK
CLAK
CLAK
THE PAIN...IT'S EVEN WORSE THAN I EXPECTED.
CLAK
CLAK
CLAK
CLAK

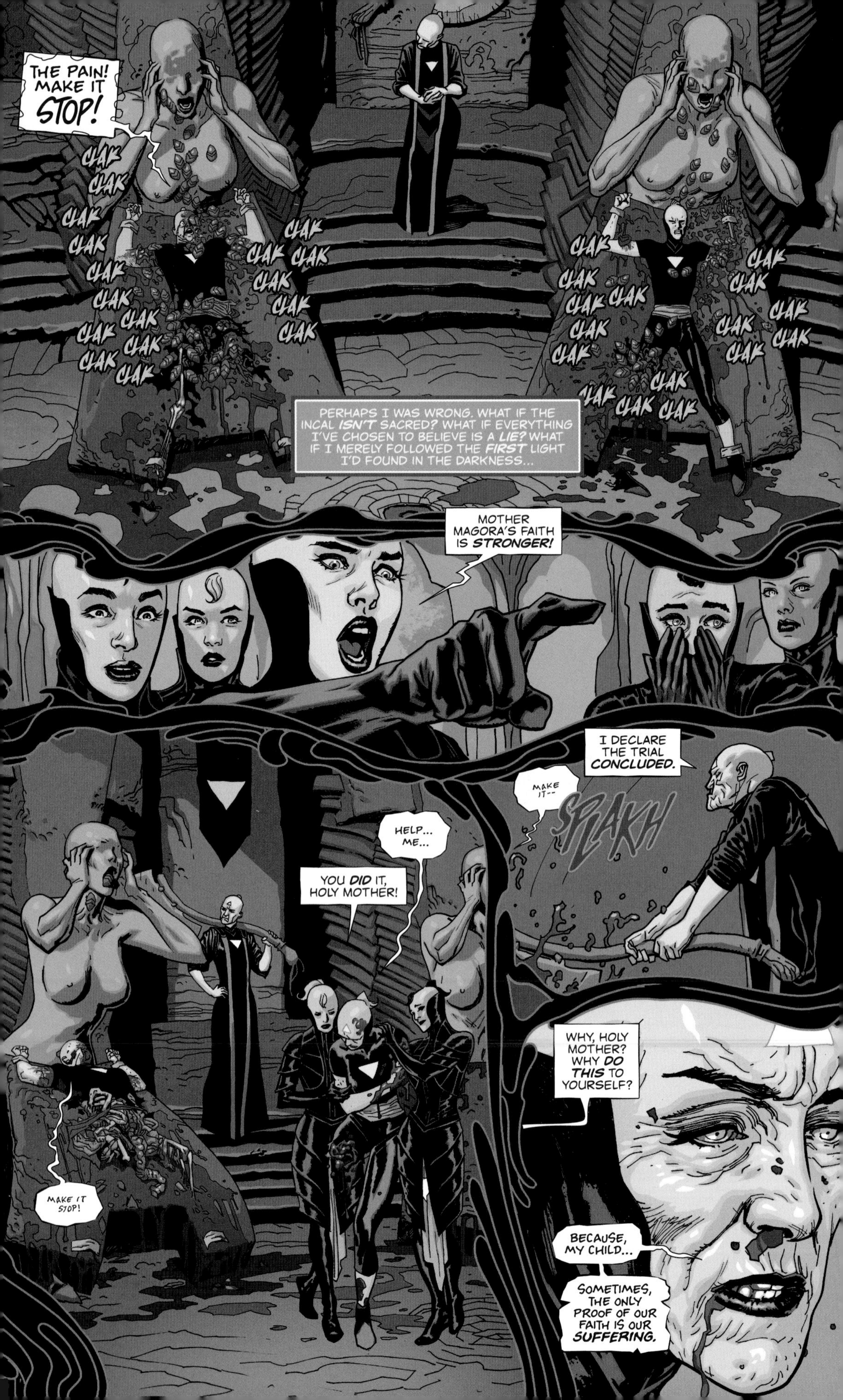
THE PAIN! MAKE IT STOP!
CLAK CLAK CLAK CLAK CLAK CLAK CLAK CLAK CLAK CLAK
CLAK CLAK CLAK CLAK CLAK CLAK
CLAK CLAK CLAK CLAK CLAK CLAK CLAK CLAK CLAK CLAK CLAK CLAK CLAK
PERHAPS I WAS WRONG. WHAT IF THE INCAL ISN'T SACRED? WHAT IF EVERYTHING I'VE CHOSEN TO BELIEVE IS A LIE? WHAT IF I MERELY FOLLOWED THE FIRST LIGHT I'D FOUND IN THE DARKNESS...
MOTHER MAGORA'S FAITH IS STRONGER!
HELP... ME...
YOU DID IT, HOLY MOTHER!
MAKE IT STOP!
I DECLARE THE TRIAL CONCLUDED.
MAKE IT--
SPLAKH
WHY, HOLY MOTHER? WHY DO THIS TO YOURSELF?
BECAUSE, MY CHILD...
SOMETIMES, THE ONLY PROOF OF OUR FAITH IS OUR SUFFERING.

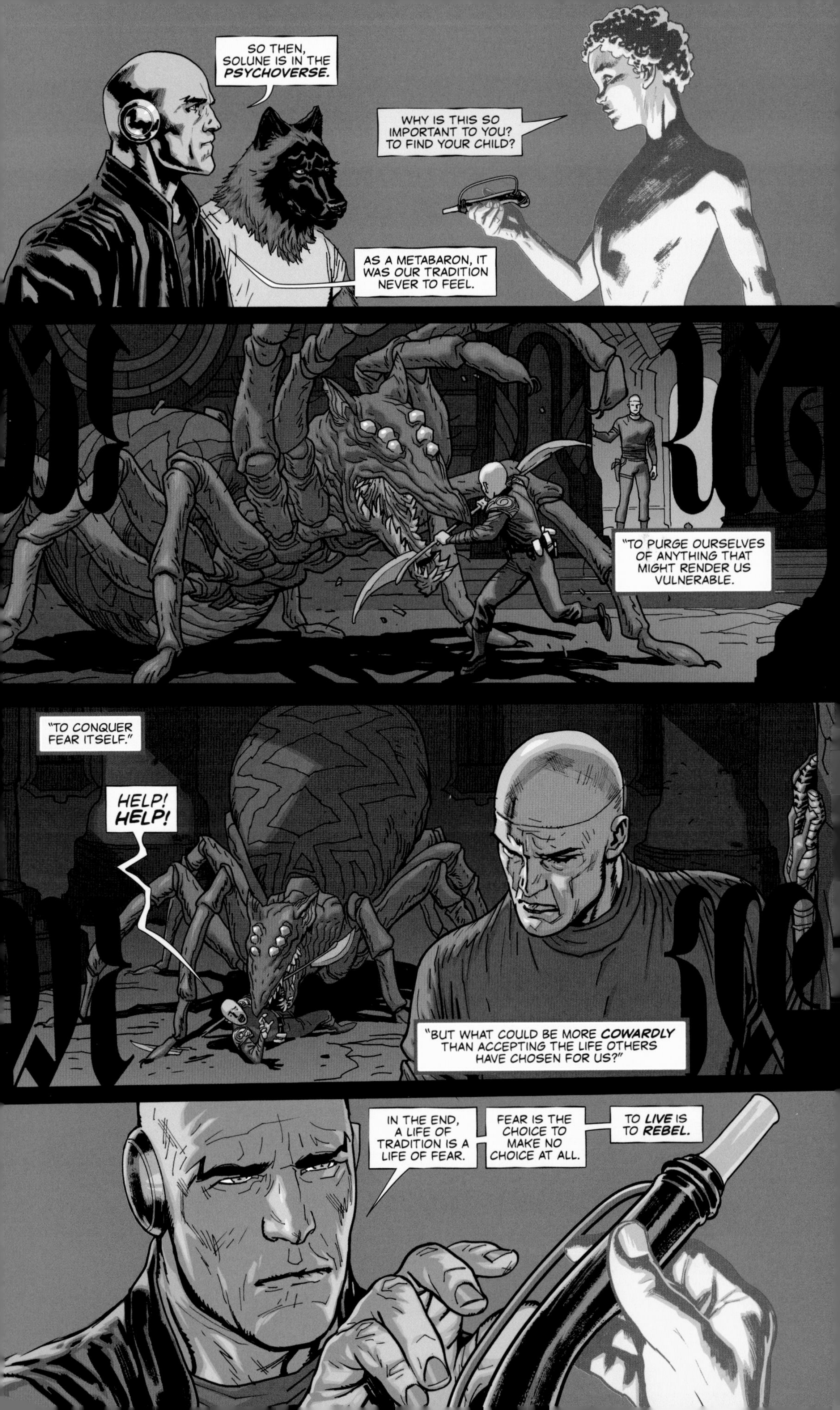

SO THEN, SOLUNE IS IN THE *PSYCHOVERSE.*
WHY IS THIS SO IMPORTANT TO YOU? TO FIND YOUR CHILD?
AS A METABARON, IT WAS OUR TRADITION NEVER TO FEEL.
"TO PURGE OURSELVES OF ANYTHING THAT MIGHT RENDER US VULNERABLE.
"TO CONQUER FEAR ITSELF."
HELP! ***HELP!***
"BUT WHAT COULD BE MORE ***COWARDLY*** THAN ACCEPTING THE LIFE OTHERS HAVE CHOSEN FOR US?"
IN THE END, A LIFE OF TRADITION IS A LIFE OF FEAR.
FEAR IS THE CHOICE TO MAKE NO CHOICE AT ALL.
TO ***LIVE*** IS TO ***REBEL.***

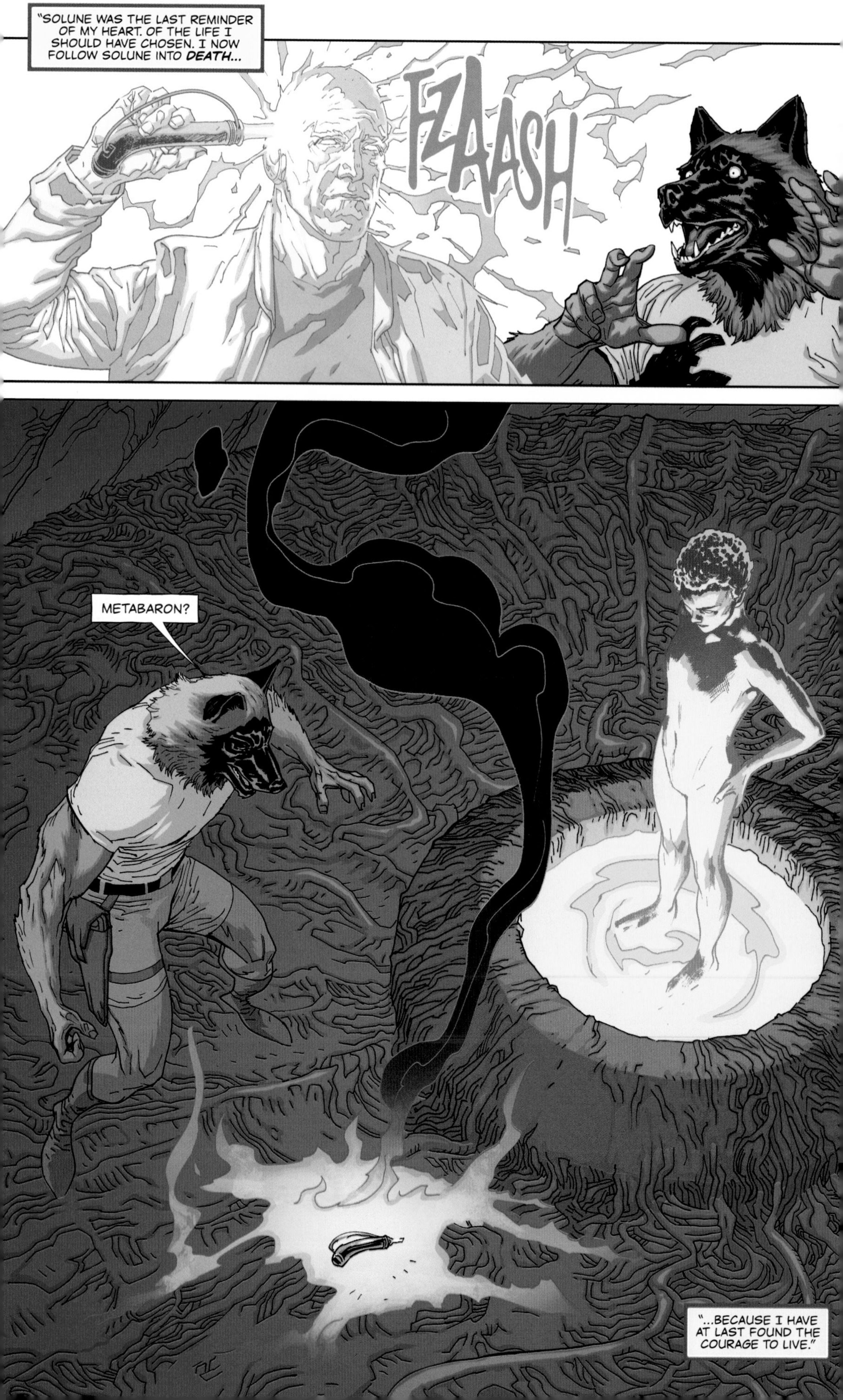
"SOLUNE WAS THE LAST REMINDER OF MY HEART. OF THE LIFE I SHOULD HAVE CHOSEN. I NOW FOLLOW SOLUNE INTO DEATH...
FZAASH
METABARON?
"...BECAUSE I HAVE AT LAST FOUND THE COURAGE TO LIVE."

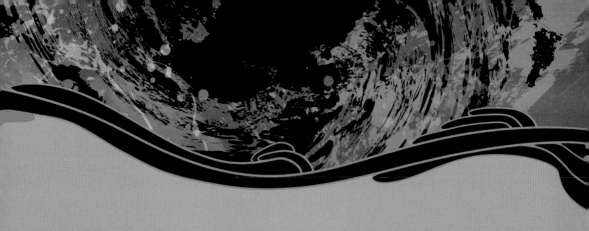

CHAPTER 4

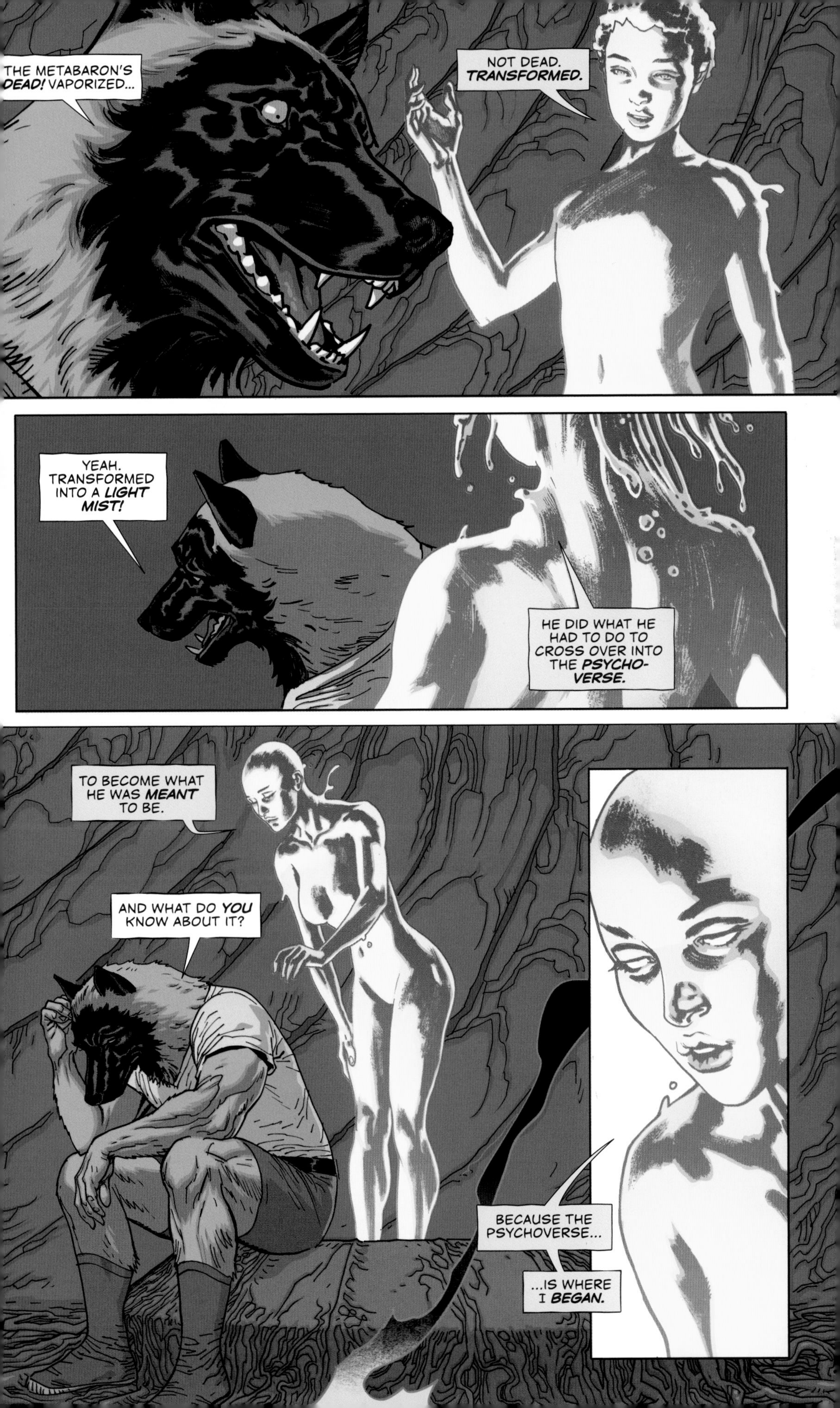
THE METABARON'S DEAD! VAPORIZED...
NOT DEAD. TRANSFORMED.
YEAH. TRANSFORMED INTO A LIGHT MIST!
HE DID WHAT HE HAD TO DO TO CROSS OVER INTO THE PSYCHO-VERSE.
TO BECOME WHAT HE WAS MEANT TO BE.
AND WHAT DO YOU KNOW ABOUT IT?
BECAUSE THE PSYCHOVERSE...
...IS WHERE I BEGAN.

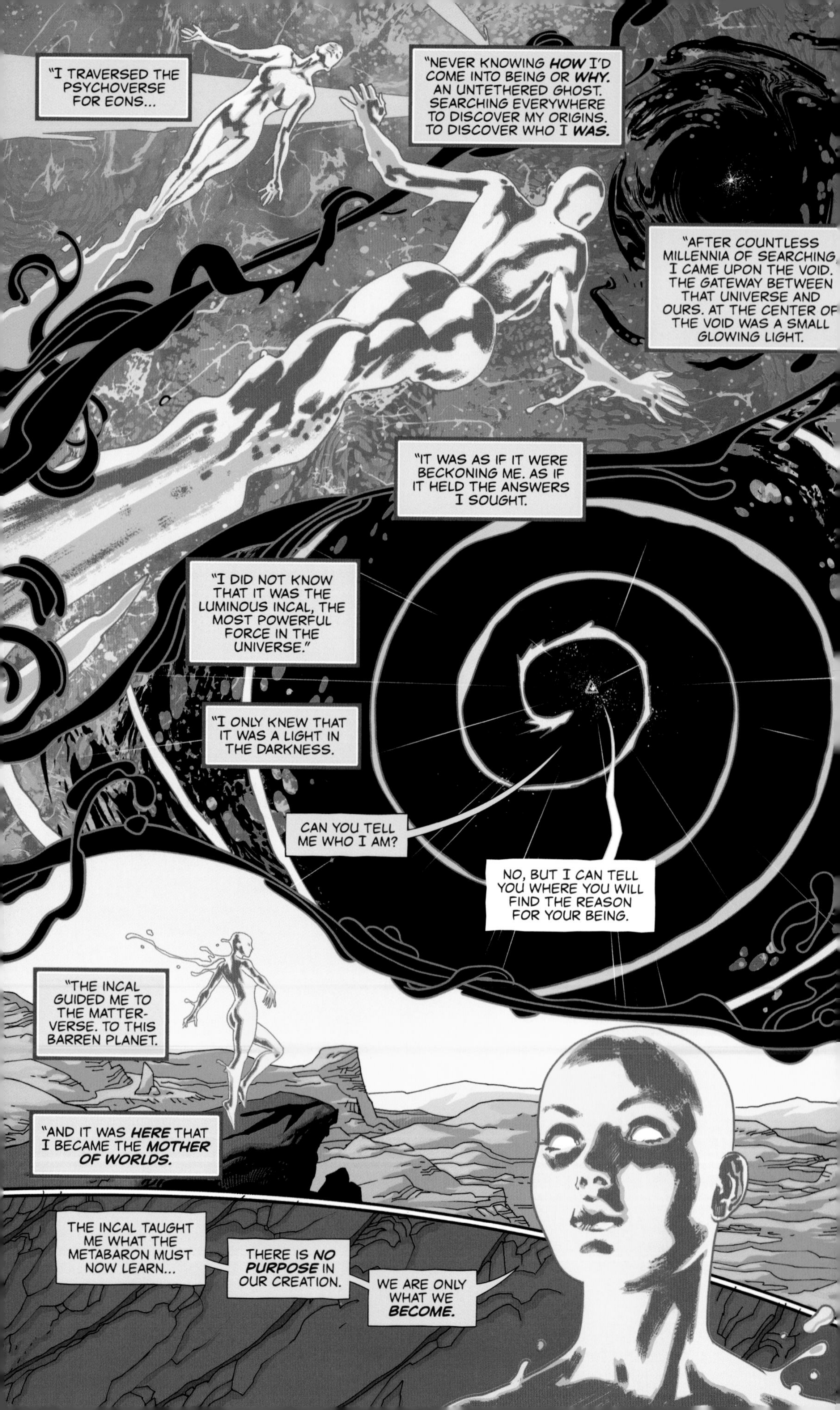

"I TRAVERSED THE PSYCHOVERSE FOR EONS...
"NEVER KNOWING **HOW** I'D COME INTO BEING OR **WHY.** AN UNTETHERED GHOST. SEARCHING EVERYWHERE TO DISCOVER MY ORIGINS. TO DISCOVER WHO I **WAS.**
"AFTER COUNTLESS MILLENNIA OF SEARCHING I CAME UPON THE VOID. THE GATEWAY BETWEEN THAT UNIVERSE AND OURS. AT THE CENTER OF THE VOID WAS A SMALL GLOWING LIGHT.
"IT WAS AS IF IT WERE BECKONING ME. AS IF IT HELD THE ANSWERS I SOUGHT.
"I DID NOT KNOW THAT IT WAS THE LUMINOUS INCAL, THE MOST POWERFUL FORCE IN THE UNIVERSE."
"I ONLY KNEW THAT IT WAS A LIGHT IN THE DARKNESS.
CAN YOU TELL ME WHO I AM?
NO, BUT I CAN TELL YOU WHERE YOU WILL FIND THE REASON FOR YOUR BEING.
"THE INCAL GUIDED ME TO THE MATTER-VERSE. TO THIS BARREN PLANET.
"AND IT WAS **HERE** THAT I BECAME THE **MOTHER OF WORLDS.**
THE INCAL TAUGHT ME WHAT THE METABARON MUST NOW LEARN...
THERE IS **NO PURPOSE** IN OUR CREATION.
WE ARE ONLY WHAT WE **BECOME.**

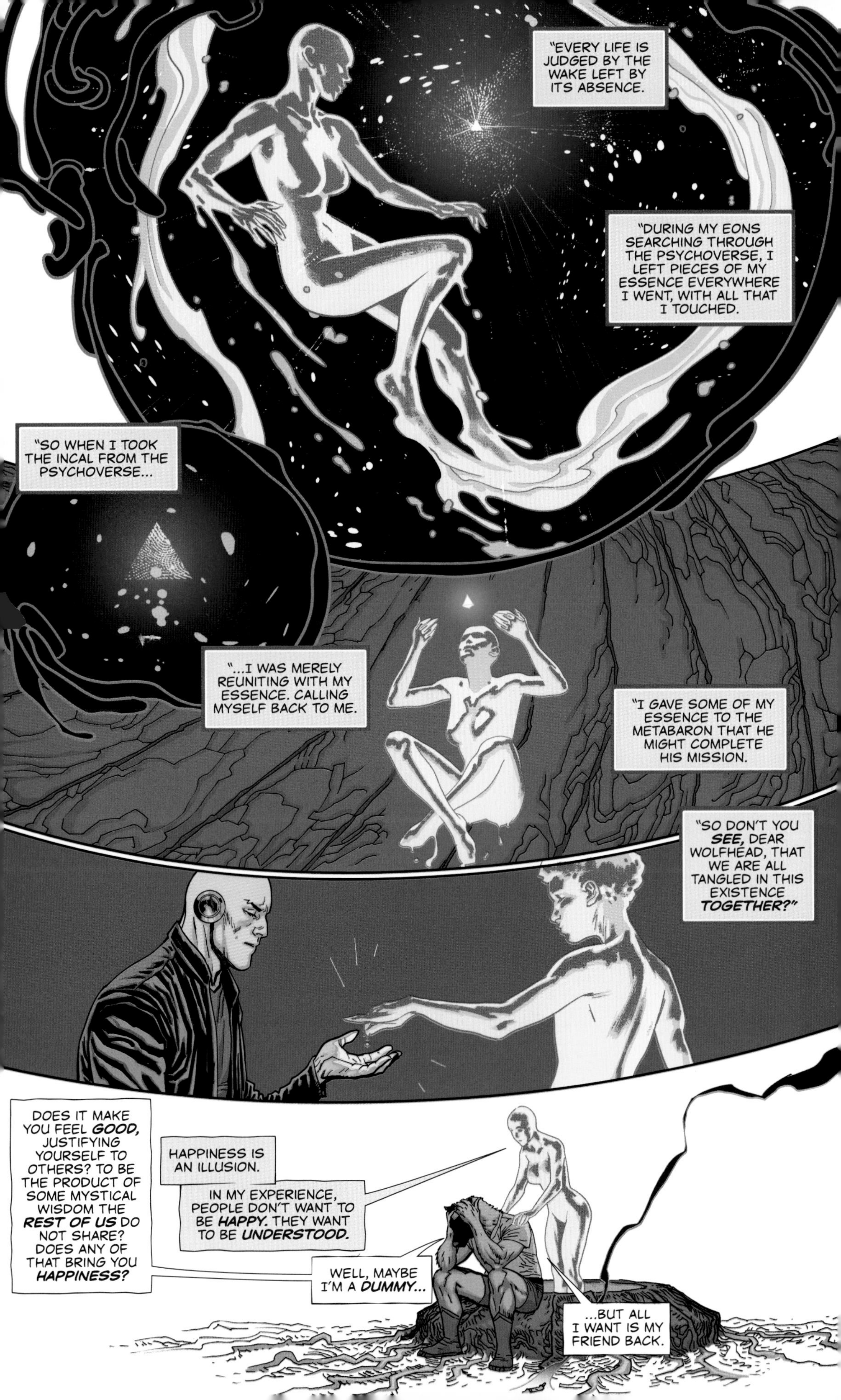
"EVERY LIFE IS JUDGED BY THE WAKE LEFT BY ITS ABSENCE.
"DURING MY EONS SEARCHING THROUGH THE PSYCHOVERSE, I LEFT PIECES OF MY ESSENCE EVERYWHERE I WENT, WITH ALL THAT I TOUCHED.
"SO WHEN I TOOK THE INCAL FROM THE PSYCHOVERSE...
"...I WAS MERELY REUNITING WITH MY ESSENCE. CALLING MYSELF BACK TO ME.
"I GAVE SOME OF MY ESSENCE TO THE METABARON THAT HE MIGHT COMPLETE HIS MISSION.
"SO DON'T YOU SEE, DEAR WOLFHEAD, THAT WE ARE ALL TANGLED IN THIS EXISTENCE TOGETHER?"
DOES IT MAKE YOU FEEL GOOD, JUSTIFYING YOURSELF TO OTHERS? TO BE THE PRODUCT OF SOME MYSTICAL WISDOM THE REST OF US DO NOT SHARE? DOES ANY OF THAT BRING YOU HAPPINESS?
HAPPINESS IS AN ILLUSION.
IN MY EXPERIENCE, PEOPLE DON'T WANT TO BE HAPPY. THEY WANT TO BE UNDERSTOOD.
WELL, MAYBE I'M A DUMMY...
...BUT ALL I WANT IS MY FRIEND BACK.

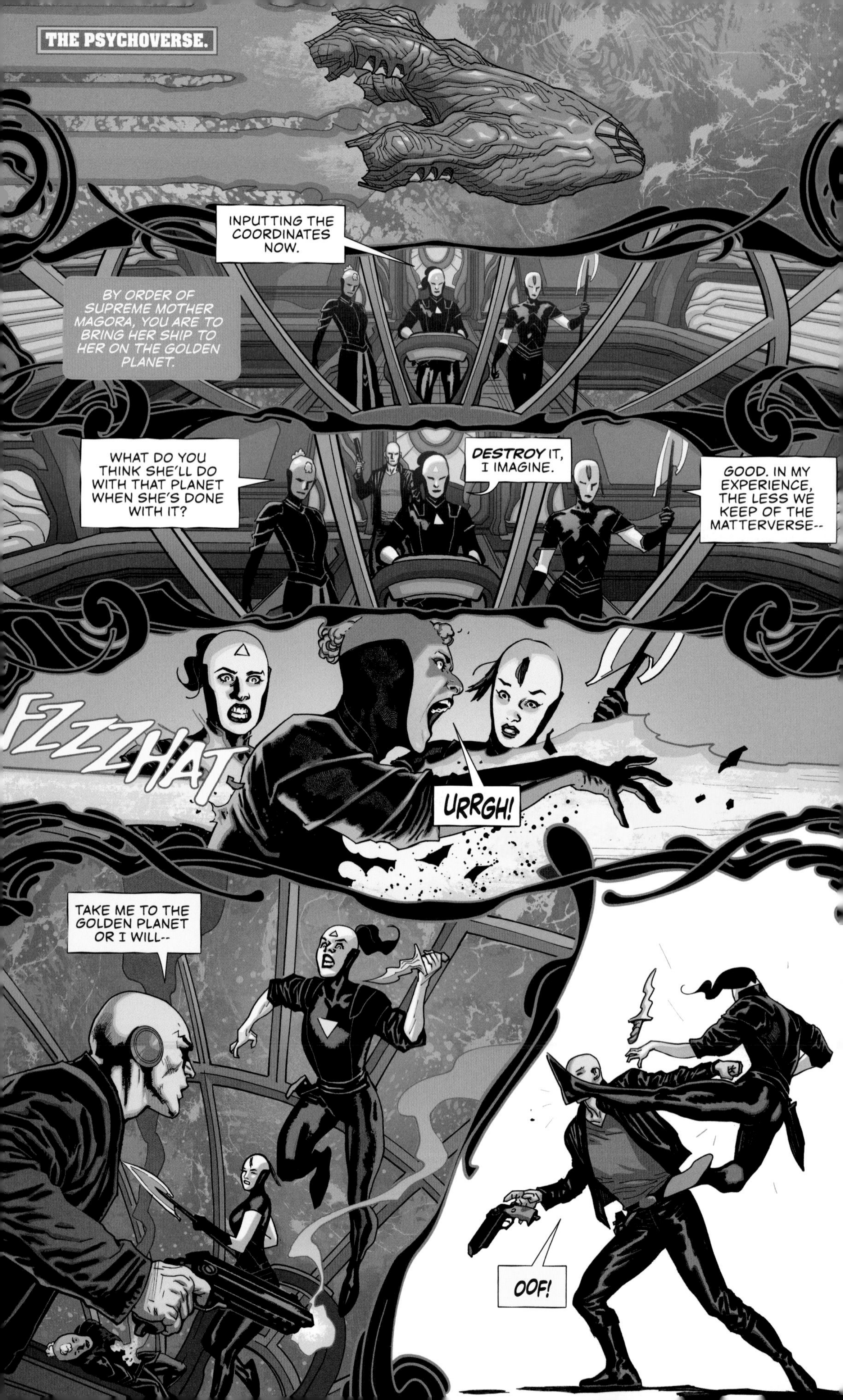
THE PSYCHOVERSE.
INPUTTING THE COORDINATES NOW.
BY ORDER OF SUPREME MOTHER MAGORA, YOU ARE TO BRING HER SHIP TO HER ON THE GOLDEN PLANET.
WHAT DO YOU THINK SHE'LL DO WITH THAT PLANET WHEN SHE'S DONE WITH IT?
DESTROY IT, I IMAGINE.
GOOD. IN MY EXPERIENCE, THE LESS WE KEEP OF THE MATTERVERSE--
FZZZHAT
URRGH!
TAKE ME TO THE GOLDEN PLANET OR I WILL--
OOF!

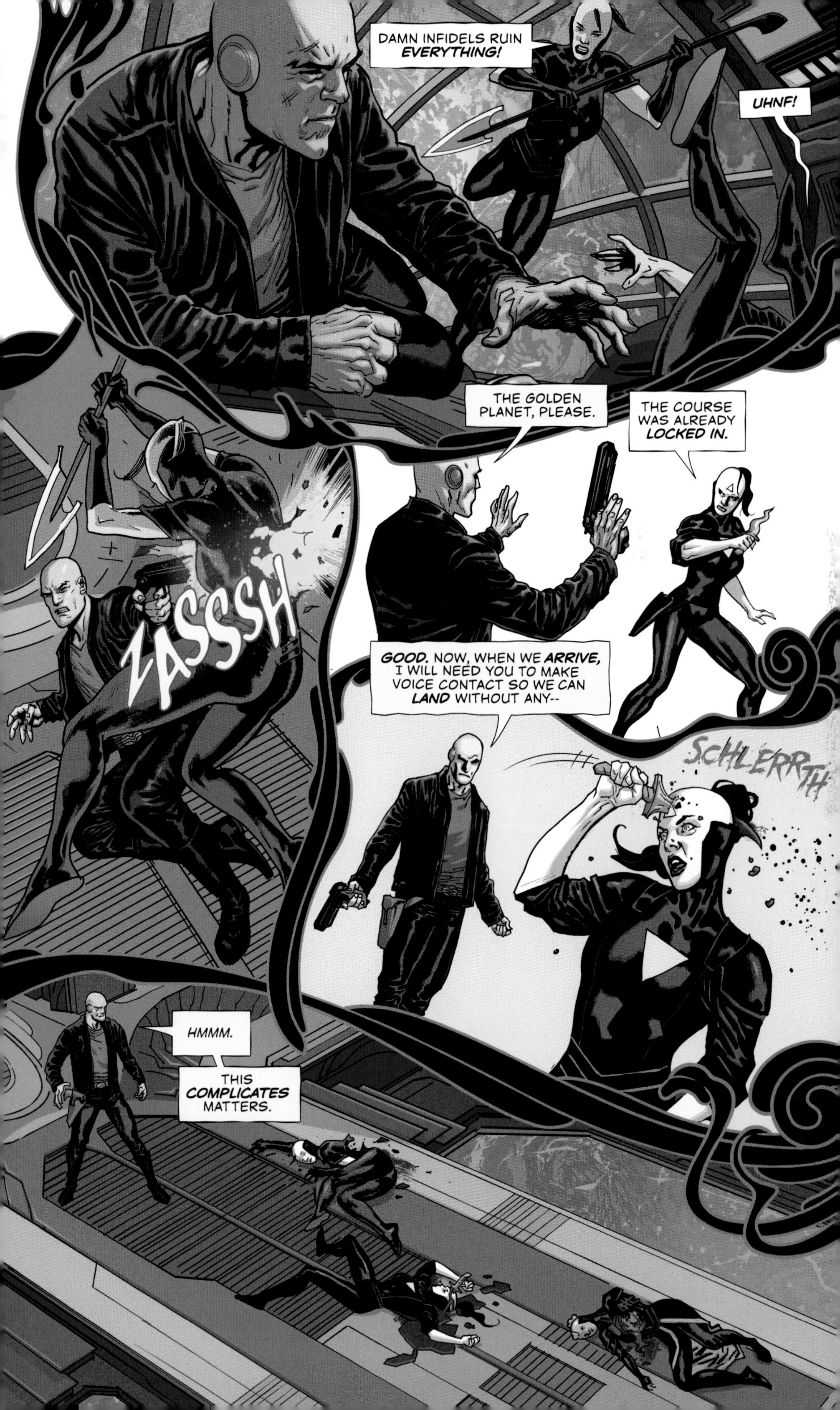
DAMN INFIDELS RUIN EVERYTHING!
UHNF!
ZASSSH
THE GOLDEN PLANET, PLEASE.
THE COURSE WAS ALREADY LOCKED IN.
GOOD. NOW, WHEN WE ARRIVE, I WILL NEED YOU TO MAKE VOICE CONTACT SO WE CAN LAND WITHOUT ANY--
SCHLERRTH
HMMM.
THIS COMPLICATES MATTERS.

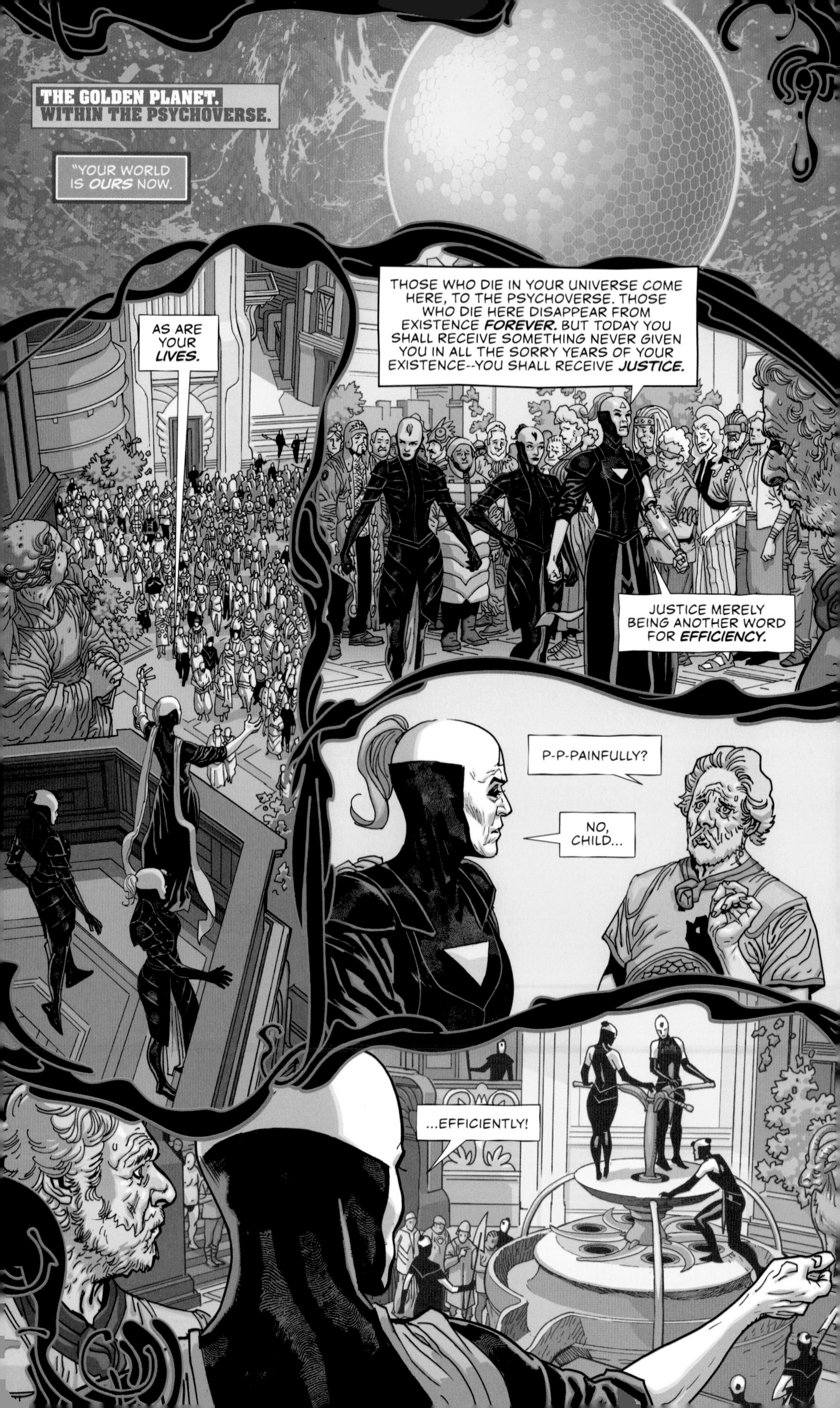
THE GOLDEN PLANET. WITHIN THE PSYCHOVERSE.
"YOUR WORLD IS OURS NOW.
AS ARE YOUR LIVES.
THOSE WHO DIE IN YOUR UNIVERSE COME HERE, TO THE PSYCHOVERSE. THOSE WHO DIE HERE DISAPPEAR FROM EXISTENCE FOREVER. BUT TODAY YOU SHALL RECEIVE SOMETHING NEVER GIVEN YOU IN ALL THE SORRY YEARS OF YOUR EXISTENCE--YOU SHALL RECEIVE JUSTICE.
JUSTICE MERELY BEING ANOTHER WORD FOR EFFICIENCY.
P-P-PAINFULLY?
NO, CHILD...
...EFFICIENTLY!

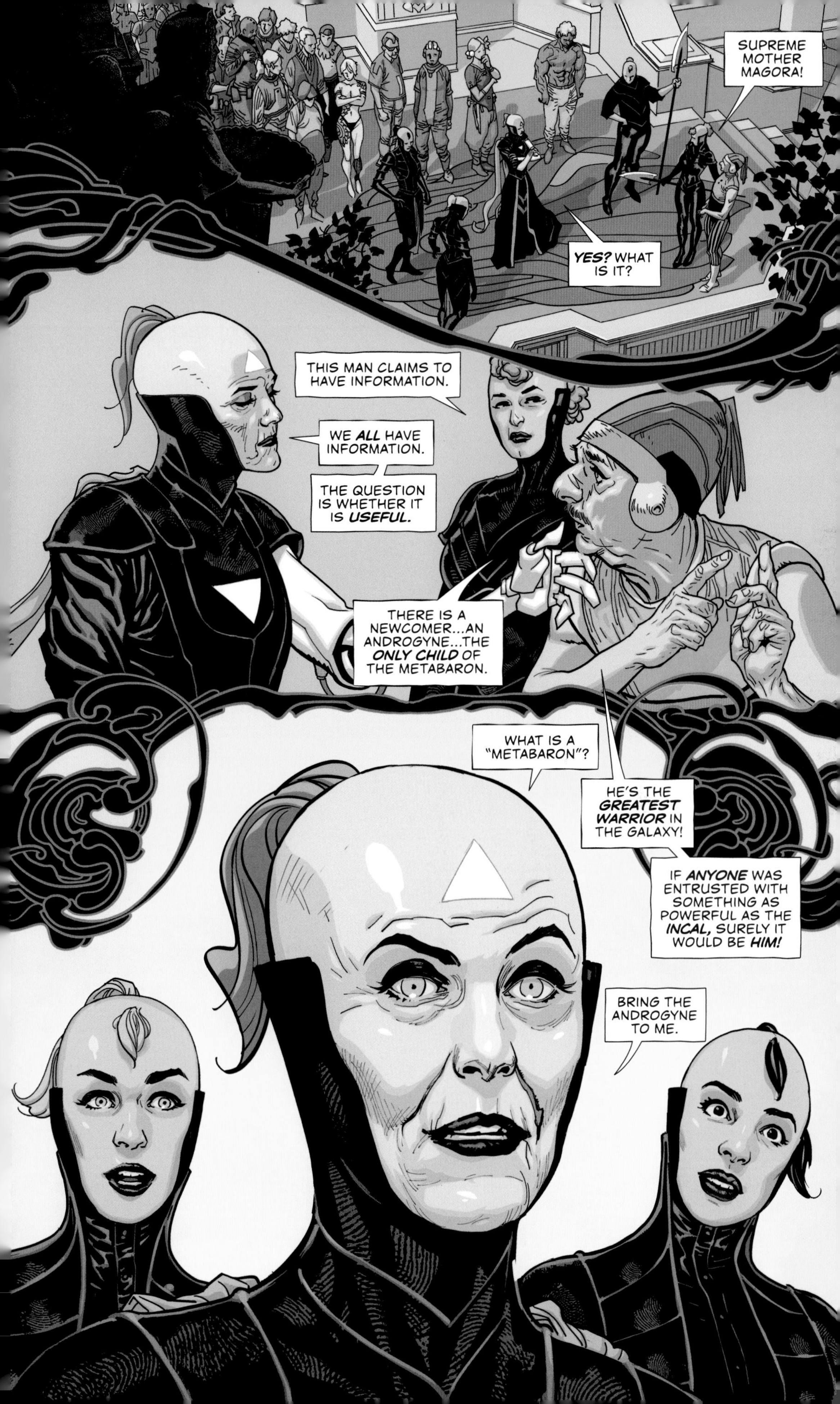
SUPREME MOTHER MAGORA!
YES? WHAT IS IT?
THIS MAN CLAIMS TO HAVE INFORMATION.
WE ALL HAVE INFORMATION.
THE QUESTION IS WHETHER IT IS USEFUL.
THERE IS A NEWCOMER...AN ANDROGYNE...THE ONLY CHILD OF THE METABARON.
WHAT IS A "METABARON"?
HE'S THE GREATEST WARRIOR IN THE GALAXY!
IF ANYONE WAS ENTRUSTED WITH SOMETHING AS POWERFUL AS THE INCAL, SURELY IT WOULD BE HIM!
BRING THE ANDROGYNE TO ME.

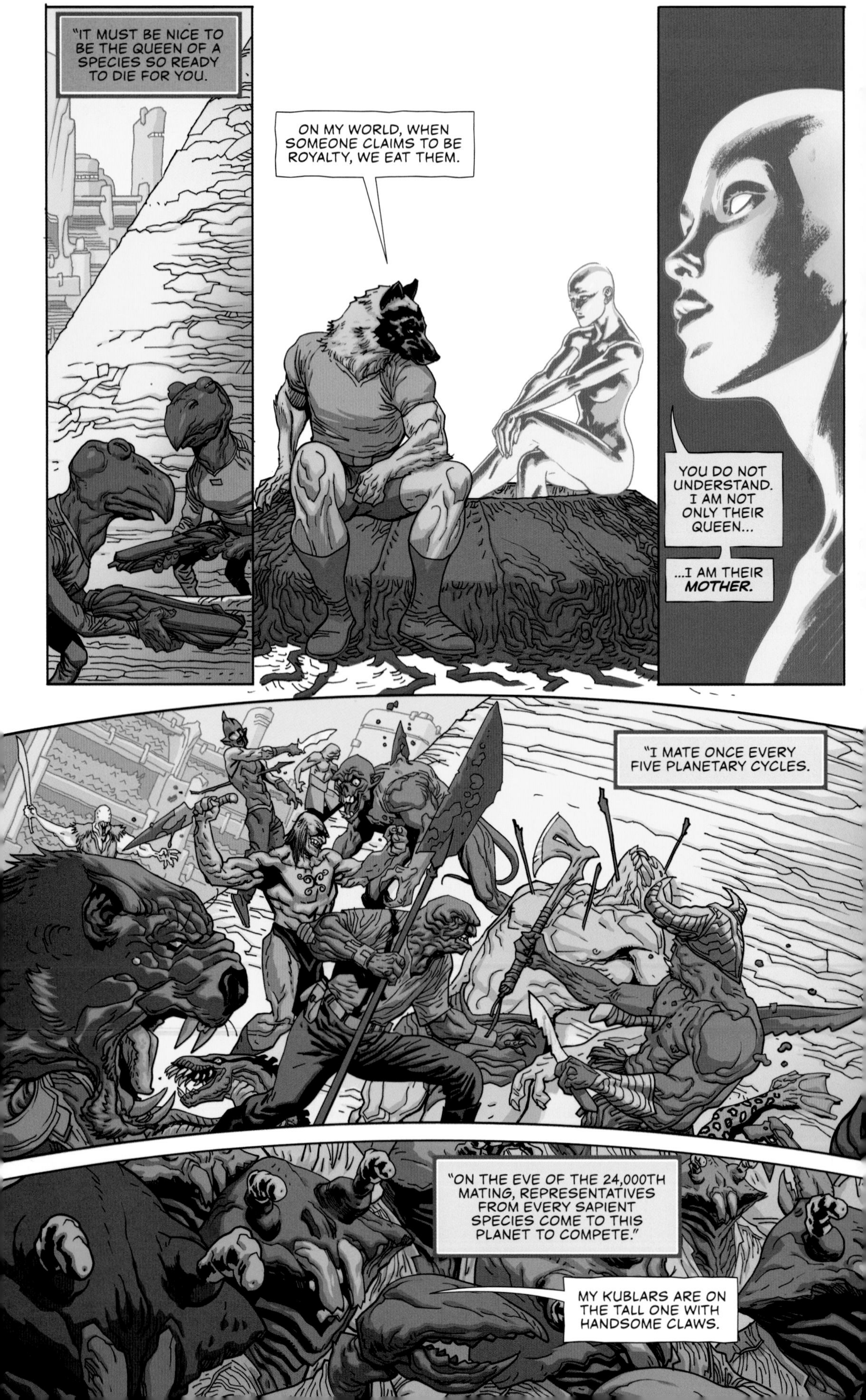
"IT MUST BE NICE TO BE THE QUEEN OF A SPECIES SO READY TO DIE FOR YOU.
ON MY WORLD, WHEN SOMEONE CLAIMS TO BE ROYALTY, WE EAT THEM.
YOU DO NOT UNDERSTAND. I AM NOT ONLY THEIR QUEEN...
...I AM THEIR *MOTHER.*
"I MATE ONCE EVERY FIVE PLANETARY CYCLES.
"ON THE EVE OF THE 24,000TH MATING, REPRESENTATIVES FROM EVERY SAPIENT SPECIES COME TO THIS PLANET TO COMPETE."
MY KUBLARS ARE ON THE TALL ONE WITH HANDSOME CLAWS.

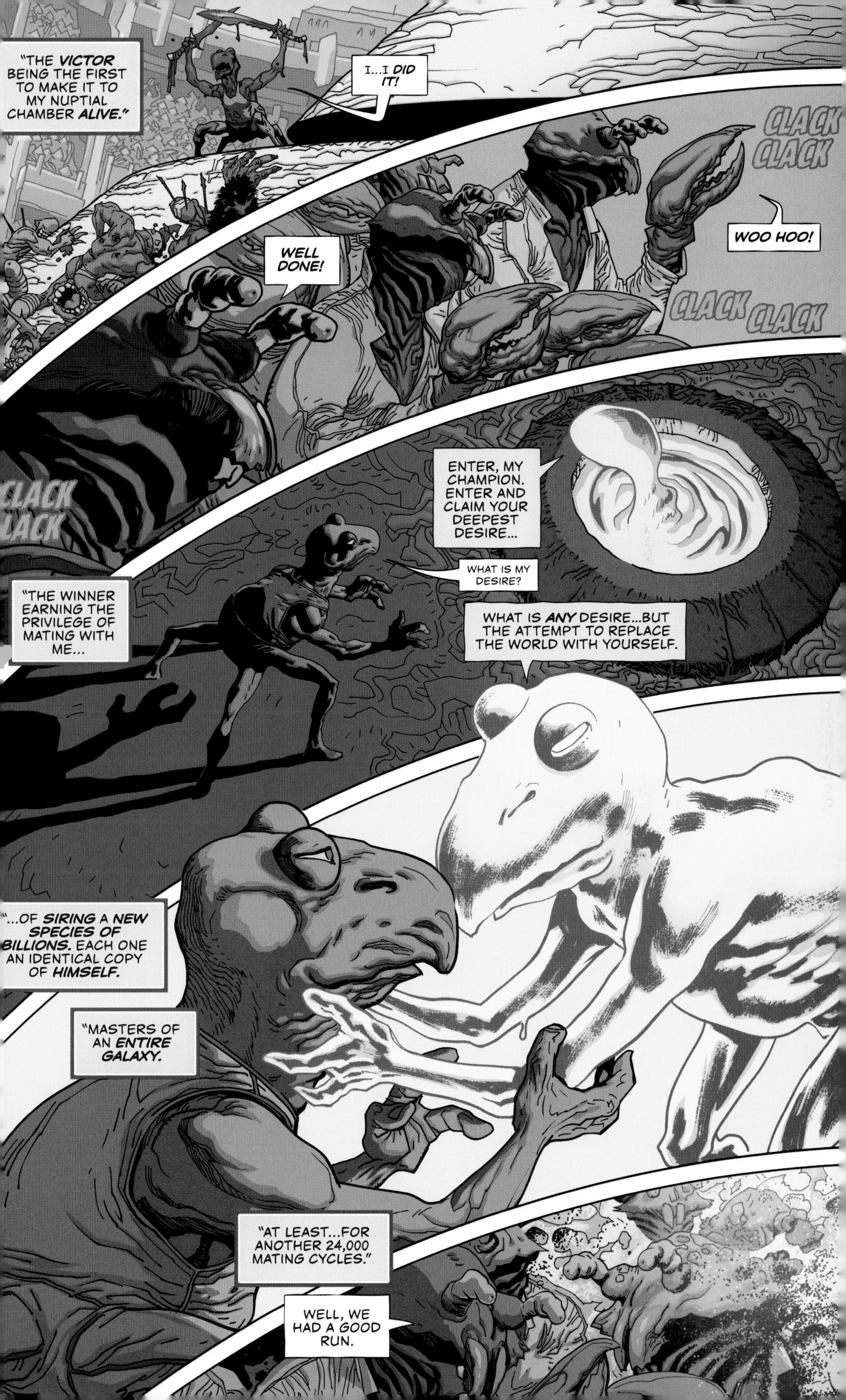
"THE VICTOR BEING THE FIRST TO MAKE IT TO MY NUPTIAL CHAMBER ALIVE."
I...I DID IT!
CLACK CLACK
WOO HOO!
WELL DONE!
CLACK CLACK
CLACK CLACK
ENTER, MY CHAMPION. ENTER AND CLAIM YOUR DEEPEST DESIRE...
WHAT IS MY DESIRE?
"THE WINNER EARNING THE PRIVILEGE OF MATING WITH ME...
WHAT IS ANY DESIRE...BUT THE ATTEMPT TO REPLACE THE WORLD WITH YOURSELF.
"...OF SIRING A NEW SPECIES OF BILLIONS. EACH ONE AN IDENTICAL COPY OF HIMSELF.
"MASTERS OF AN ENTIRE GALAXY.
"AT LEAST...FOR ANOTHER 24,000 MATING CYCLES."
WELL, WE HAD A GOOD RUN.

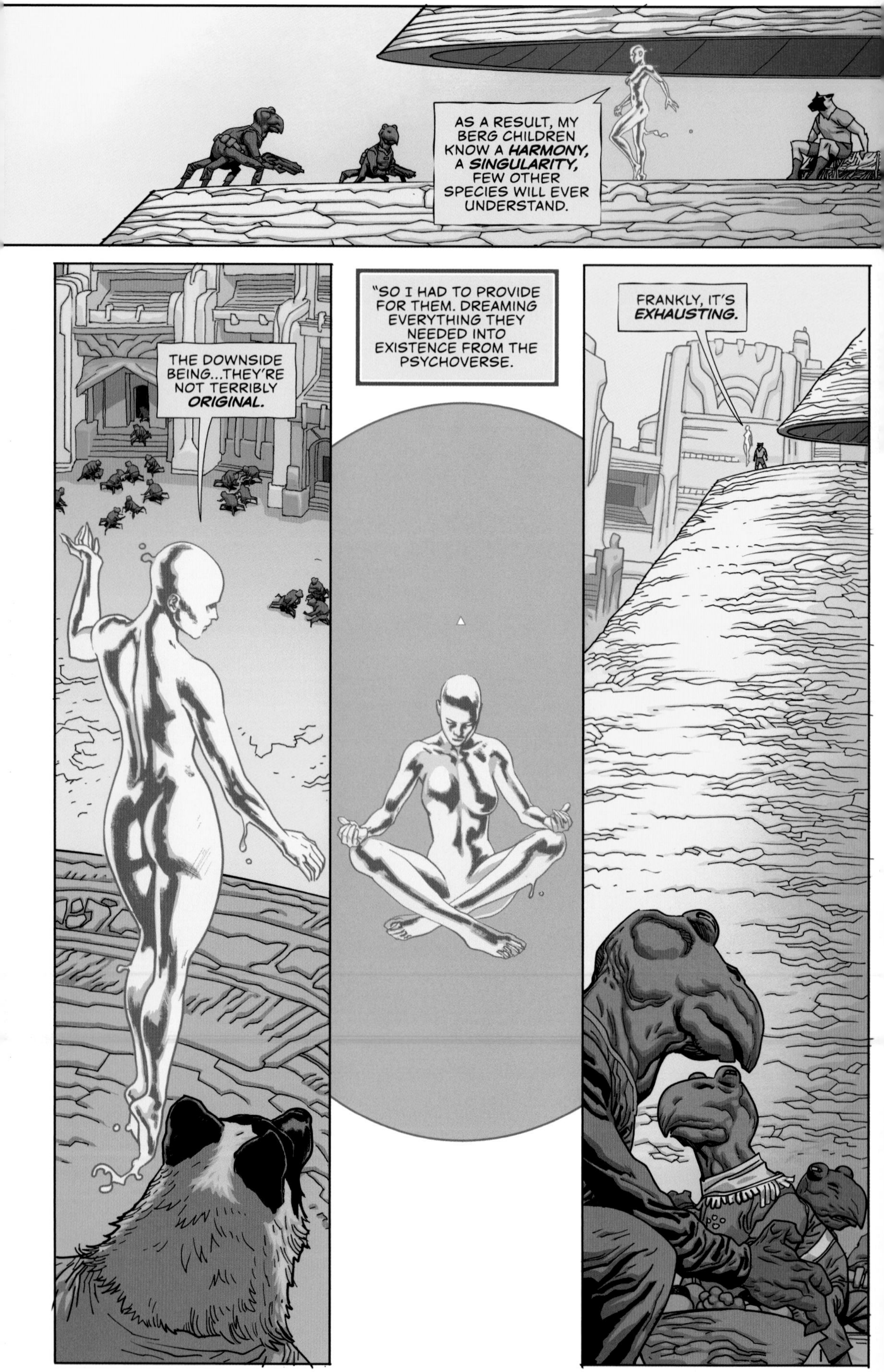

AS A RESULT, MY BERG CHILDREN KNOW A **HARMONY,** A **SINGULARITY,** FEW OTHER SPECIES WILL EVER UNDERSTAND.
THE DOWNSIDE BEING...THEY'RE NOT TERRIBLY **ORIGINAL.**
"SO I HAD TO PROVIDE FOR THEM. DREAMING EVERYTHING THEY NEEDED INTO EXISTENCE FROM THE PSYCHOVERSE.
FRANKLY, IT'S **EXHAUSTING.**

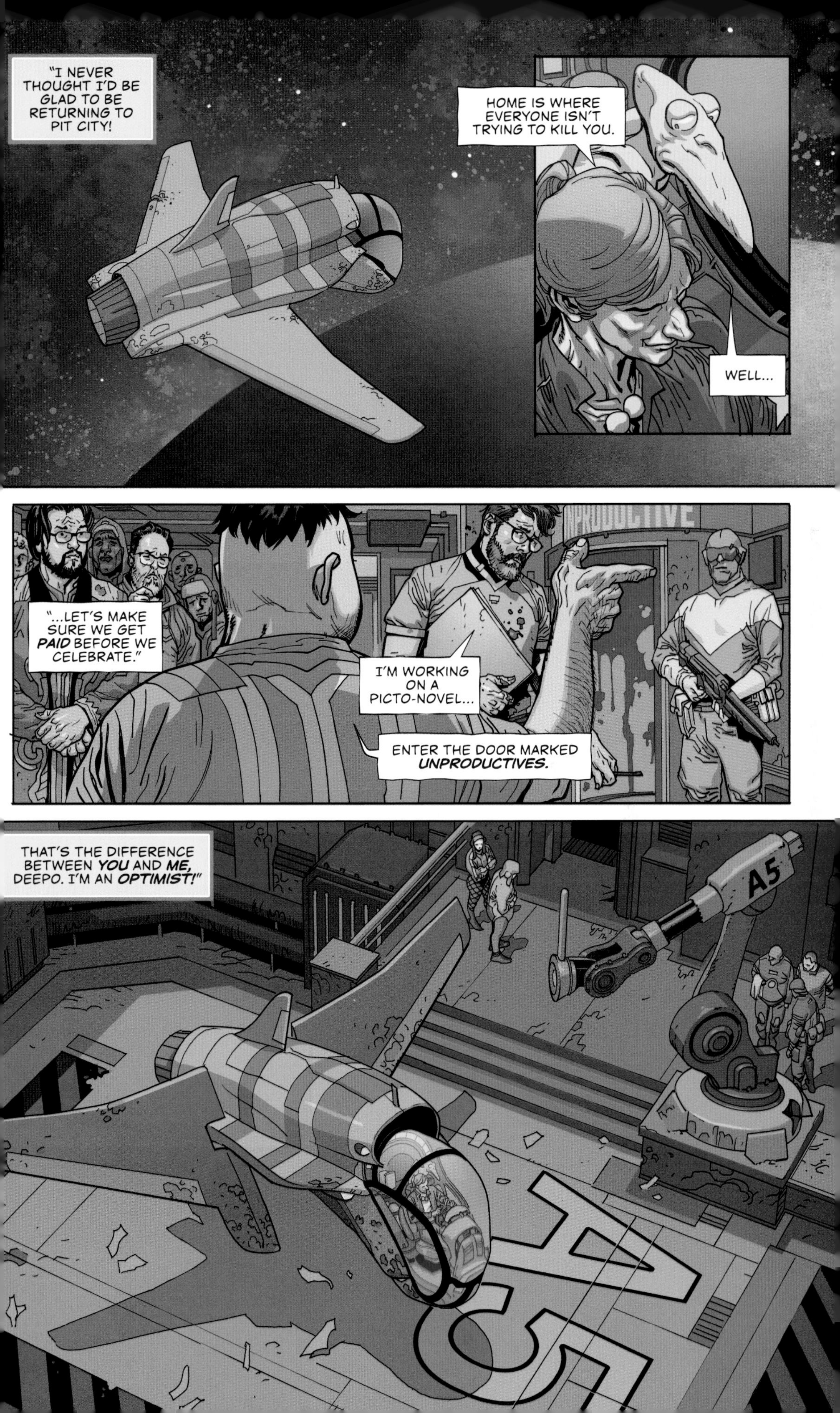
"I NEVER THOUGHT I'D BE GLAD TO BE RETURNING TO PIT CITY!
HOME IS WHERE EVERYONE ISN'T TRYING TO KILL YOU.
WELL...
"...LET'S MAKE SURE WE GET PAID BEFORE WE CELEBRATE."
I'M WORKING ON A PICTO-NOVEL...
ENTER THE DOOR MARKED UNPRODUCTIVES.
THAT'S THE DIFFERENCE BETWEEN YOU AND ME, DEEPO. I'M AN OPTIMIST!"
A5

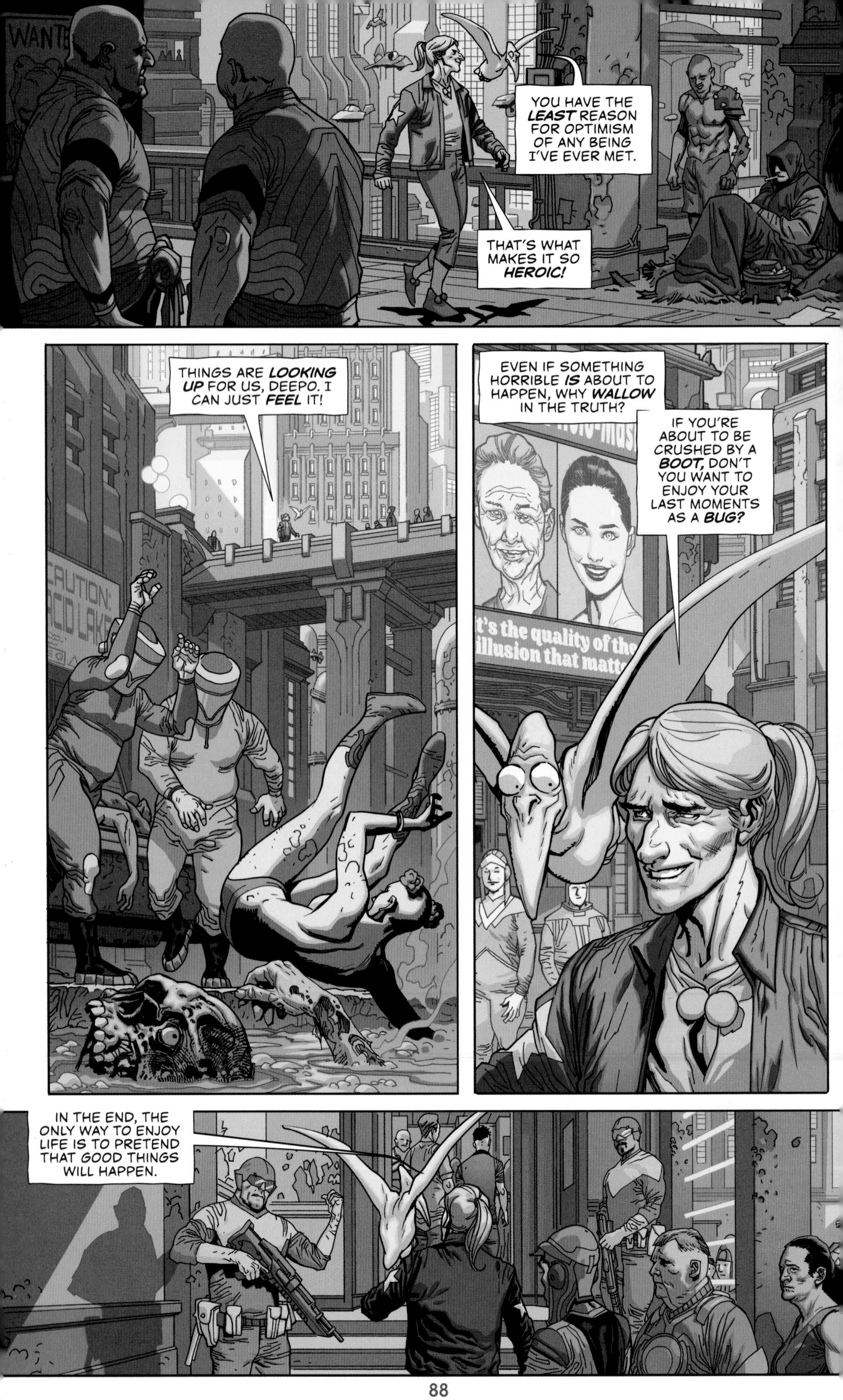
YOU HAVE THE LEAST REASON FOR OPTIMISM OF ANY BEING I'VE EVER MET.
THAT'S WHAT MAKES IT SO HEROIC!
THINGS ARE LOOKING UP FOR US, DEEPO. I CAN JUST FEEL IT!
EVEN IF SOMETHING HORRIBLE IS ABOUT TO HAPPEN, WHY WALLOW IN THE TRUTH?
IF YOU'RE ABOUT TO BE CRUSHED BY A BOOT, DON'T YOU WANT TO ENJOY YOUR LAST MOMENTS AS A BUG?
IN THE END, THE ONLY WAY TO ENJOY LIFE IS TO PRETEND THAT GOOD THINGS WILL HAPPEN.

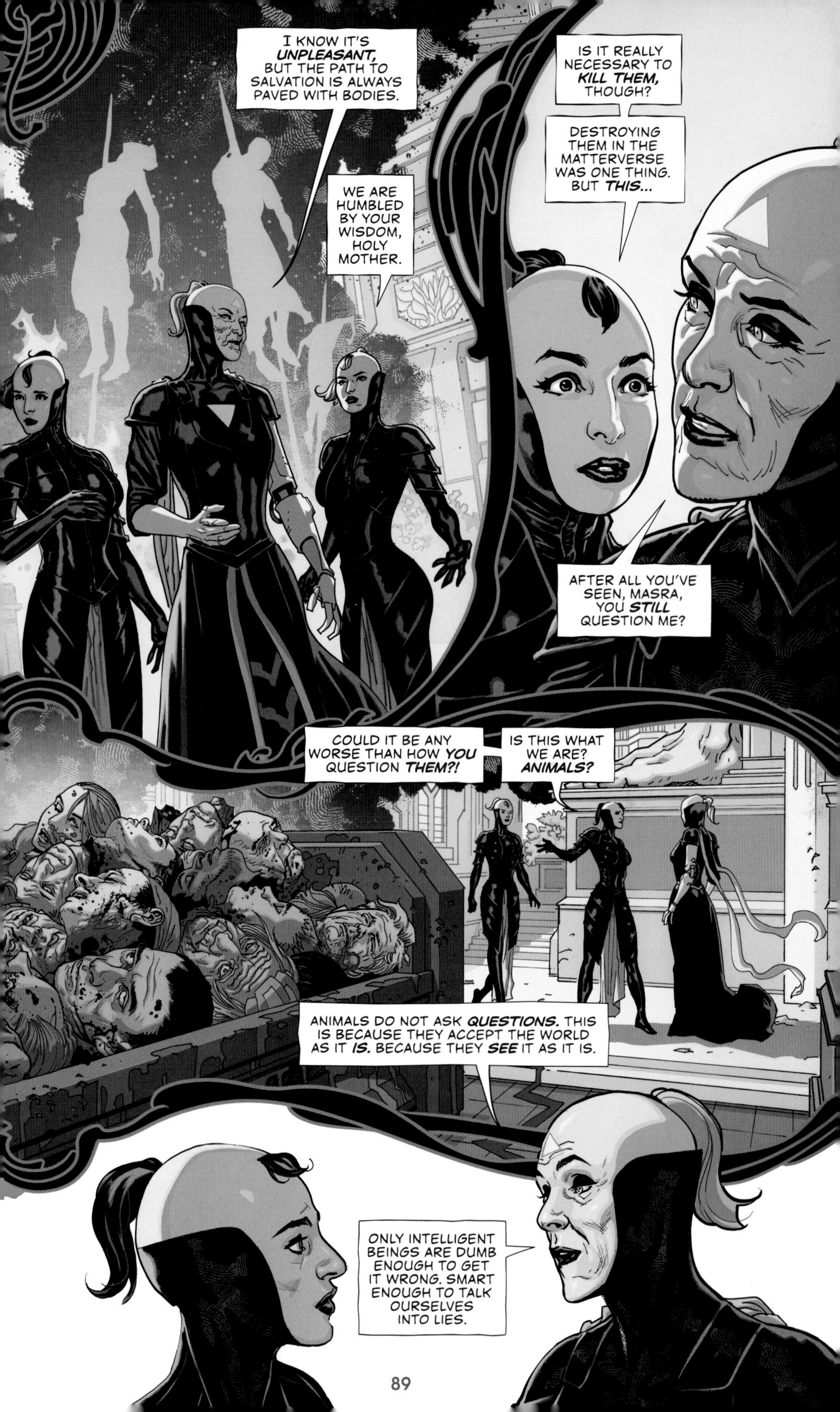

I KNOW IT'S ***UNPLEASANT,*** BUT THE PATH TO SALVATION IS ALWAYS PAVED WITH BODIES.
WE ARE HUMBLED BY YOUR WISDOM, HOLY MOTHER.
IS IT REALLY NECESSARY TO ***KILL THEM,*** THOUGH?
DESTROYING THEM IN THE MATTERVERSE WAS ONE THING. BUT ***THIS...***
AFTER ALL YOU'VE SEEN, MASRA, YOU ***STILL*** QUESTION ME?
COULD IT BE ANY WORSE THAN HOW ***YOU*** QUESTION ***THEM?!***
IS THIS WHAT WE ARE? ***ANIMALS?***
ANIMALS DO NOT ASK ***QUESTIONS.*** THIS IS BECAUSE THEY ACCEPT THE WORLD AS IT ***IS.*** BECAUSE THEY ***SEE*** IT AS IT IS.
ONLY INTELLIGENT BEINGS ARE DUMB ENOUGH TO GET IT WRONG. SMART ENOUGH TO TALK OURSELVES INTO LIES.

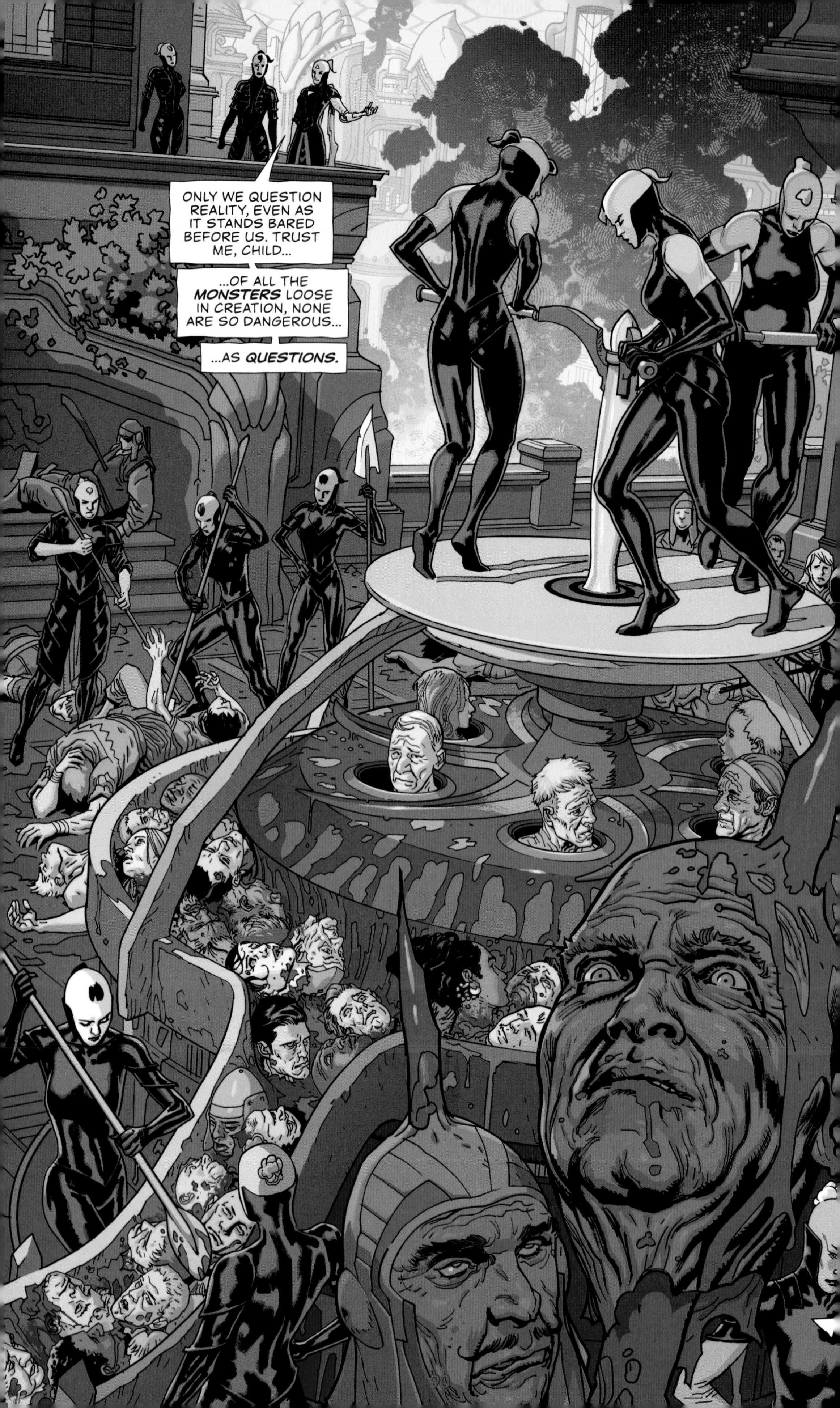
ONLY WE QUESTION REALITY, EVEN AS IT STANDS BARED BEFORE US. TRUST ME, CHILD...
...OF ALL THE **MONSTERS** LOOSE IN CREATION, NONE ARE SO DANGEROUS...
...AS **QUESTIONS.**

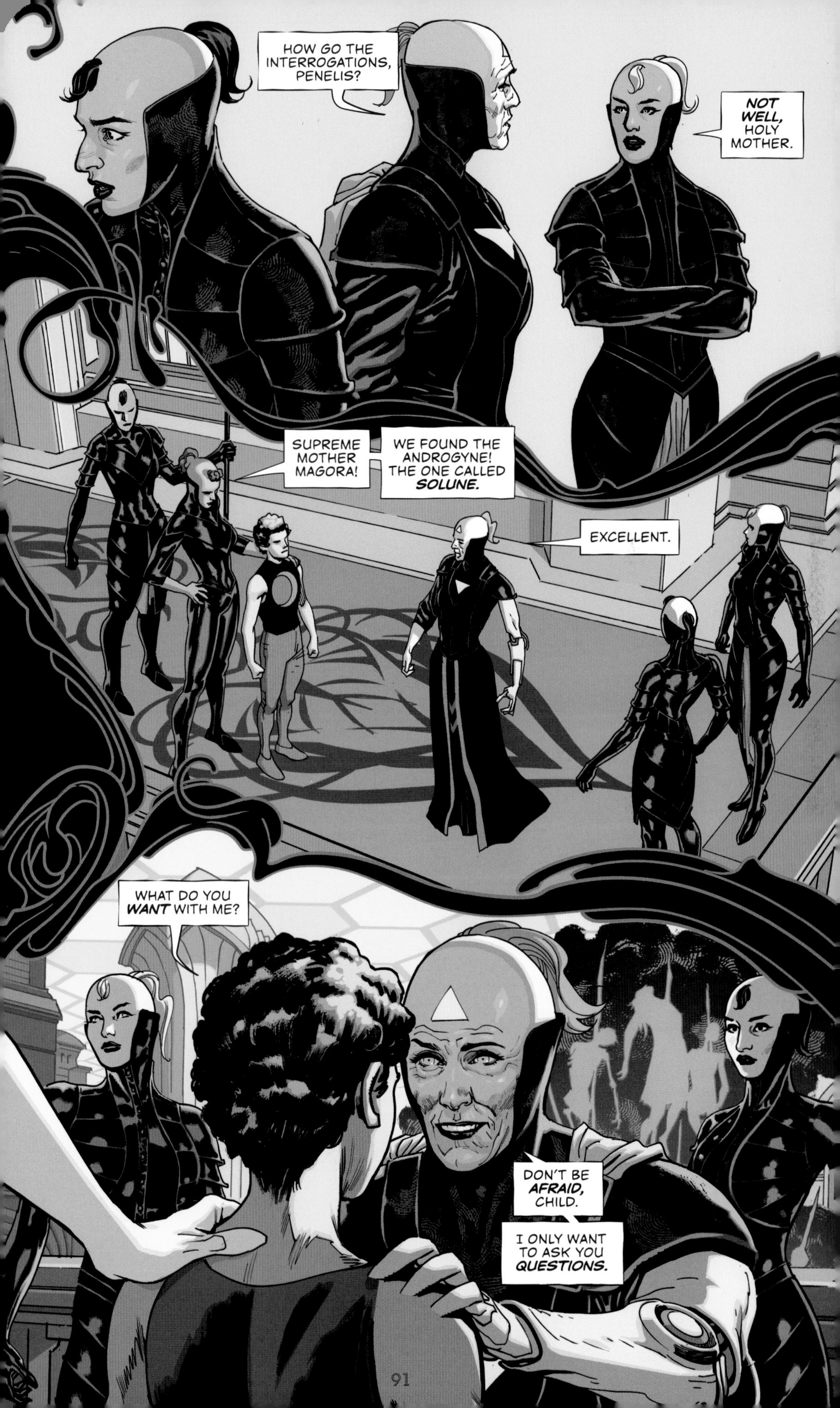
HOW GO THE INTERROGATIONS, PENELIS?
NOT WELL, HOLY MOTHER.
SUPREME MOTHER MAGORA!
WE FOUND THE ANDROGYNE! THE ONE CALLED *SOLUNE.*
EXCELLENT.
WHAT DO YOU *WANT* WITH ME?
DON'T BE *AFRAID,* CHILD.
I ONLY WANT TO ASK YOU *QUESTIONS.*

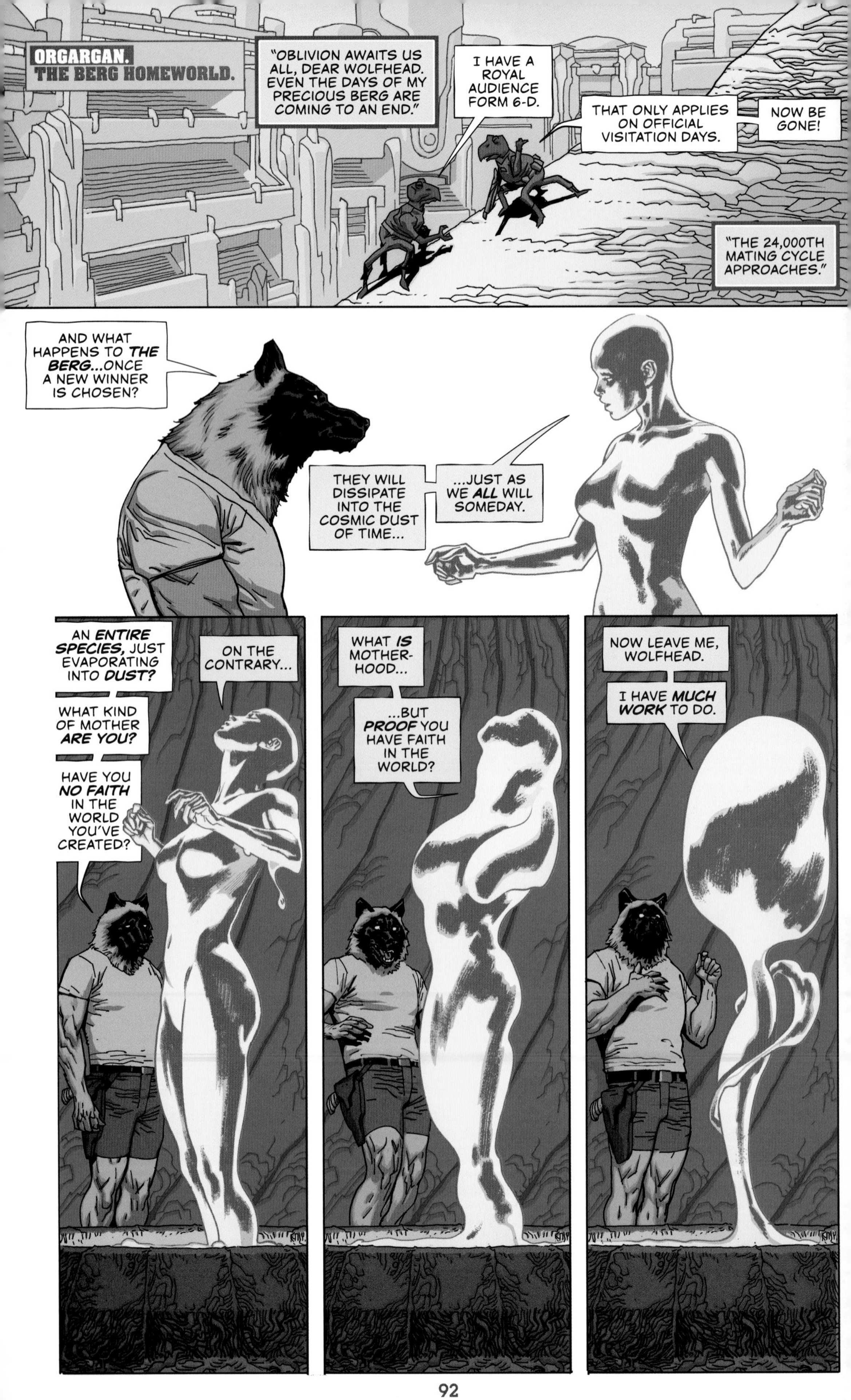
ORGARGAN.
THE BERG HOMEWORLD.
"OBLIVION AWAITS US ALL, DEAR WOLFHEAD. EVEN THE DAYS OF MY PRECIOUS BERG ARE COMING TO AN END."
I HAVE A ROYAL AUDIENCE FORM 6-D.
THAT ONLY APPLIES ON OFFICIAL VISITATION DAYS.
NOW BE GONE!
"THE 24,000TH MATING CYCLE APPROACHES."
AND WHAT HAPPENS TO THE BERG...ONCE A NEW WINNER IS CHOSEN?
THEY WILL DISSIPATE INTO THE COSMIC DUST OF TIME...
...JUST AS WE ALL WILL SOMEDAY.
AN ENTIRE SPECIES, JUST EVAPORATING INTO DUST?
WHAT KIND OF MOTHER ARE YOU?
HAVE YOU NO FAITH IN THE WORLD YOU'VE CREATED?
ON THE CONTRARY...
WHAT IS MOTHER-HOOD...
...BUT PROOF YOU HAVE FAITH IN THE WORLD?
NOW LEAVE ME, WOLFHEAD.
I HAVE MUCH WORK TO DO.

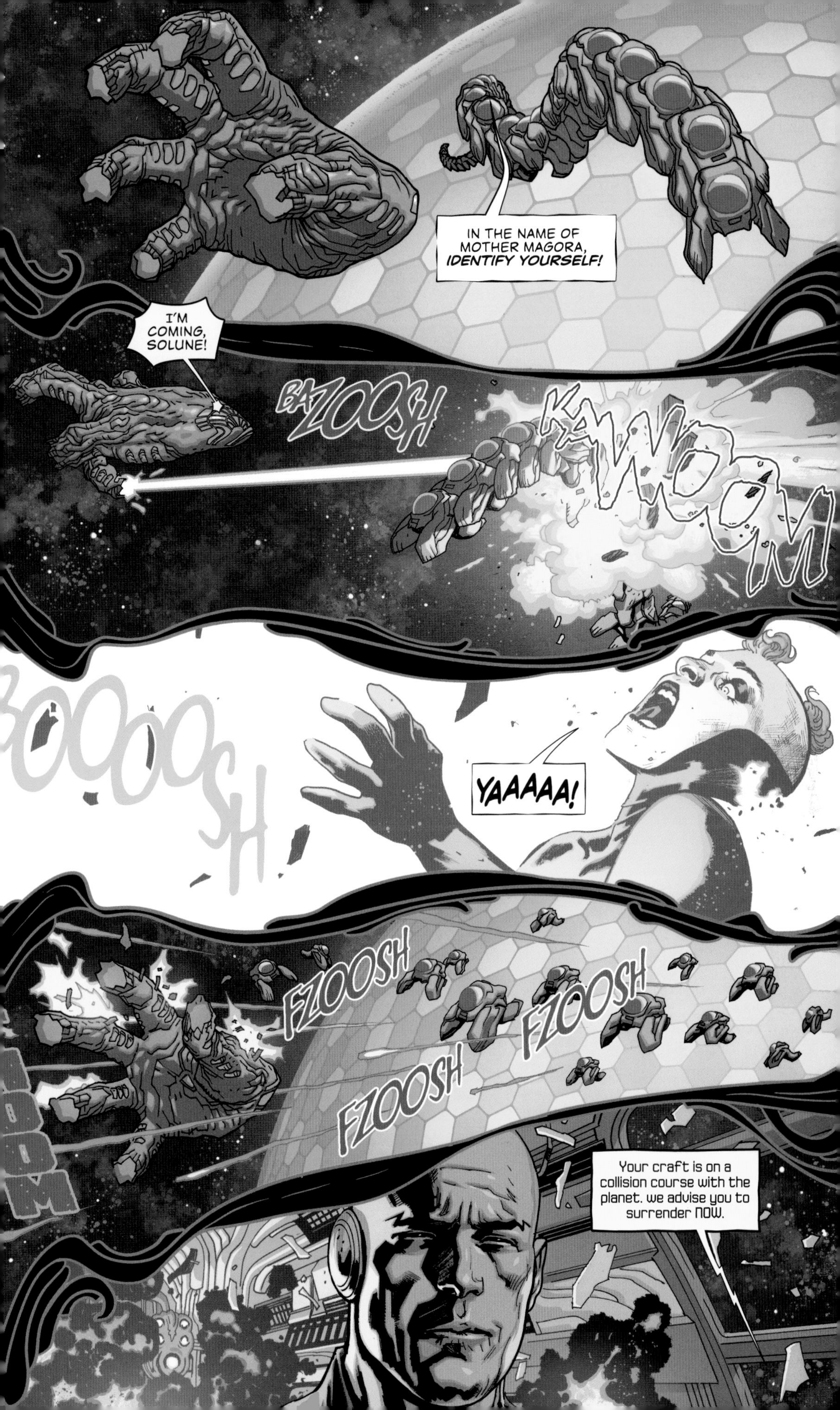
IN THE NAME OF MOTHER MAGORA, IDENTIFY YOURSELF!
I'M COMING, SOLUNE!
BAZOOSH
KAWOOOM
BOOOOSH
YAAAAA!
FZOOSH
FZOOSH
FZOOSH
BOOOM
Your craft is on a collision course with the planet. we advise you to surrender NOW.

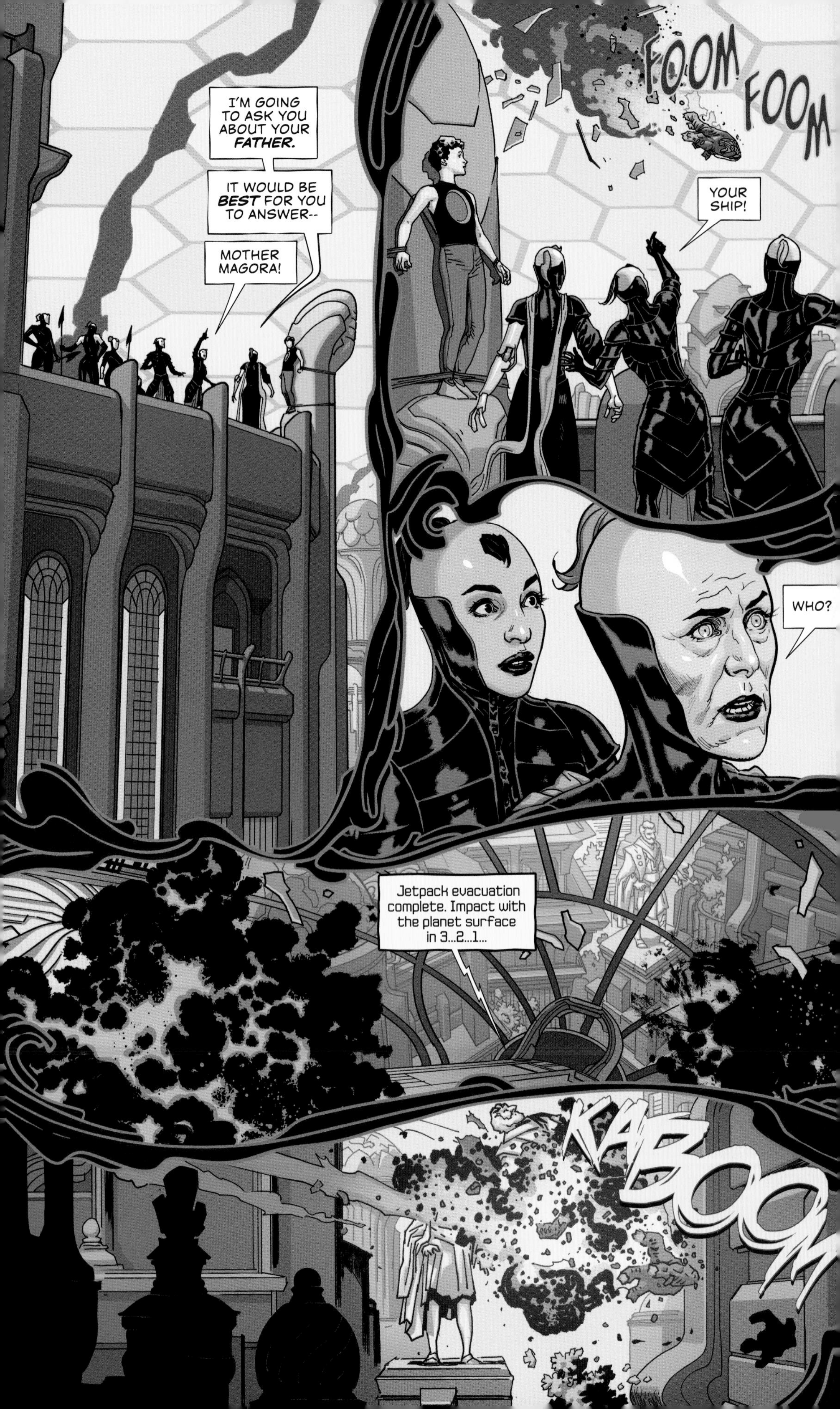

I'M GOING TO ASK YOU ABOUT YOUR **FATHER.**
IT WOULD BE **BEST** FOR YOU TO ANSWER--
MOTHER MAGORA!
FOOM
FOOM
YOUR SHIP!
WHO?
Jetpack evacuation complete. Impact with the planet surface in 3...2...1...
KABOOM

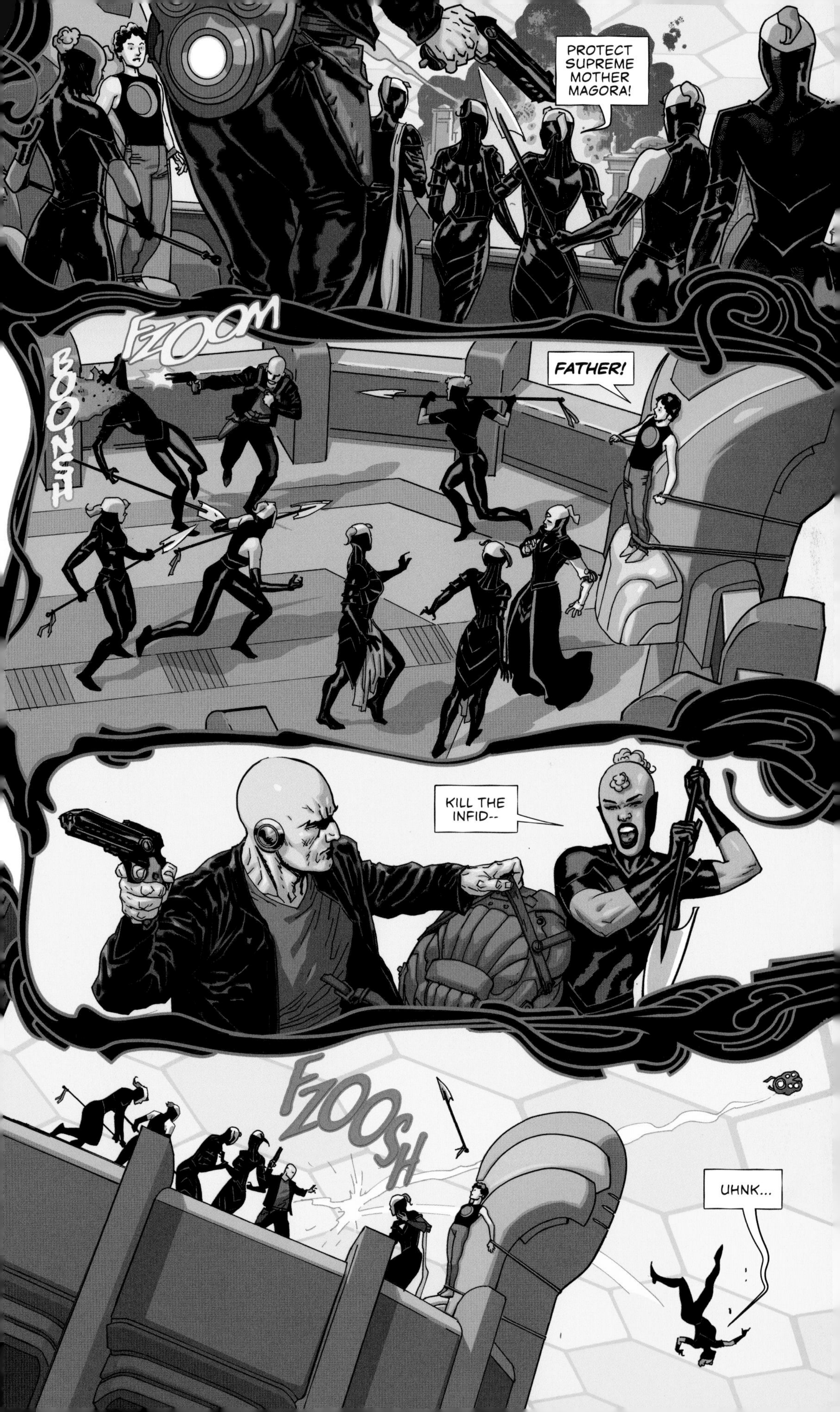
PROTECT SUPREME MOTHER MAGORA!
FZOOM
BOOONSH
FATHER!
KILL THE INFID--
FZOOSH
UHNK...

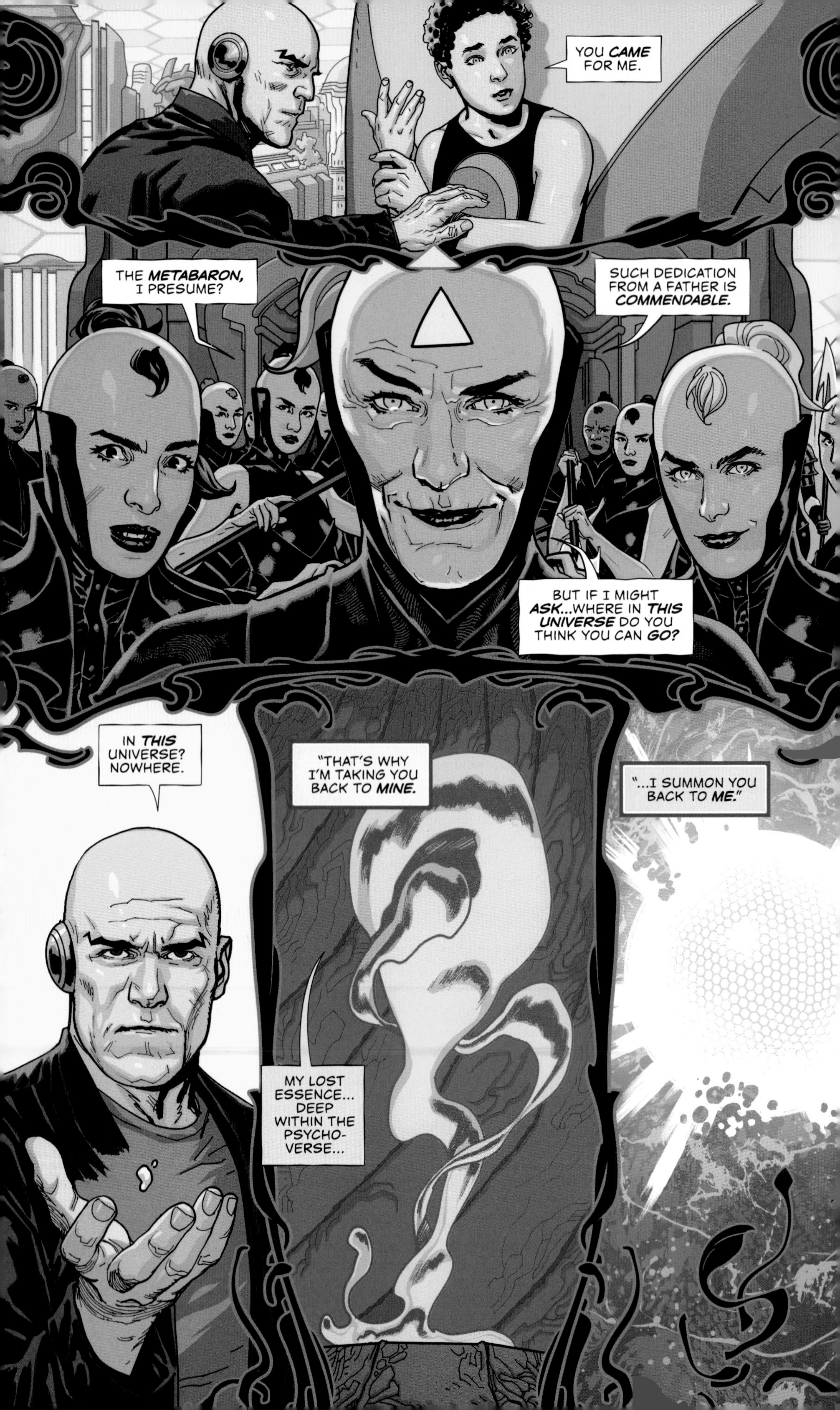
YOU CAME FOR ME.
THE METABARON, I PRESUME?
SUCH DEDICATION FROM A FATHER IS COMMENDABLE.
BUT IF I MIGHT ASK...WHERE IN THIS UNIVERSE DO YOU THINK YOU CAN GO?
IN THIS UNIVERSE? NOWHERE.
"THAT'S WHY I'M TAKING YOU BACK TO MINE.
MY LOST ESSENCE... DEEP WITHIN THE PSYCHO-VERSE...
"...I SUMMON YOU BACK TO ME."

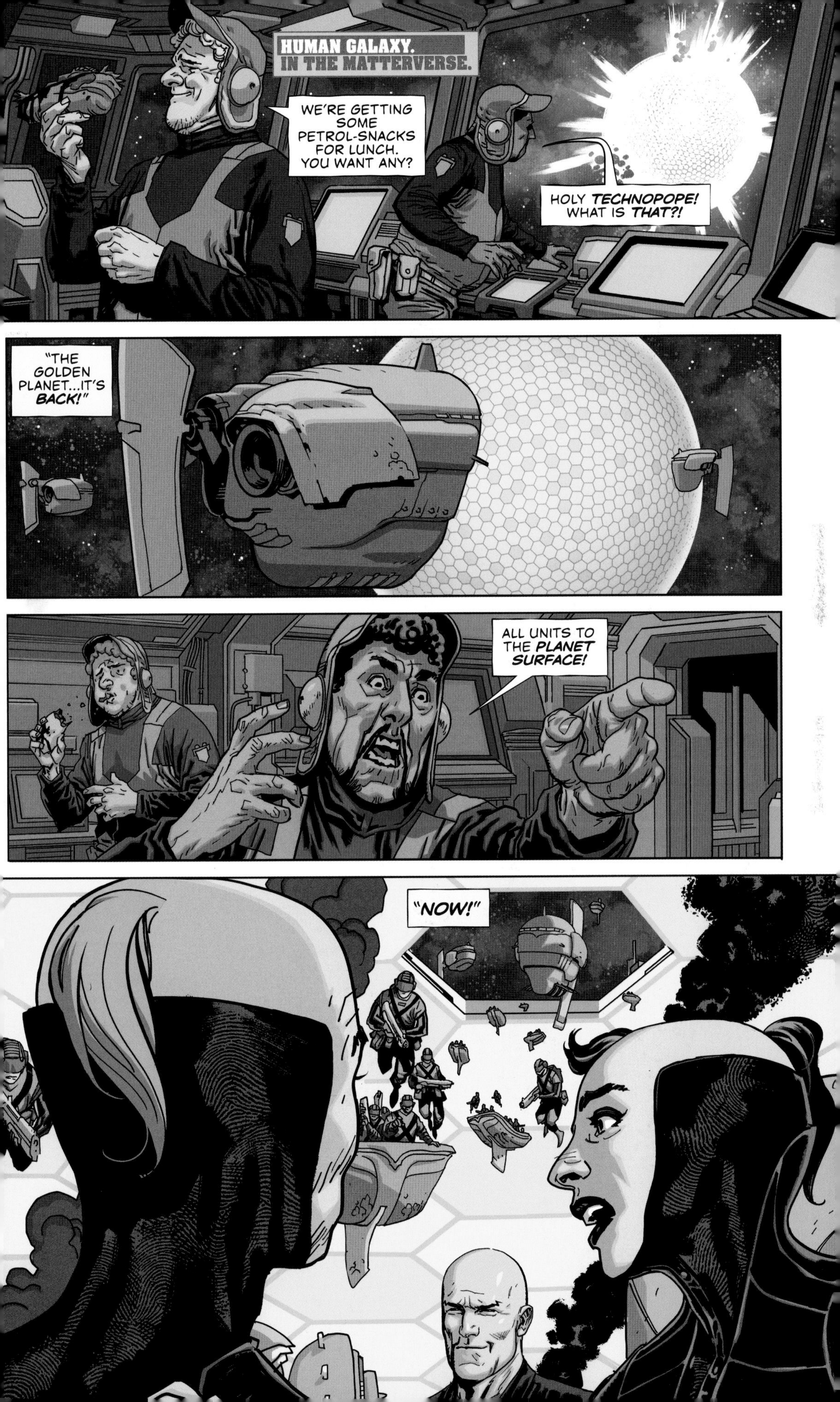
HUMAN GALAXY.
IN THE MATTERVERSE.
WE'RE GETTING SOME PETROL-SNACKS FOR LUNCH. YOU WANT ANY?
HOLY TECHNOPOPE! WHAT IS THAT?!
"THE GOLDEN PLANET...IT'S BACK!"
ALL UNITS TO THE PLANET SURFACE!
"NOW!"

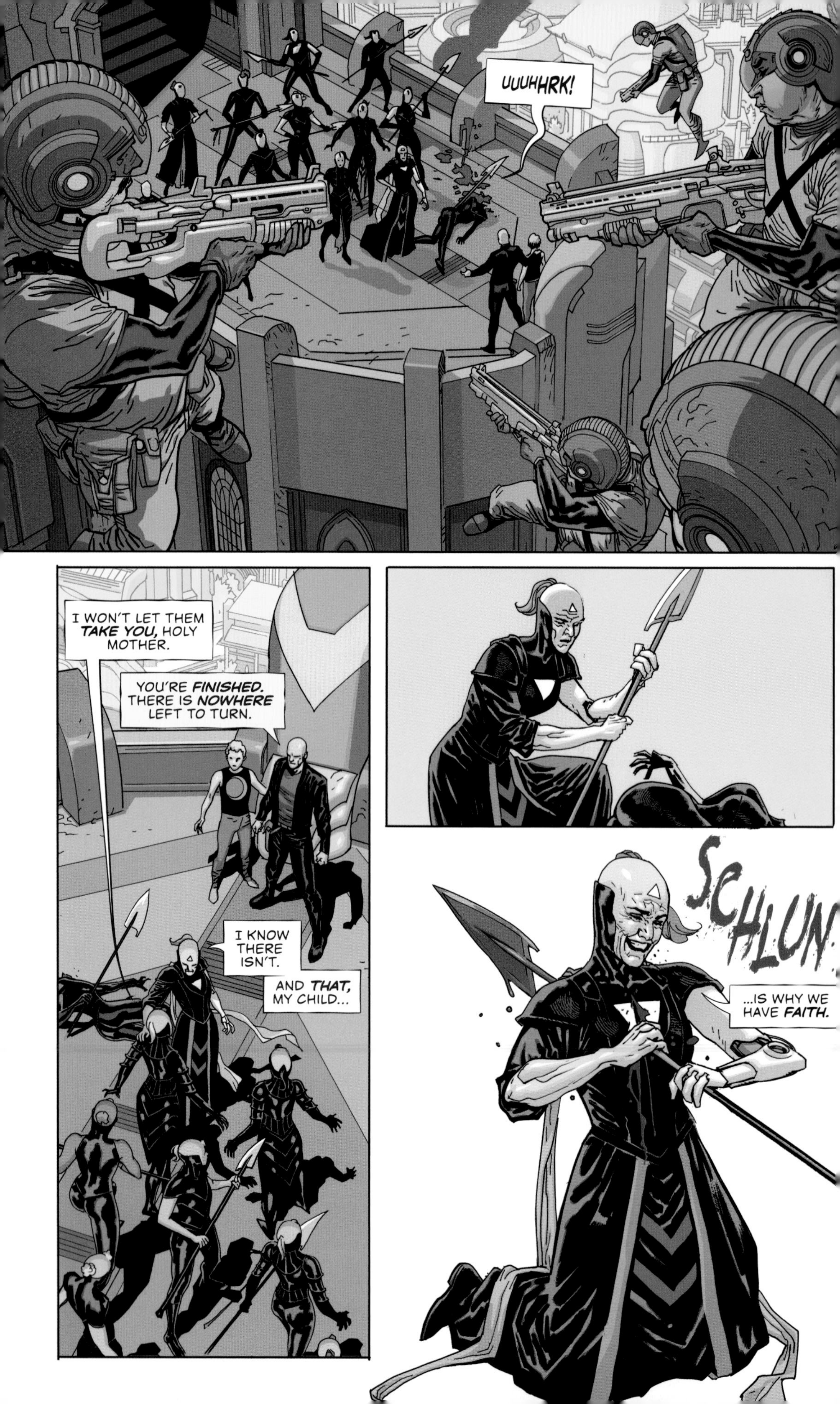
UUUHHRK!
I WON'T LET THEM TAKE YOU, HOLY MOTHER.
YOU'RE FINISHED. THERE IS NOWHERE LEFT TO TURN.
I KNOW THERE ISN'T.
AND THAT, MY CHILD...
SCHLUNK
...IS WHY WE HAVE FAITH.

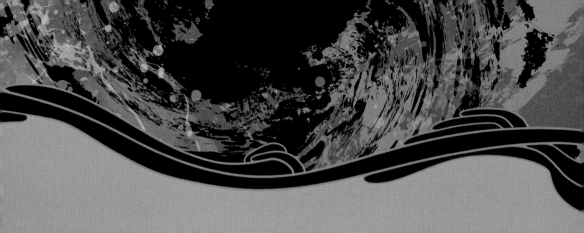

CHAPTER 5

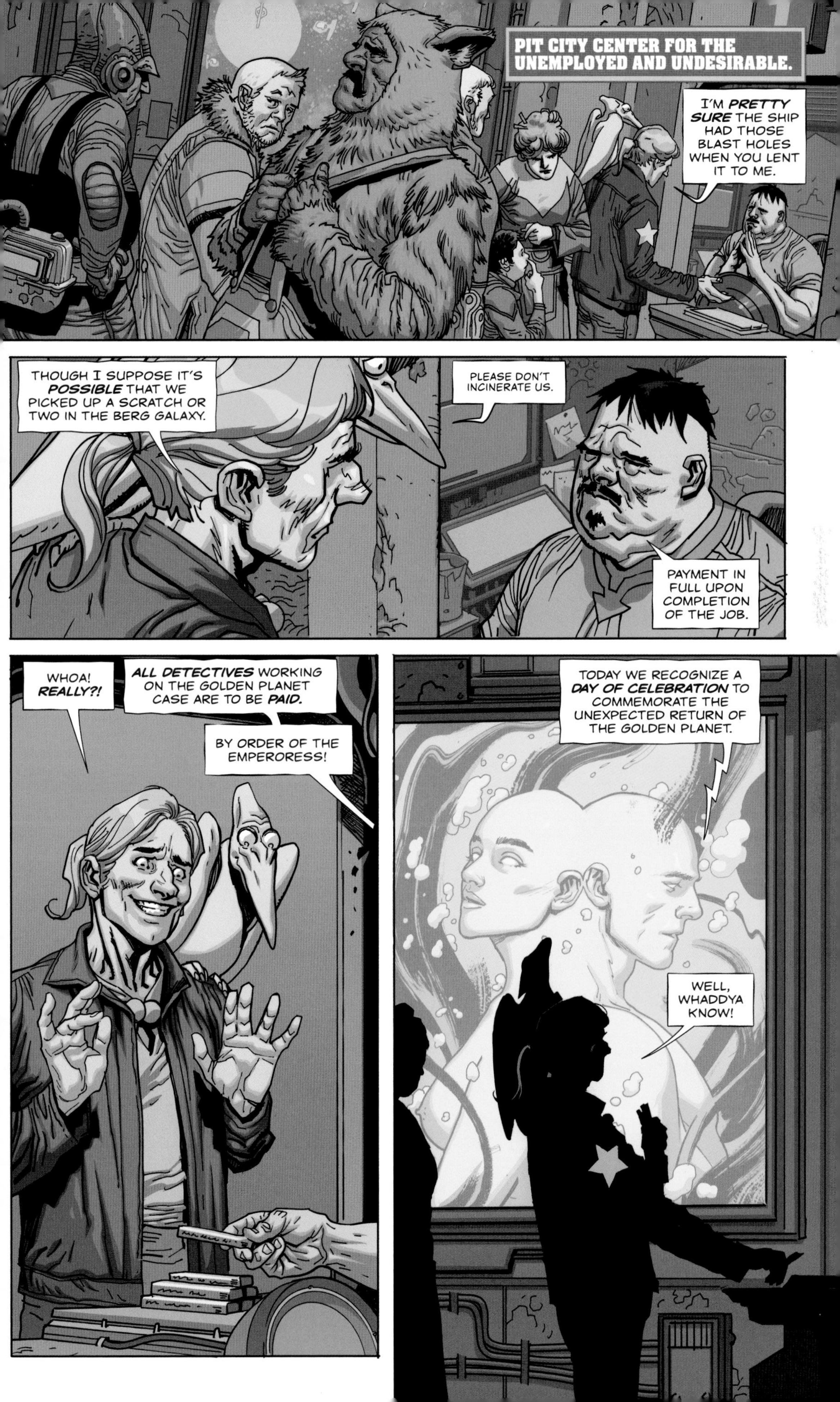
PIT CITY CENTER FOR THE UNEMPLOYED AND UNDESIRABLE.
I'M PRETTY SURE THE SHIP HAD THOSE BLAST HOLES WHEN YOU LENT IT TO ME.
THOUGH I SUPPOSE IT'S POSSIBLE THAT WE PICKED UP A SCRATCH OR TWO IN THE BERG GALAXY.
PLEASE DON'T INCINERATE US.
PAYMENT IN FULL UPON COMPLETION OF THE JOB.
WHOA! REALLY?!
ALL DETECTIVES WORKING ON THE GOLDEN PLANET CASE ARE TO BE PAID.
BY ORDER OF THE EMPERORESS!
TODAY WE RECOGNIZE A DAY OF CELEBRATION TO COMMEMORATE THE UNEXPECTED RETURN OF THE GOLDEN PLANET.
WELL, WHADDYA KNOW!

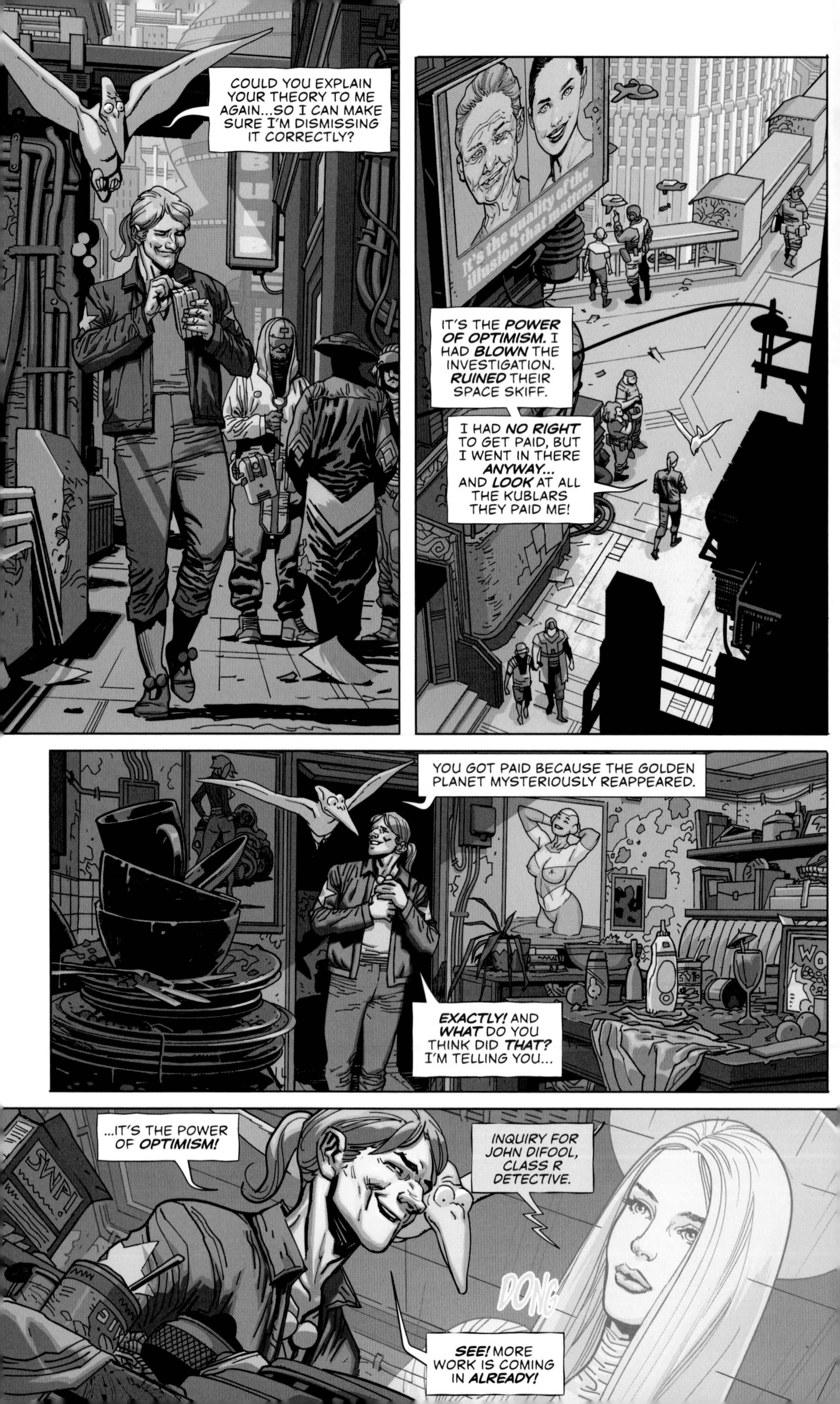

COULD YOU EXPLAIN YOUR THEORY TO ME AGAIN...SO I CAN MAKE SURE I'M DISMISSING IT CORRECTLY?
It's the quality of the illusion that matters
IT'S THE POWER OF OPTIMISM. I HAD BLOWN THE INVESTIGATION. RUINED THEIR SPACE SKIFF.
I HAD NO RIGHT TO GET PAID, BUT I WENT IN THERE ANYWAY... AND LOOK AT ALL THE KUBLARS THEY PAID ME!
YOU GOT PAID BECAUSE THE GOLDEN PLANET MYSTERIOUSLY REAPPEARED.
EXACTLY! AND WHAT DO YOU THINK DID THAT? I'M TELLING YOU...
...IT'S THE POWER OF OPTIMISM!
INQUIRY FOR JOHN DIFOOL, CLASS R DETECTIVE.
DONG
SEE! MORE WORK IS COMING IN ALREADY!

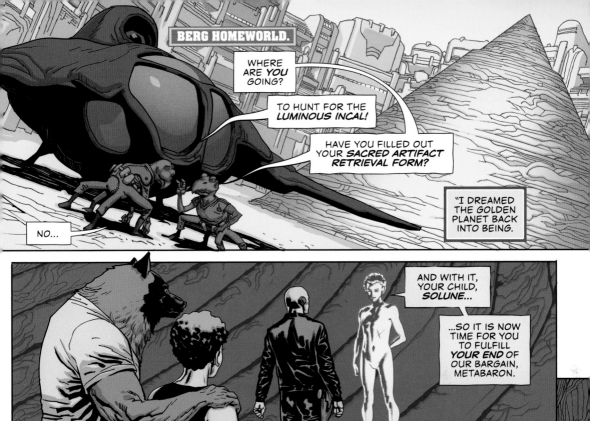

WHERE ARE *YOU* GOING?

TO HUNT FOR THE *LUMINOUS INCAL!*

HAVE YOU FILLED OUT YOUR *SACRED ARTIFACT RETRIEVAL FORM?*

NO...

"I DREAMED THE GOLDEN PLANET BACK INTO BEING.

AND WITH IT, YOUR CHILD, *SOLUNE*...

...SO IT IS NOW TIME FOR YOU TO FULFILL *YOUR END* OF OUR BARGAIN, METABARON.

TO FIND THE *LUMINOUS INCAL* AND RETURN IT TO ME.

AND YOUR *BERG* WHO ARE ALREADY HUNTING IT?

THEY *MEAN* WELL, BUT *REALLY*...THIS TASK REQUIRES A MAN OF *YOUR* TALENTS.

NOW *GO*, METABARON.

IT IS TIME FOR ME TO *REST.*

AND FOR YOU TO PAY YOUR *DEBTS.*

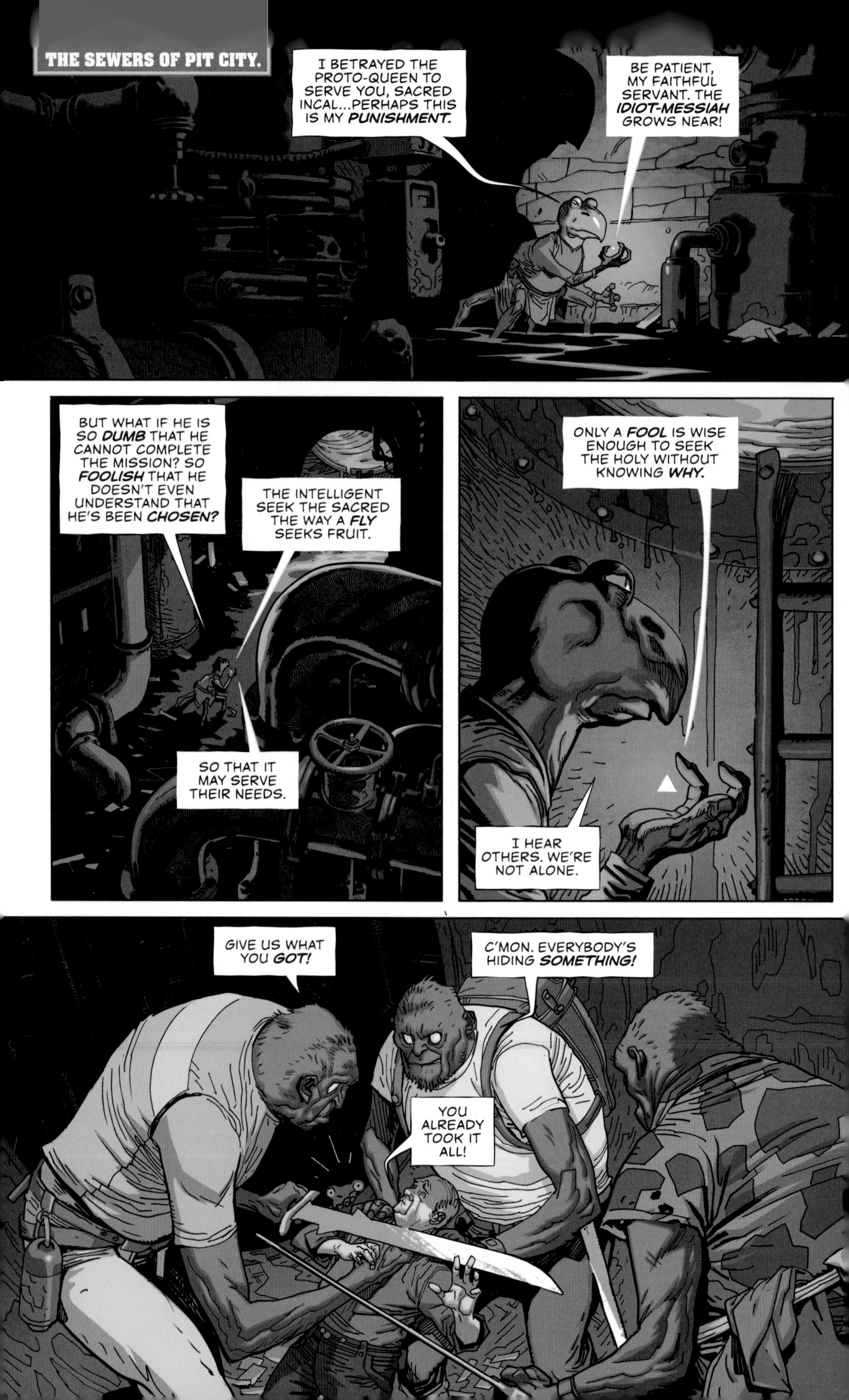
THE SEWERS OF PIT CITY.
I BETRAYED THE PROTO-QUEEN TO SERVE YOU, SACRED INCAL...PERHAPS THIS IS MY PUNISHMENT.
BE PATIENT, MY FAITHFUL SERVANT. THE IDIOT-MESSIAH GROWS NEAR!
BUT WHAT IF HE IS SO DUMB THAT HE CANNOT COMPLETE THE MISSION? SO FOOLISH THAT HE DOESN'T EVEN UNDERSTAND THAT HE'S BEEN CHOSEN?
THE INTELLIGENT SEEK THE SACRED THE WAY A FLY SEEKS FRUIT.
SO THAT IT MAY SERVE THEIR NEEDS.
ONLY A FOOL IS WISE ENOUGH TO SEEK THE HOLY WITHOUT KNOWING WHY.
I HEAR OTHERS. WE'RE NOT ALONE.
GIVE US WHAT YOU GOT!
C'MON. EVERYBODY'S HIDING SOMETHING!
YOU ALREADY TOOK IT ALL!

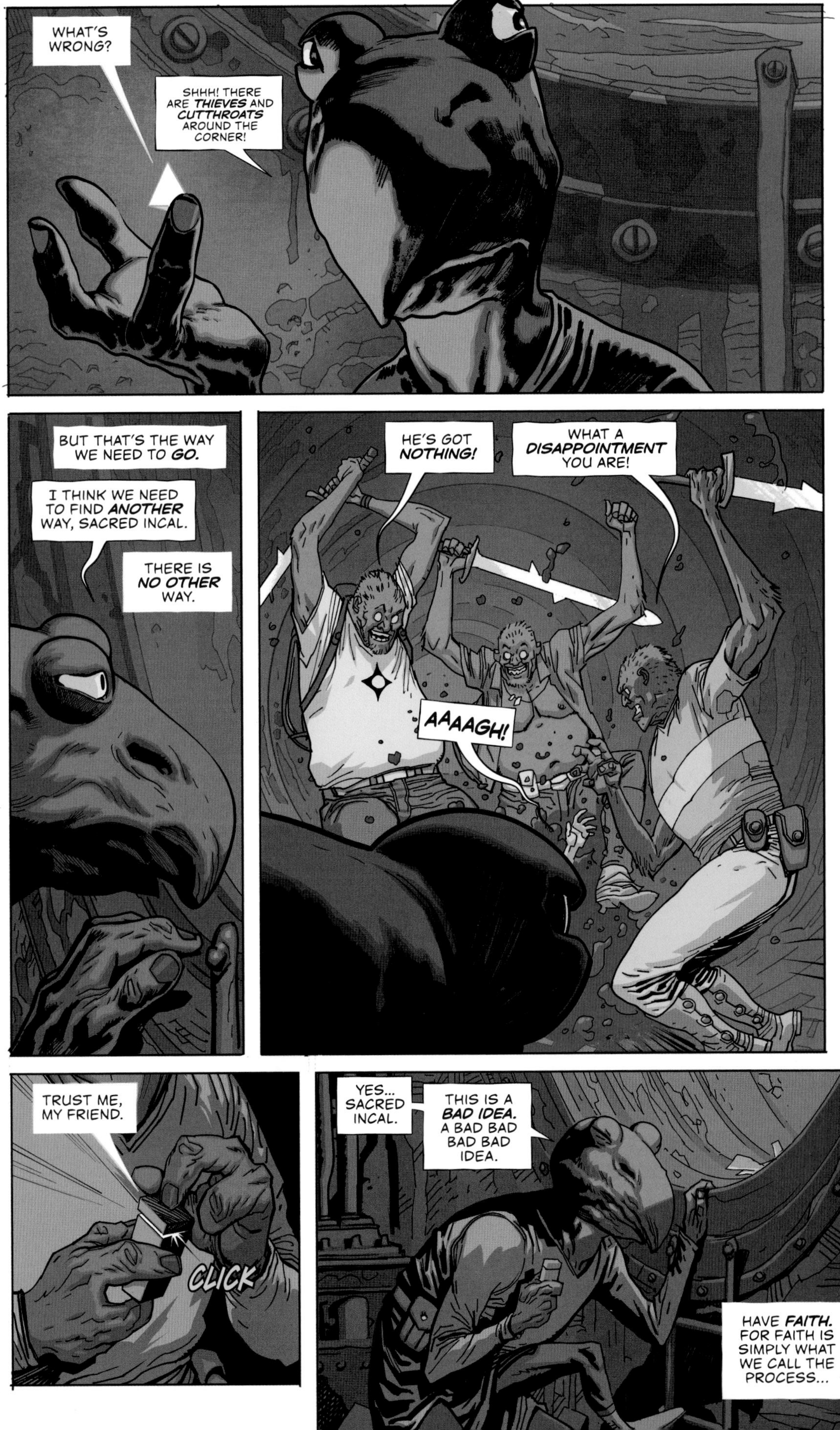
WHAT'S WRONG?
SHHH! THERE ARE THIEVES AND CUTTHROATS AROUND THE CORNER!
BUT THAT'S THE WAY WE NEED TO GO.
I THINK WE NEED TO FIND ANOTHER WAY, SACRED INCAL.
THERE IS NO OTHER WAY.
HE'S GOT NOTHING!
WHAT A DISAPPOINTMENT YOU ARE!
AAAAGH!
TRUST ME, MY FRIEND.
CLICK
YES... SACRED INCAL.
THIS IS A BAD IDEA. A BAD BAD BAD BAD IDEA.
HAVE FAITH. FOR FAITH IS SIMPLY WHAT WE CALL THE PROCESS...

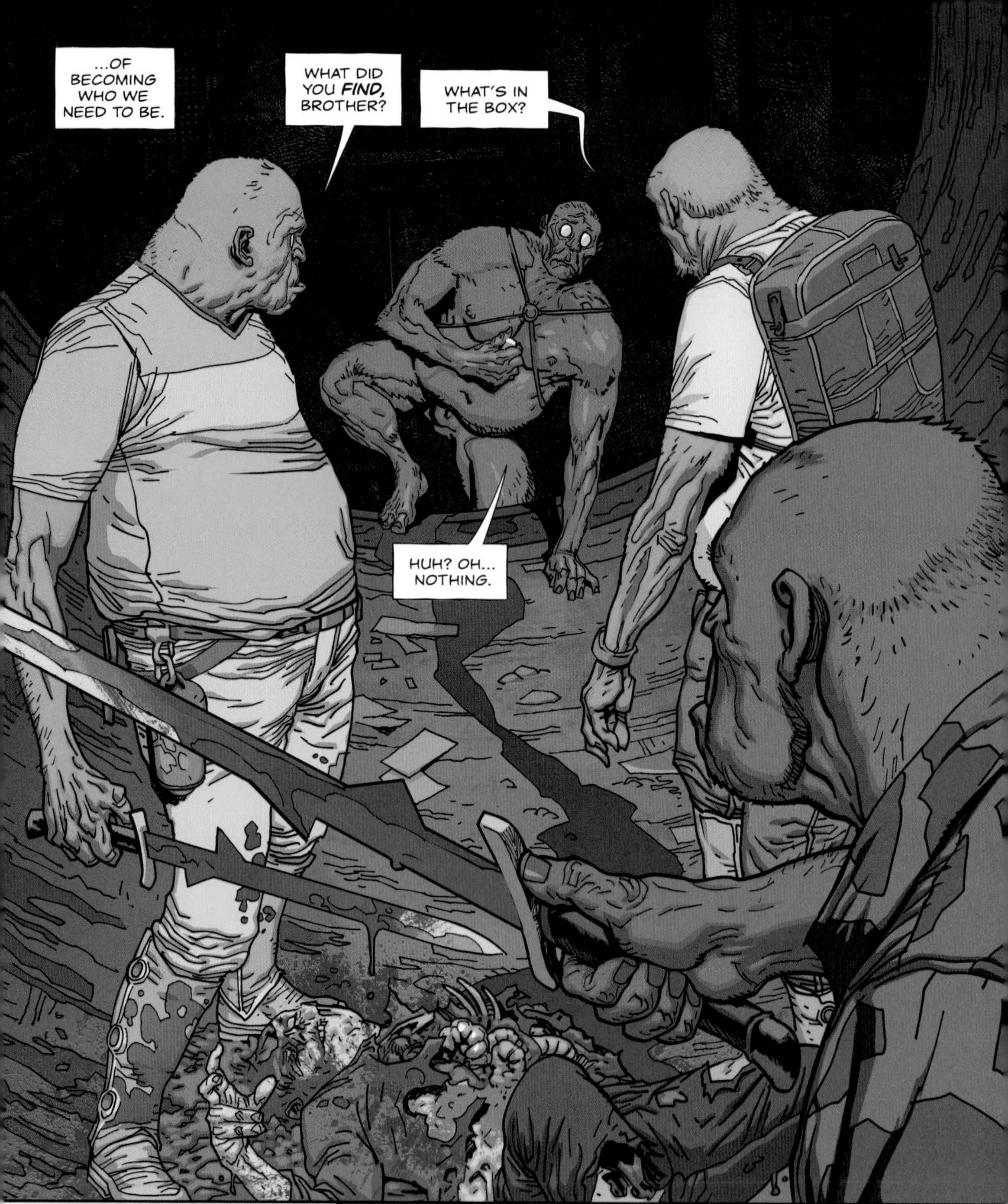
...OF BECOMING WHO WE NEED TO BE.
WHAT DID YOU **FIND,** BROTHER?
WHAT'S IN THE BOX?
HUH? OH... NOTHING.

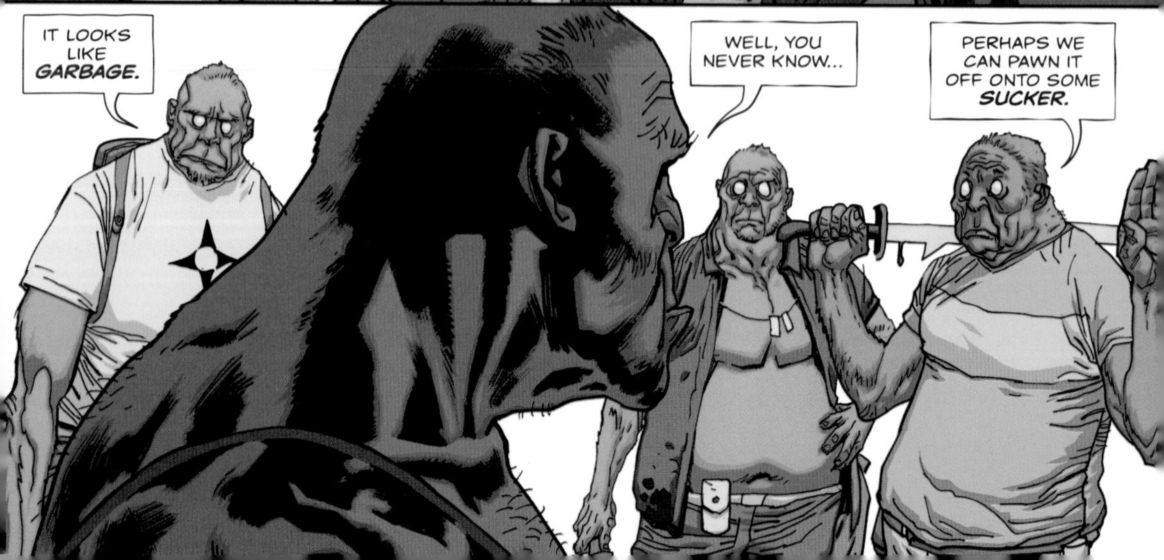
IT LOOKS LIKE **GARBAGE.**
WELL, YOU NEVER KNOW...
PERHAPS WE CAN PAWN IT OFF ONTO SOME **SUCKER.**

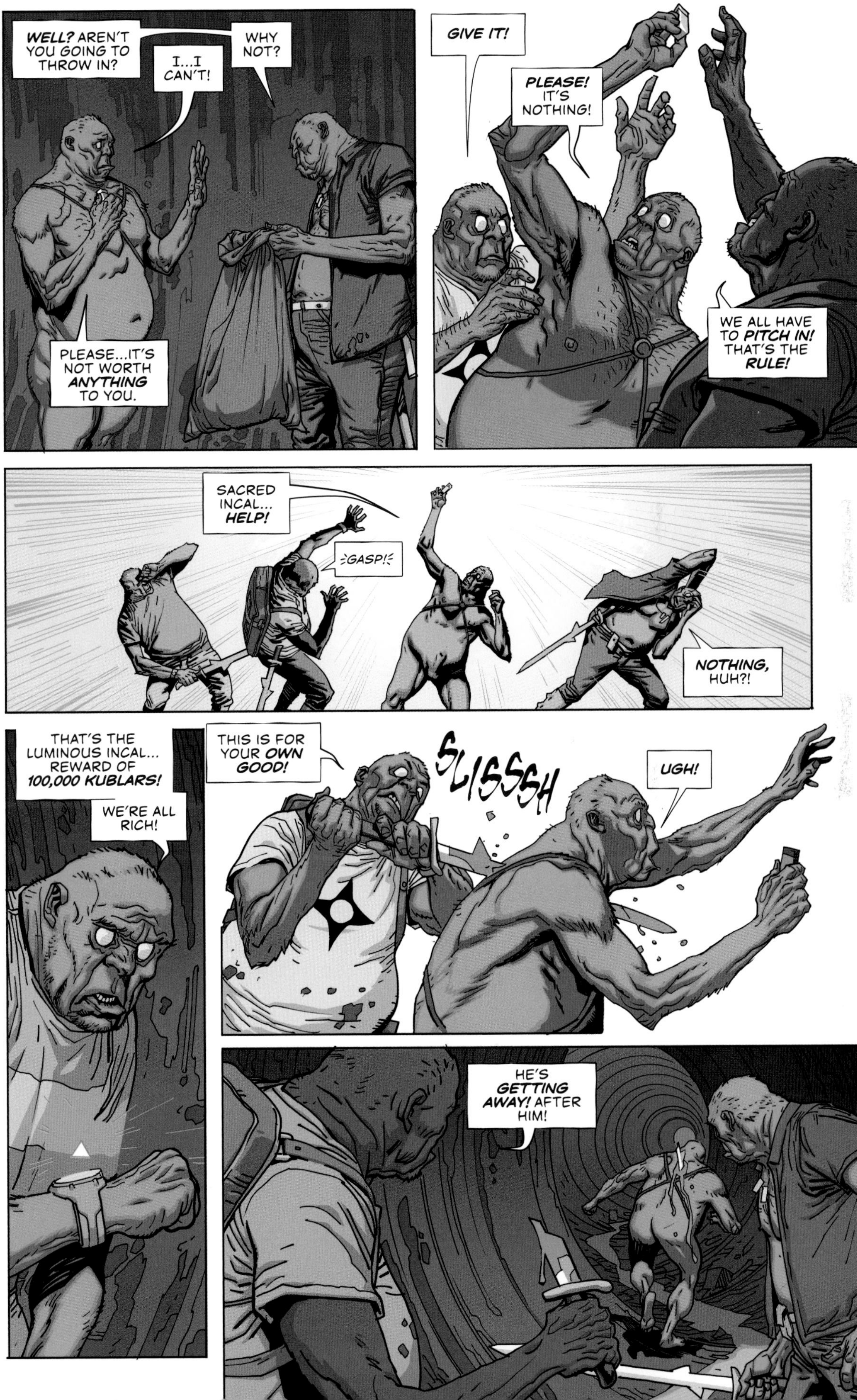
WELL? AREN'T YOU GOING TO THROW IN?
I...I CAN'T!
WHY NOT?
PLEASE...IT'S NOT WORTH ANYTHING TO YOU.
GIVE IT!
PLEASE! IT'S NOTHING!
WE ALL HAVE TO PITCH IN! THAT'S THE RULE!
SACRED INCAL... HELP!
GASP!
NOTHING, HUH?!
THAT'S THE LUMINOUS INCAL... REWARD OF 100,000 KUBLARS!
WE'RE ALL RICH!
THIS IS FOR YOUR OWN GOOD!
SLISSSH
UGH!
HE'S GETTING AWAY! AFTER HIM!

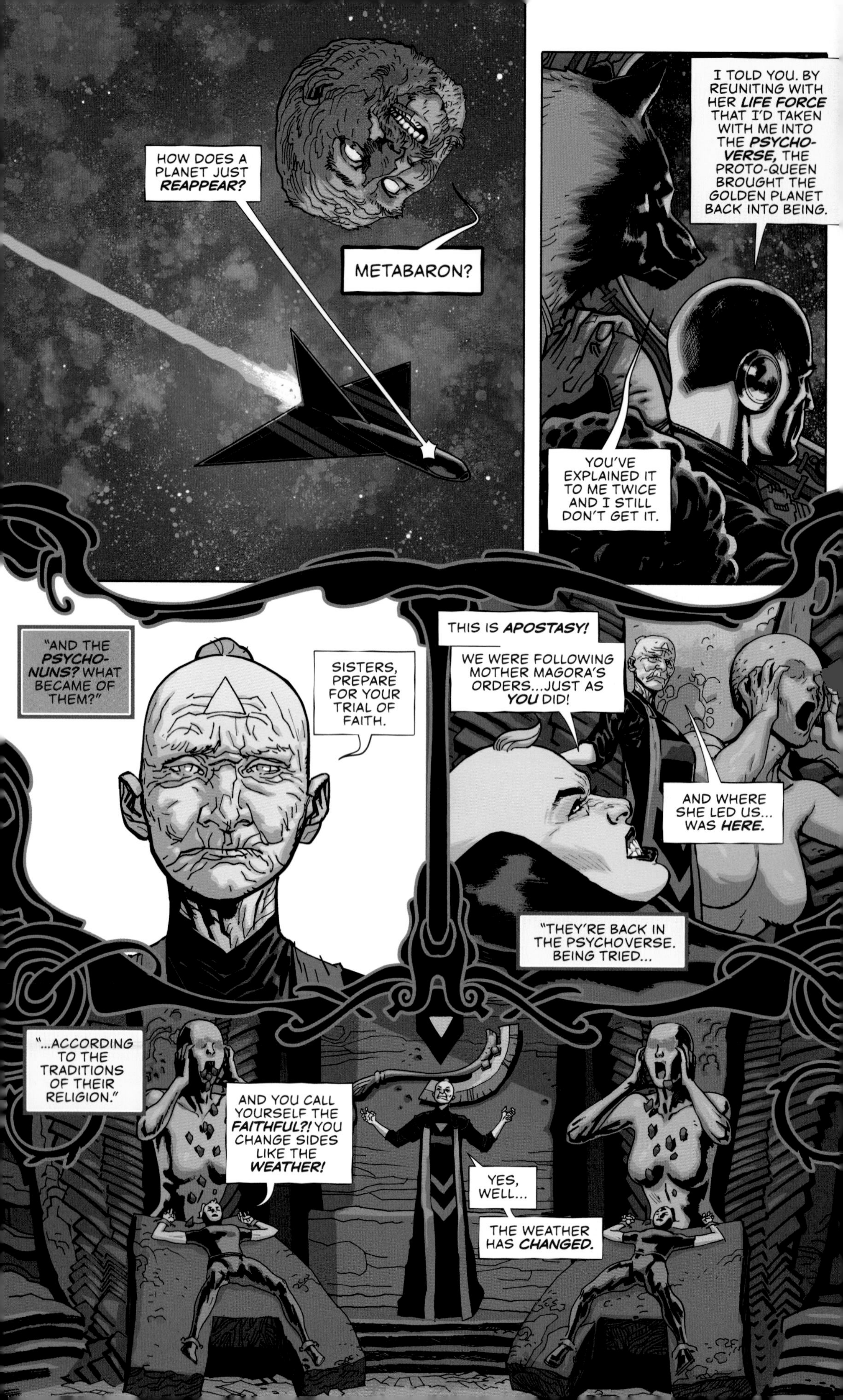
HOW DOES A PLANET JUST *REAPPEAR?*
METABARON?
I TOLD YOU. BY REUNITING WITH HER *LIFE FORCE* THAT I'D TAKEN WITH ME INTO THE *PSYCHO-VERSE,* THE PROTO-QUEEN BROUGHT THE GOLDEN PLANET BACK INTO BEING.
YOU'VE EXPLAINED IT TO ME TWICE AND I STILL DON'T GET IT.
"AND THE *PSYCHO-NUNS?* WHAT BECAME OF THEM?"
SISTERS, PREPARE FOR YOUR TRIAL OF FAITH.
THIS IS *APOSTASY!*
WE WERE FOLLOWING MOTHER MAGORA'S ORDERS...JUST AS *YOU* DID!
AND WHERE SHE LED US... WAS *HERE.*
"THEY'RE BACK IN THE PSYCHOVERSE. BEING TRIED...
"...ACCORDING TO THE TRADITIONS OF THEIR RELIGION."
AND YOU CALL YOURSELF THE *FAITHFUL?!* YOU CHANGE SIDES LIKE THE *WEATHER!*
YES, WELL...
THE WEATHER HAS *CHANGED.*

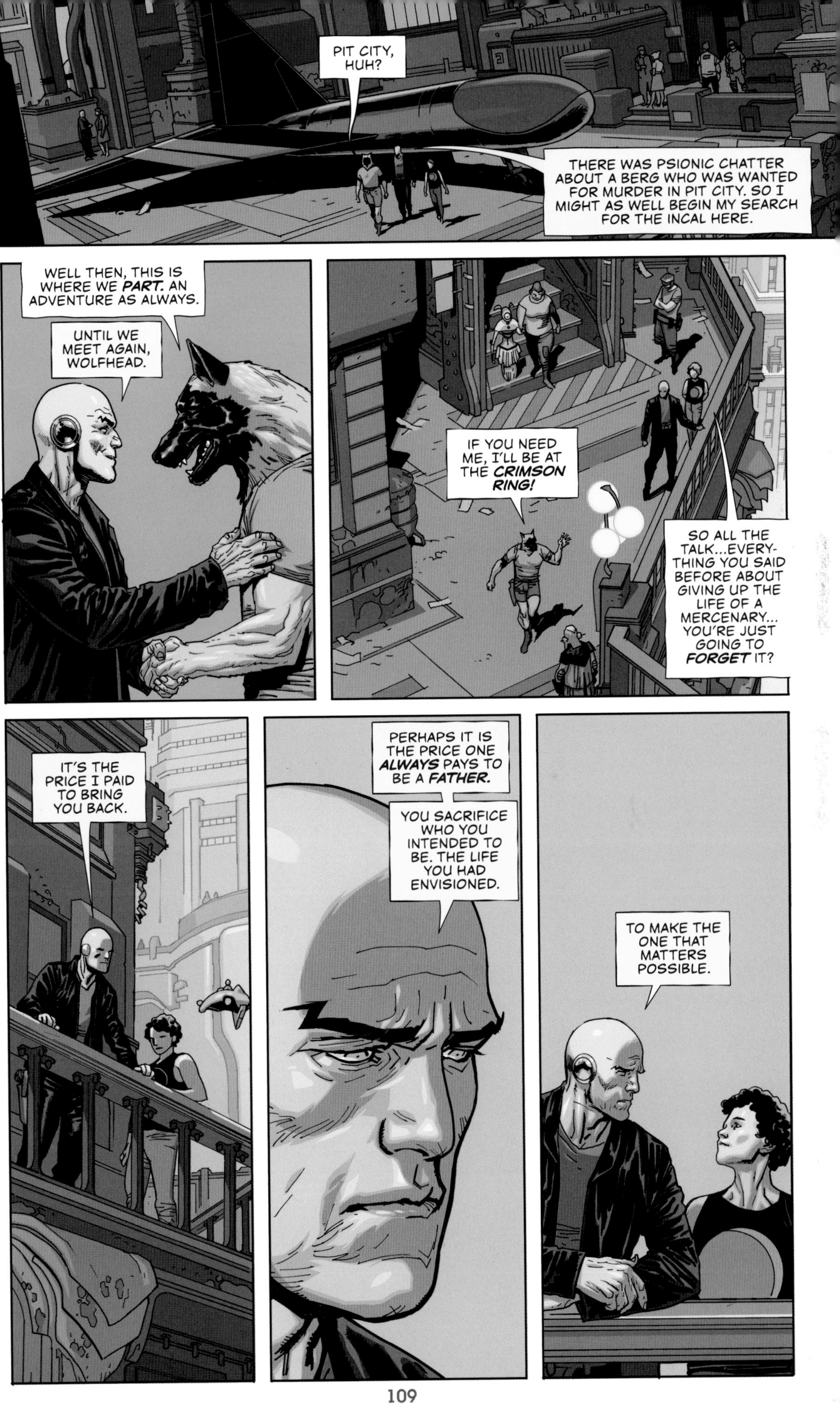
PIT CITY, HUH?
THERE WAS PSIONIC CHATTER ABOUT A BERG WHO WAS WANTED FOR MURDER IN PIT CITY. SO I MIGHT AS WELL BEGIN MY SEARCH FOR THE INCAL HERE.
WELL THEN, THIS IS WHERE WE **PART.** AN ADVENTURE AS ALWAYS.
UNTIL WE MEET AGAIN, WOLFHEAD.
IF YOU NEED ME, I'LL BE AT THE **CRIMSON RING!**
SO ALL THE TALK...EVERY-THING YOU SAID BEFORE ABOUT GIVING UP THE LIFE OF A MERCENARY... YOU'RE JUST GOING TO **FORGET** IT?
IT'S THE PRICE I PAID TO BRING YOU BACK.
PERHAPS IT IS THE PRICE ONE **ALWAYS** PAYS TO BE A **FATHER.**
YOU SACRIFICE WHO YOU INTENDED TO BE. THE LIFE YOU HAD ENVISIONED.
TO MAKE THE ONE THAT MATTERS POSSIBLE.

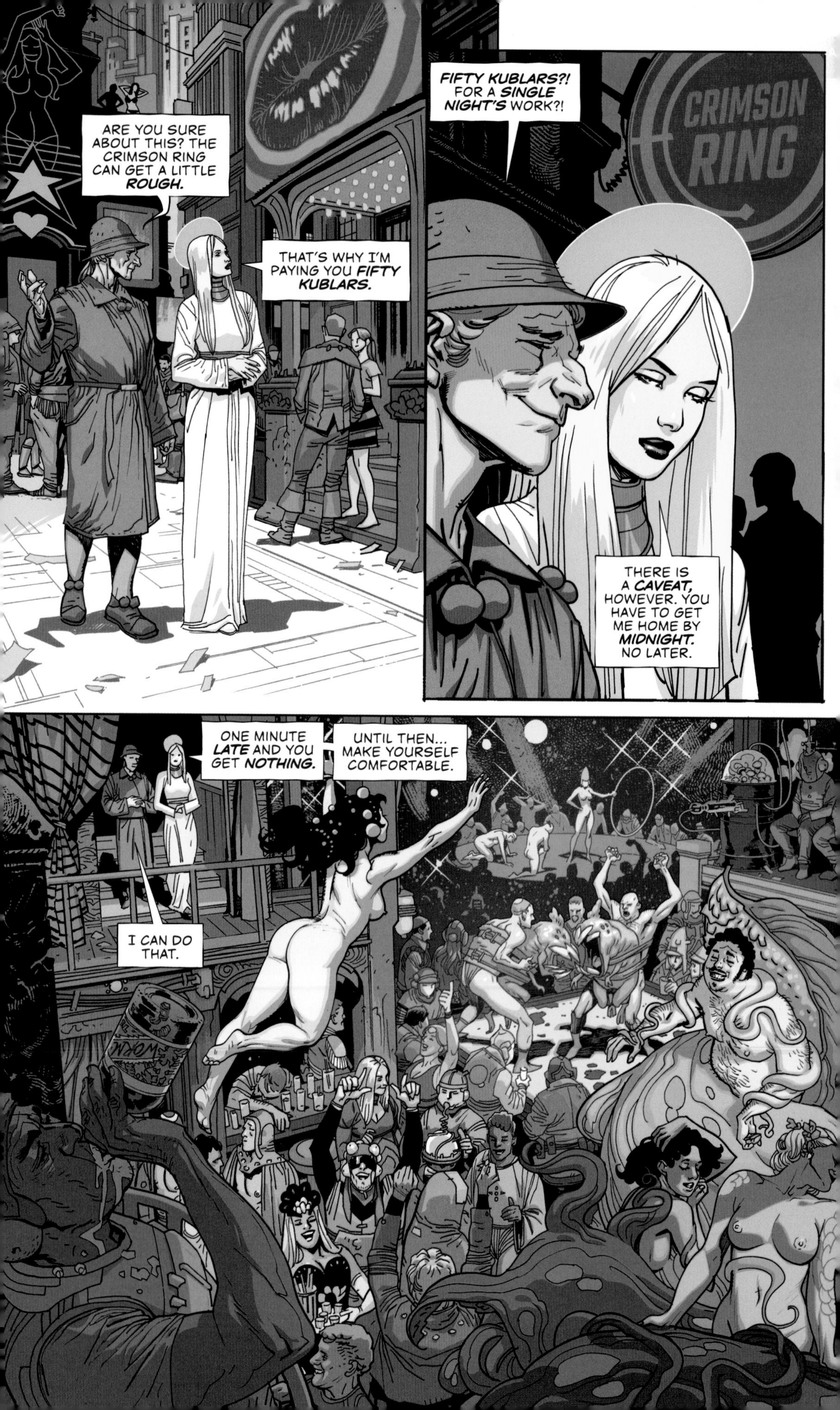
ARE YOU SURE ABOUT THIS? THE CRIMSON RING CAN GET A LITTLE *ROUGH.*
THAT'S WHY I'M PAYING YOU *FIFTY KUBLARS.*
FIFTY KUBLARS?! FOR A *SINGLE NIGHT'S* WORK?!
CRIMSON RING
THERE IS A *CAVEAT,* HOWEVER. YOU HAVE TO GET ME HOME BY *MIDNIGHT.* NO LATER.
ONE MINUTE *LATE* AND YOU GET *NOTHING.*
UNTIL THEN... MAKE YOURSELF COMFORTABLE.
I CAN DO THAT.

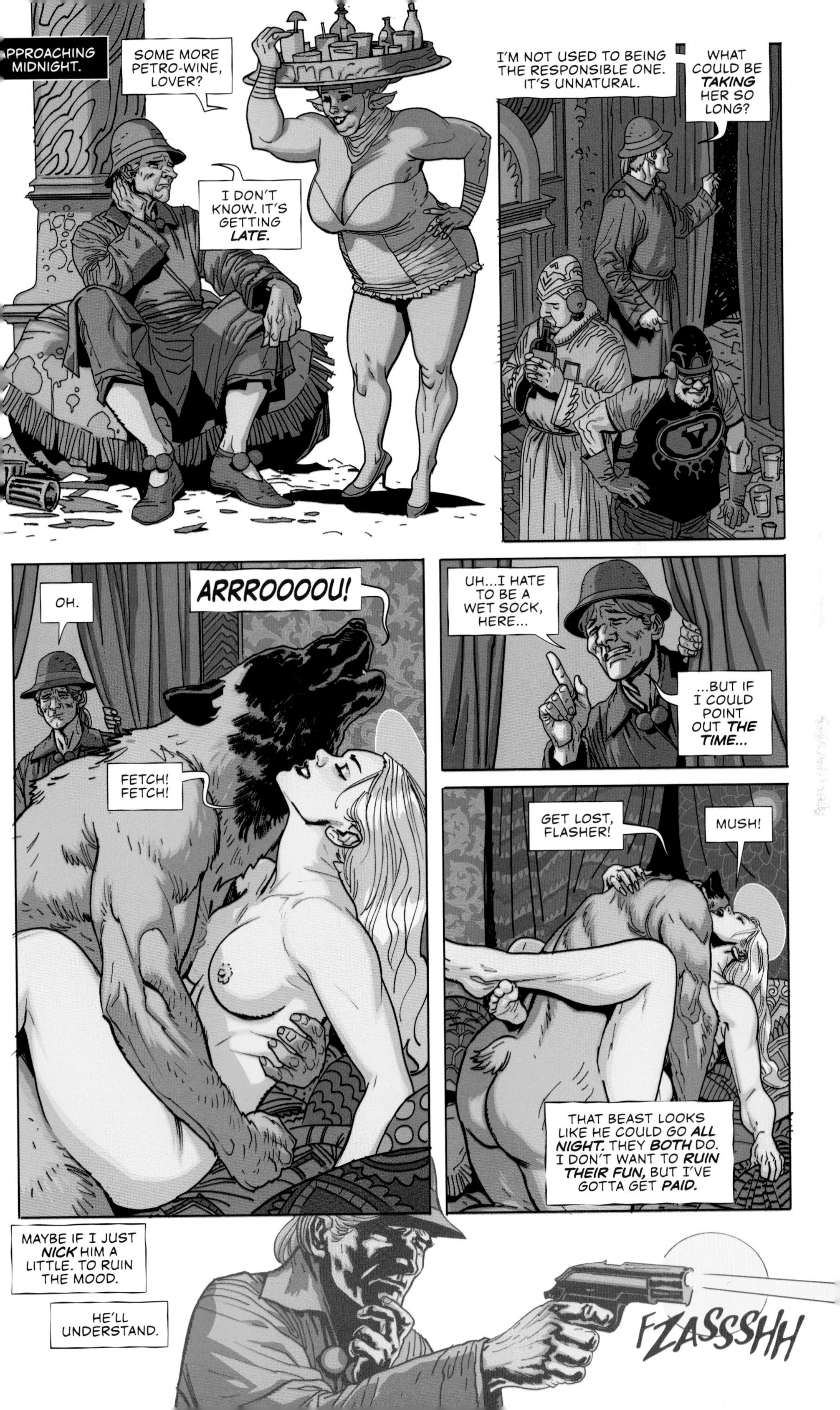
PPROACHING MIDNIGHT.
SOME MORE PETRO-WINE, LOVER?
I DON'T KNOW. IT'S GETTING LATE.
I'M NOT USED TO BEING THE RESPONSIBLE ONE. IT'S UNNATURAL.
WHAT COULD BE TAKING HER SO LONG?
OH.
ARRROOOOU!
FETCH! FETCH!
UH...I HATE TO BE A WET SOCK, HERE...
...BUT IF I COULD POINT OUT THE TIME...
GET LOST, FLASHER!
MUSH!
THAT BEAST LOOKS LIKE HE COULD GO ALL NIGHT. THEY BOTH DO. I DON'T WANT TO RUIN THEIR FUN, BUT I'VE GOTTA GET PAID.
MAYBE IF I JUST NICK HIM A LITTLE. TO RUIN THE MOOD.
HE'LL UNDERSTAND.
FZASSSHH

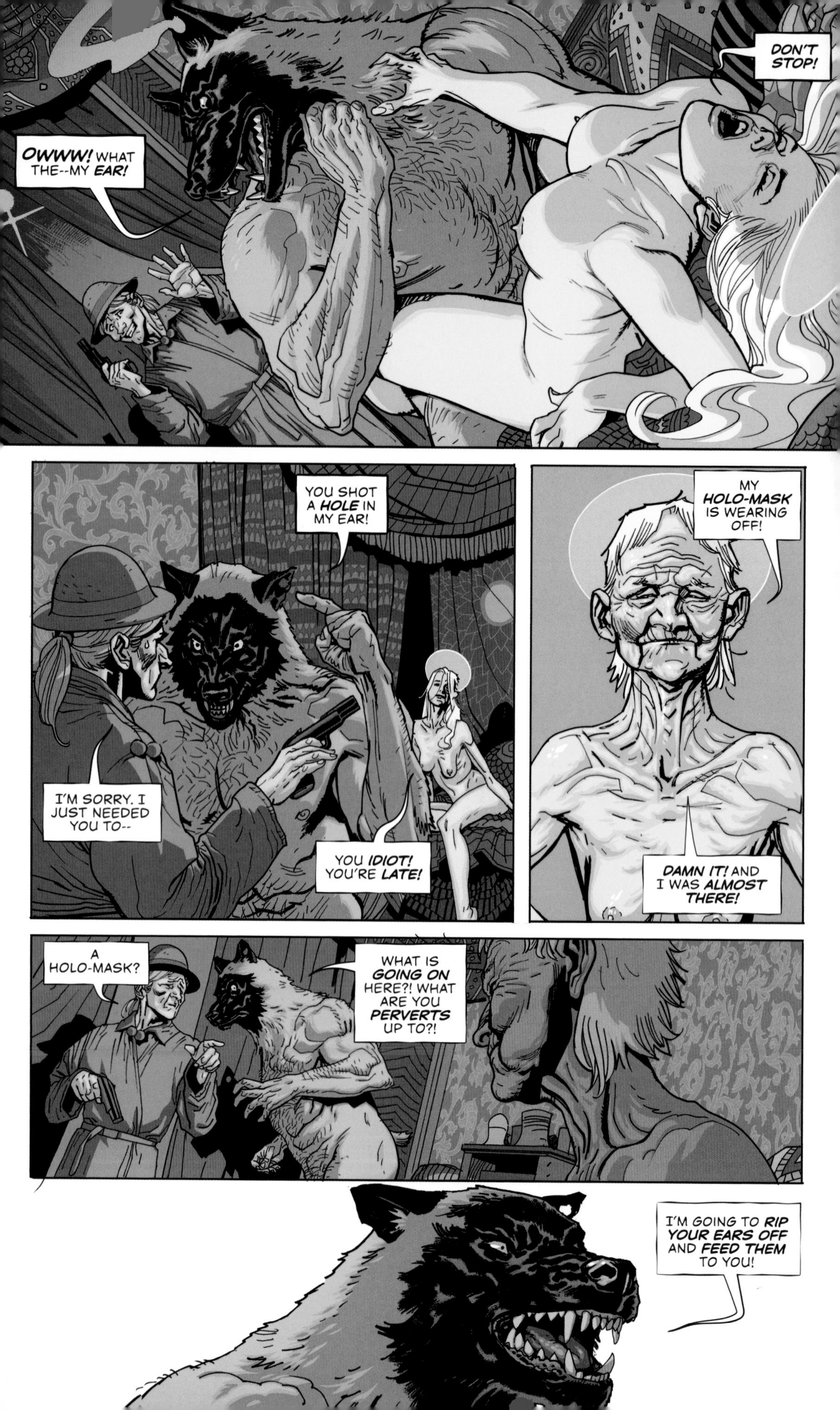
DON'T STOP!
OWWW! WHAT THE--MY EAR!
YOU SHOT A HOLE IN MY EAR!
I'M SORRY. I JUST NEEDED YOU TO--
YOU IDIOT! YOU'RE LATE!
MY HOLO-MASK IS WEARING OFF!
DAMN IT! AND I WAS ALMOST THERE!
A HOLO-MASK?
WHAT IS GOING ON HERE?! WHAT ARE YOU PERVERTS UP TO?!
I'M GOING TO RIP YOUR EARS OFF AND FEED THEM TO YOU!

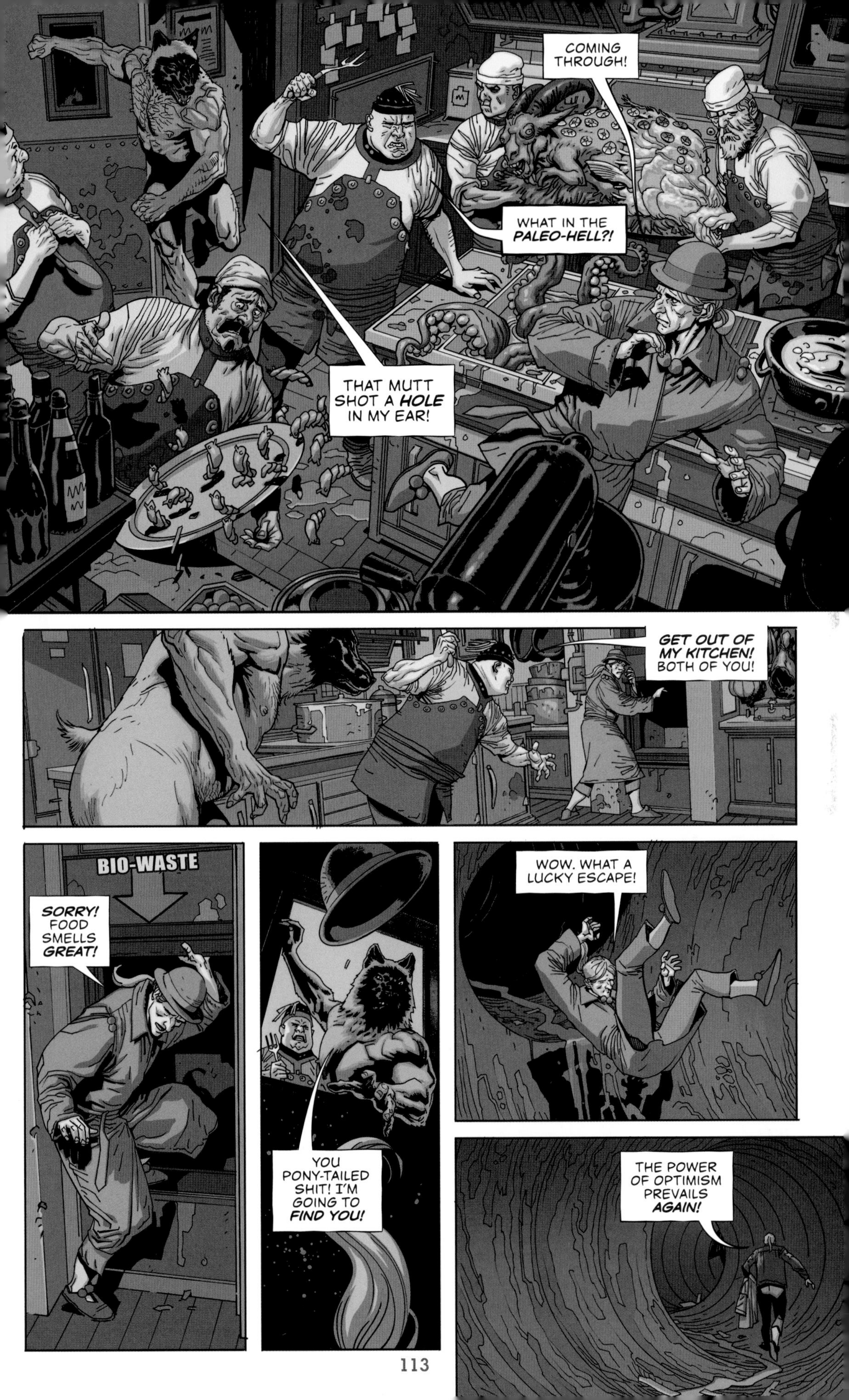
COMING THROUGH!
WHAT IN THE *PALEO-HELL?!*
THAT MUTT SHOT A *HOLE* IN MY EAR!
GET OUT OF MY KITCHEN! BOTH OF YOU!
BIO-WASTE
SORRY! FOOD SMELLS *GREAT!*
YOU PONY-TAILED SHIT! I'M GOING TO *FIND YOU!*
WOW. WHAT A LUCKY ESCAPE!
THE POWER OF OPTIMISM PREVAILS *AGAIN!*

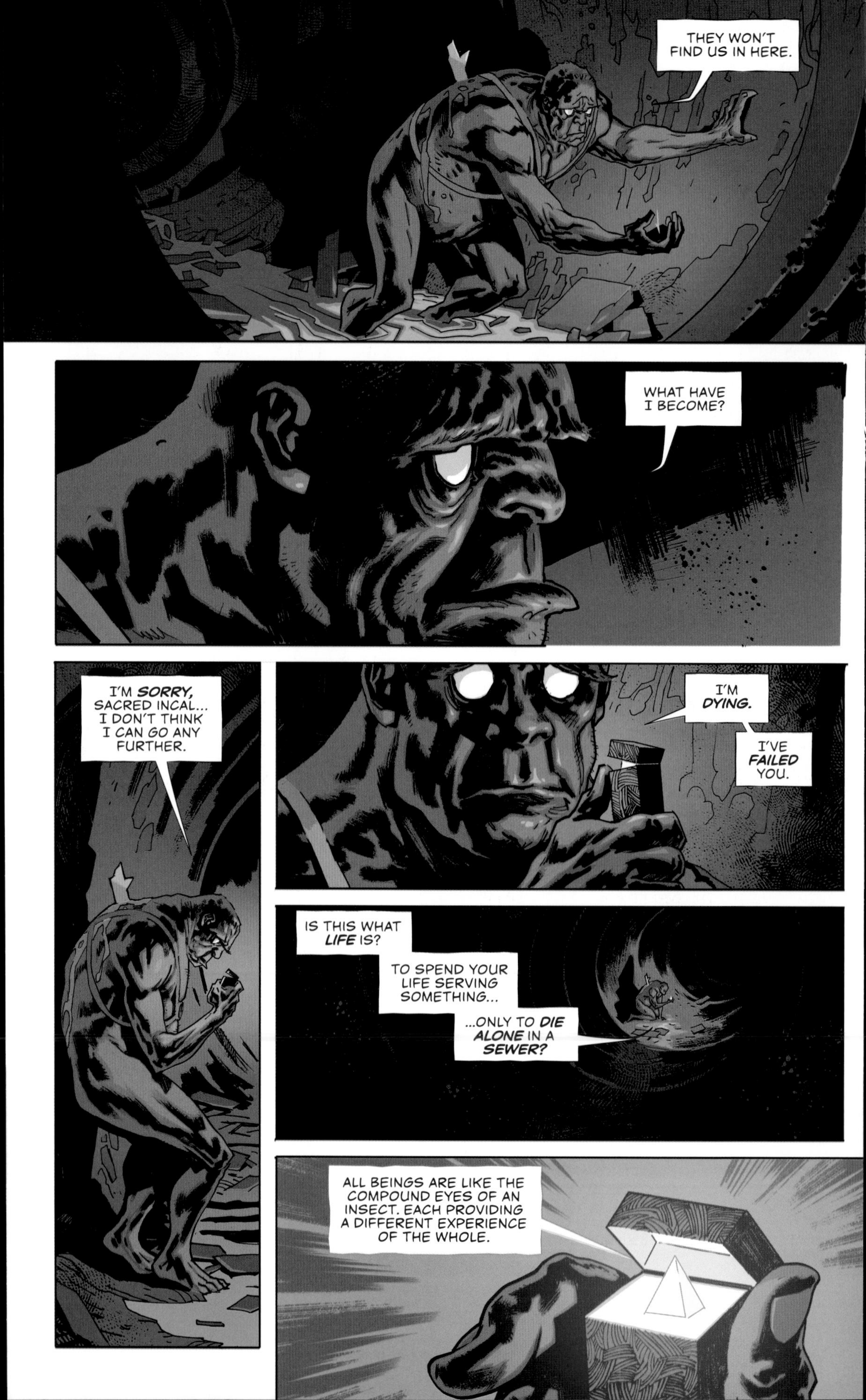
THEY WON'T FIND US IN HERE.
WHAT HAVE I BECOME?
I'M SORRY, SACRED INCAL... I DON'T THINK I CAN GO ANY FURTHER.
I'M DYING.
I'VE FAILED YOU.
IS THIS WHAT LIFE IS?
TO SPEND YOUR LIFE SERVING SOMETHING...
...ONLY TO DIE ALONE IN A SEWER?
ALL BEINGS ARE LIKE THE COMPOUND EYES OF AN INSECT. EACH PROVIDING A DIFFERENT EXPERIENCE OF THE WHOLE.

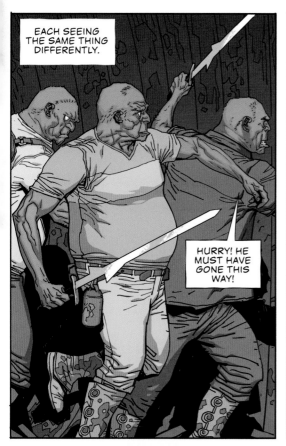

EACH SEEING THE SAME THING DIFFERENTLY.

HURRY! HE MUST HAVE GONE THIS WAY!

A SINGLE SHEET OF LIGHT SHONE THROUGH A COLANDER. ALL SERVING A COMMON PURPOSE...

I ALWAYS SEEM TO END UP IN A SEWER.

...UNKNOWN TO THEM ONLY BECAUSE OF THE ILLUSION OF SEPARATION.

BUT THE LIGHT OF CONSCIOUSNESS NEEDS TO SHINE *EVERYWHERE.* EVEN IN THE DEPTHS WHERE ALL SEEMS LOST. *ESPECIALLY* IN THE DEPTHS. YOU MERELY TOOK THE LIGHT WHERE IT NEEDED TO GO.

SO YOU DID NOT *FAIL,* MY FRIEND. NO ONE *EVER* FAILS...

AND NO ONE IS *ALONE.*

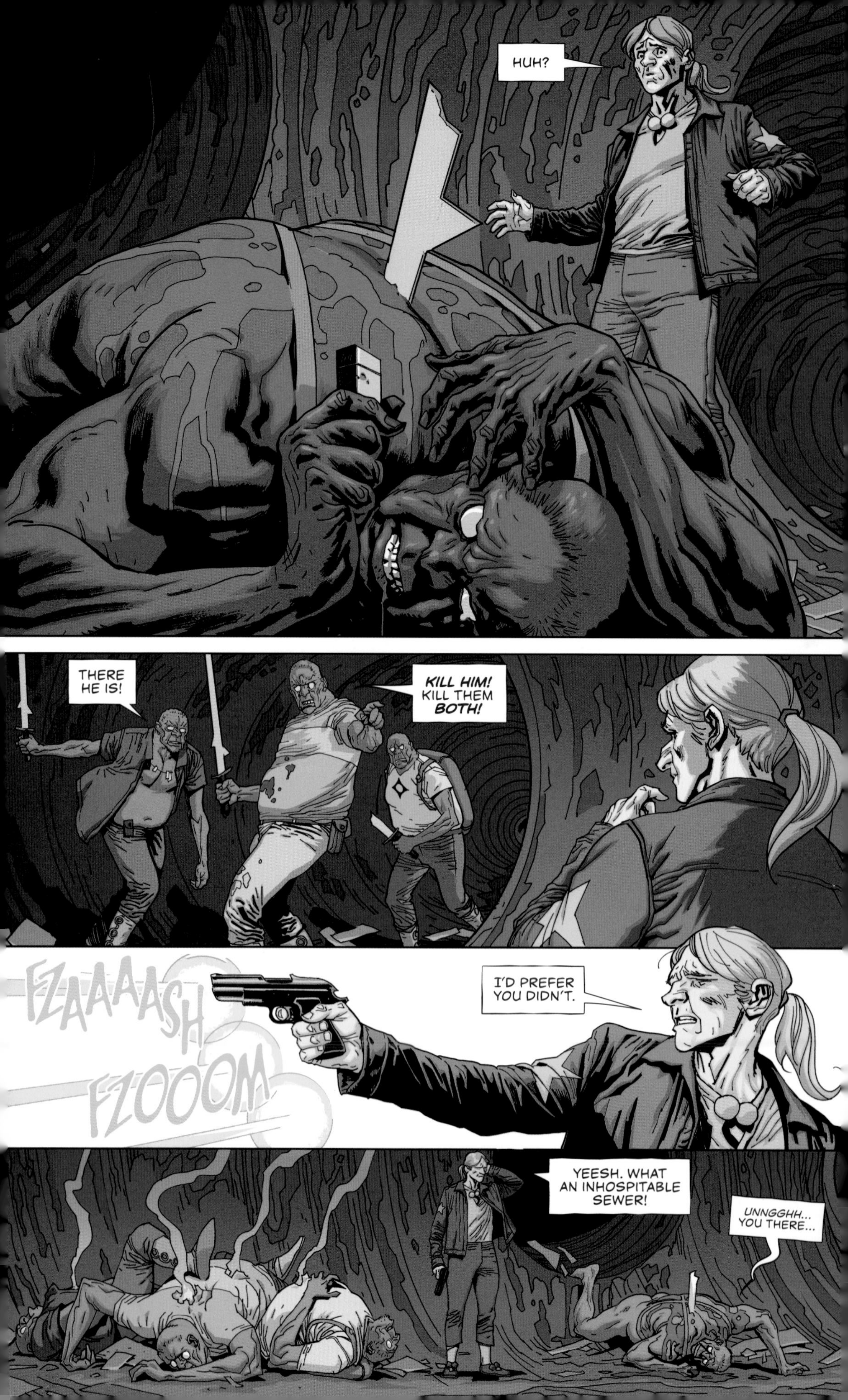
HUH?
THERE HE IS!
KILL HIM! KILL THEM BOTH!
FZAAAAASH
FZOOOM
I'D PREFER YOU DIDN'T.
YEESH. WHAT AN INHOSPITABLE SEWER!
UNNGGHH... YOU THERE...

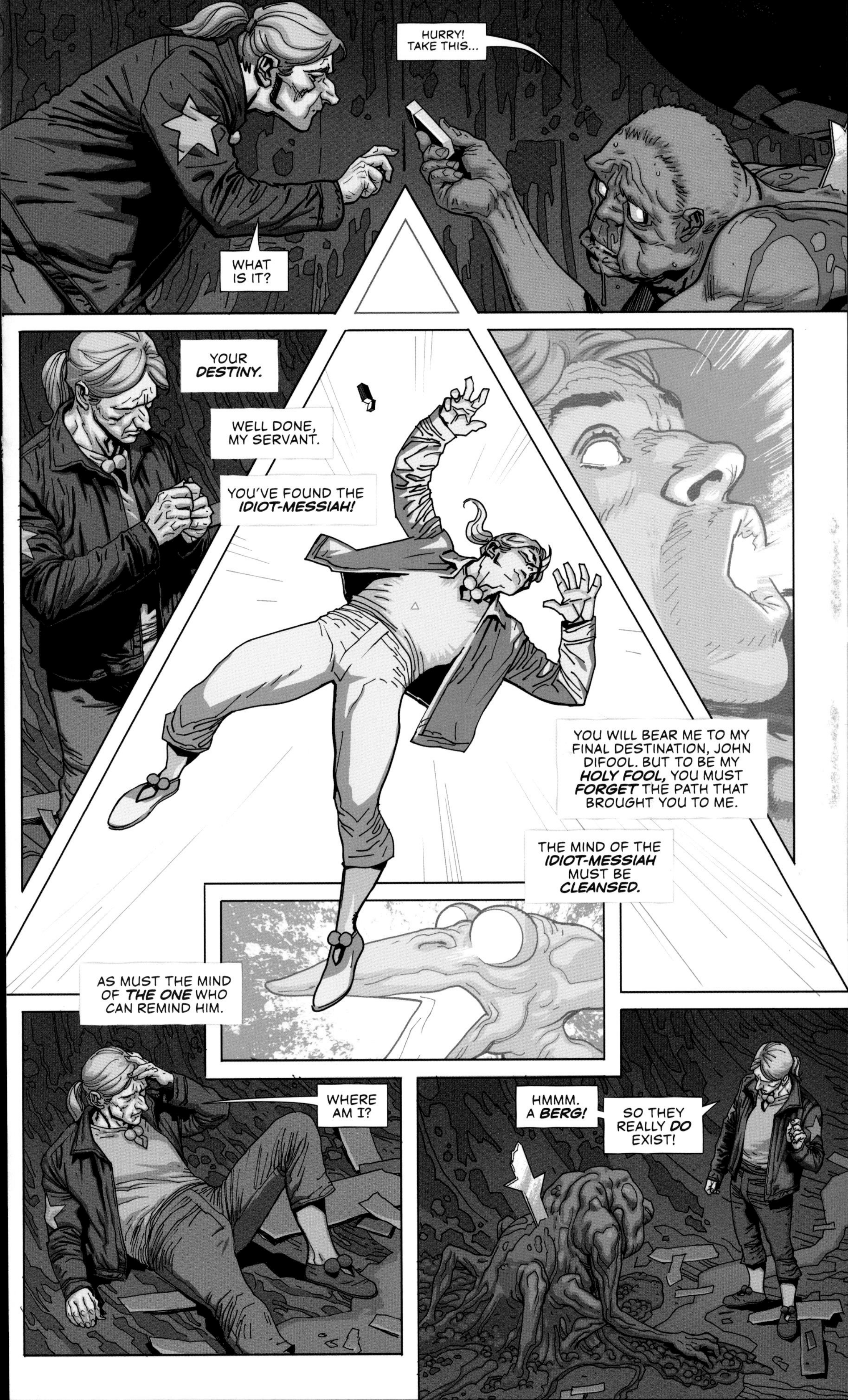
HURRY! TAKE THIS...
WHAT IS IT?
YOUR DESTINY.
WELL DONE, MY SERVANT.
YOU'VE FOUND THE IDIOT-MESSIAH!
YOU WILL BEAR ME TO MY FINAL DESTINATION, JOHN DIFOOL. BUT TO BE MY HOLY FOOL, YOU MUST FORGET THE PATH THAT BROUGHT YOU TO ME.
THE MIND OF THE IDIOT-MESSIAH MUST BE CLEANSED.
AS MUST THE MIND OF THE ONE WHO CAN REMIND HIM.
WHERE AM I?
HMMM. A BERG!
SO THEY REALLY DO EXIST!

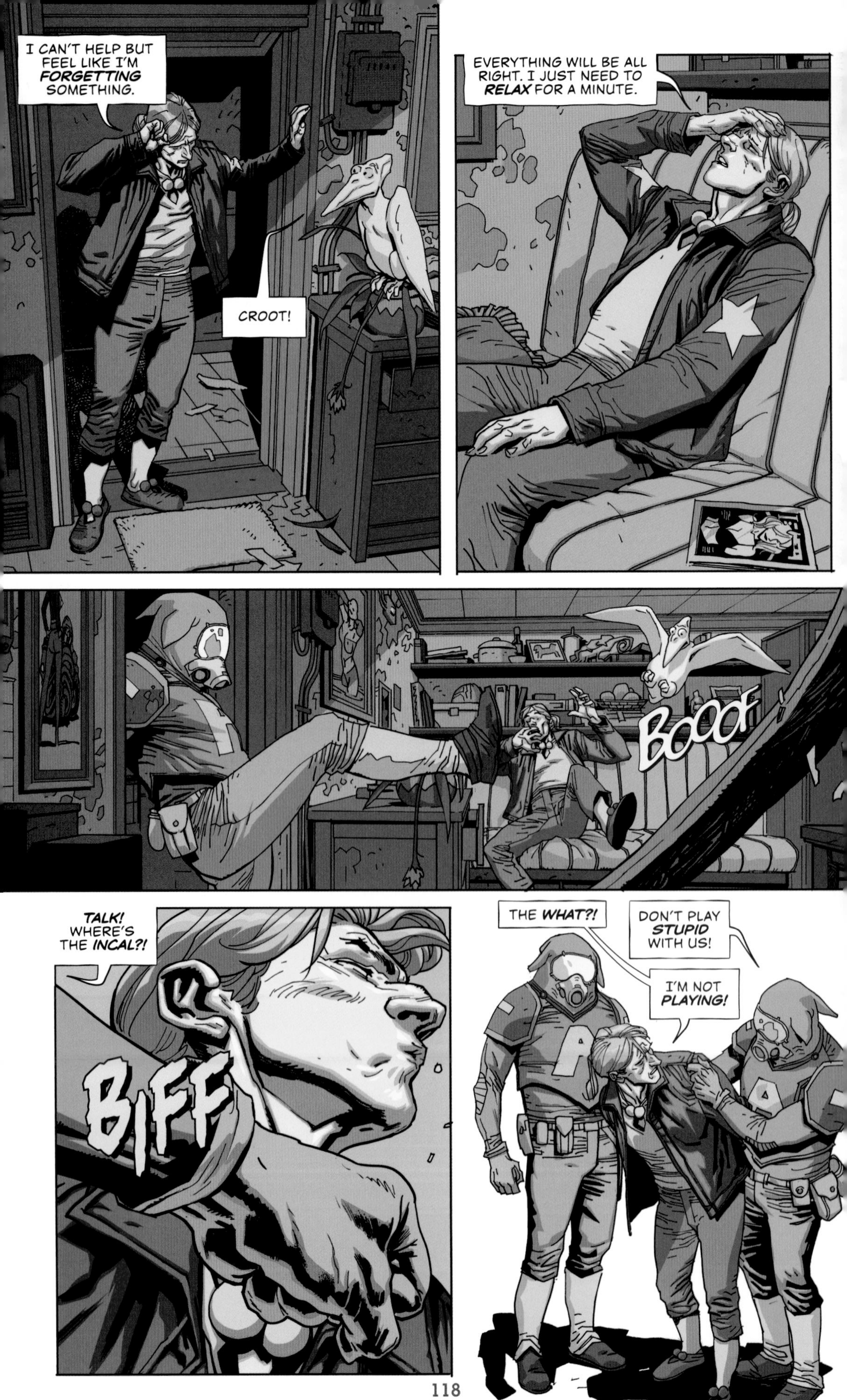
I CAN'T HELP BUT FEEL LIKE I'M **FORGETTING** SOMETHING.
CROOT!
EVERYTHING WILL BE ALL RIGHT. I JUST NEED TO **RELAX** FOR A MINUTE.
BOOOF
TALK! WHERE'S THE **INCAL?!**
BIFF
THE **WHAT?!**
DON'T PLAY **STUPID** WITH US!
I'M NOT **PLAYING!**

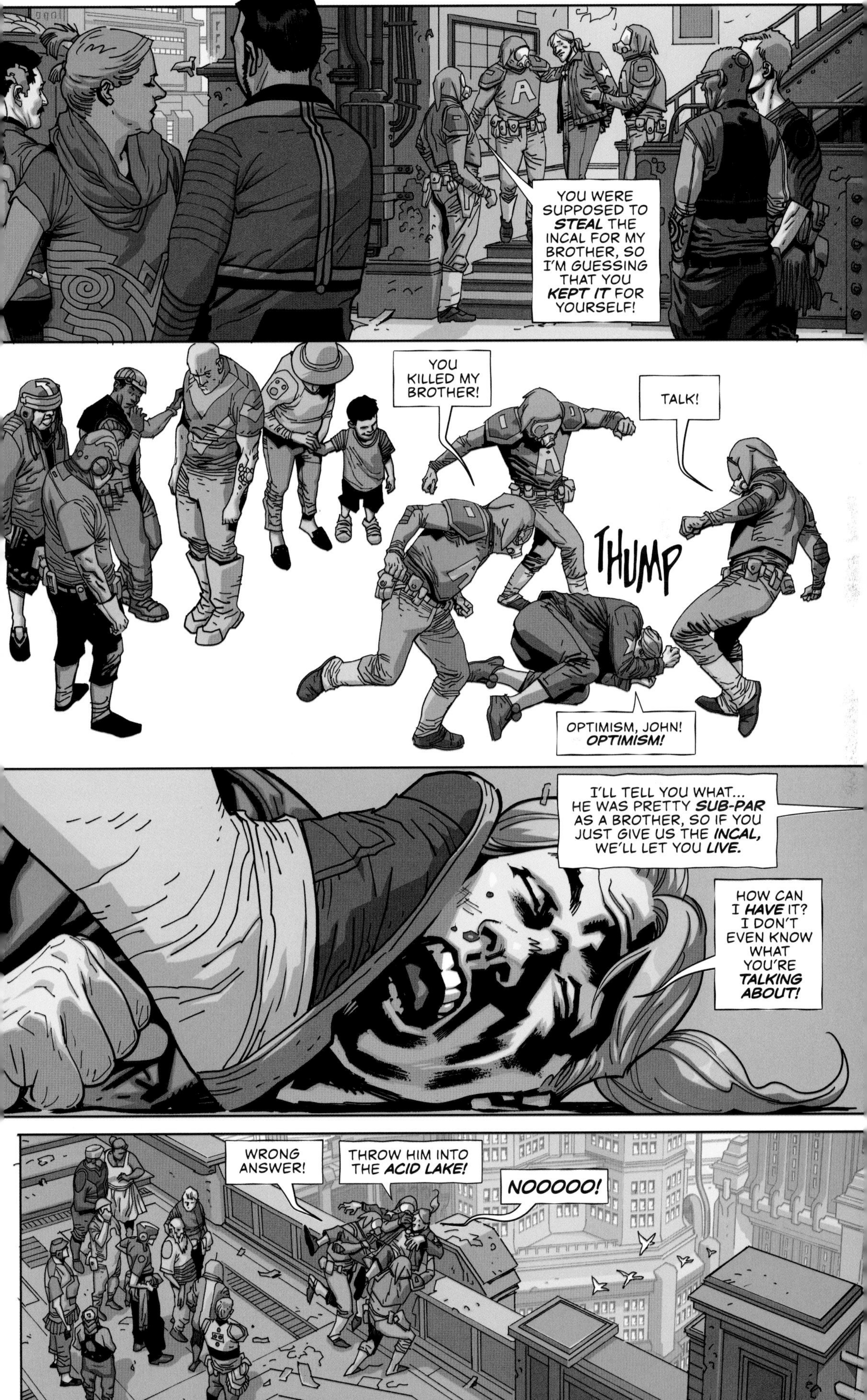
YOU WERE SUPPOSED TO STEAL THE INCAL FOR MY BROTHER, SO I'M GUESSING THAT YOU KEPT IT FOR YOURSELF!
YOU KILLED MY BROTHER!
TALK!
THUMP
OPTIMISM, JOHN! OPTIMISM!
I'LL TELL YOU WHAT... HE WAS PRETTY SUB-PAR AS A BROTHER, SO IF YOU JUST GIVE US THE INCAL, WE'LL LET YOU LIVE.
HOW CAN I HAVE IT? I DON'T EVEN KNOW WHAT YOU'RE TALKING ABOUT!
WRONG ANSWER!
THROW HIM INTO THE ACID LAKE!
NOOOOO!

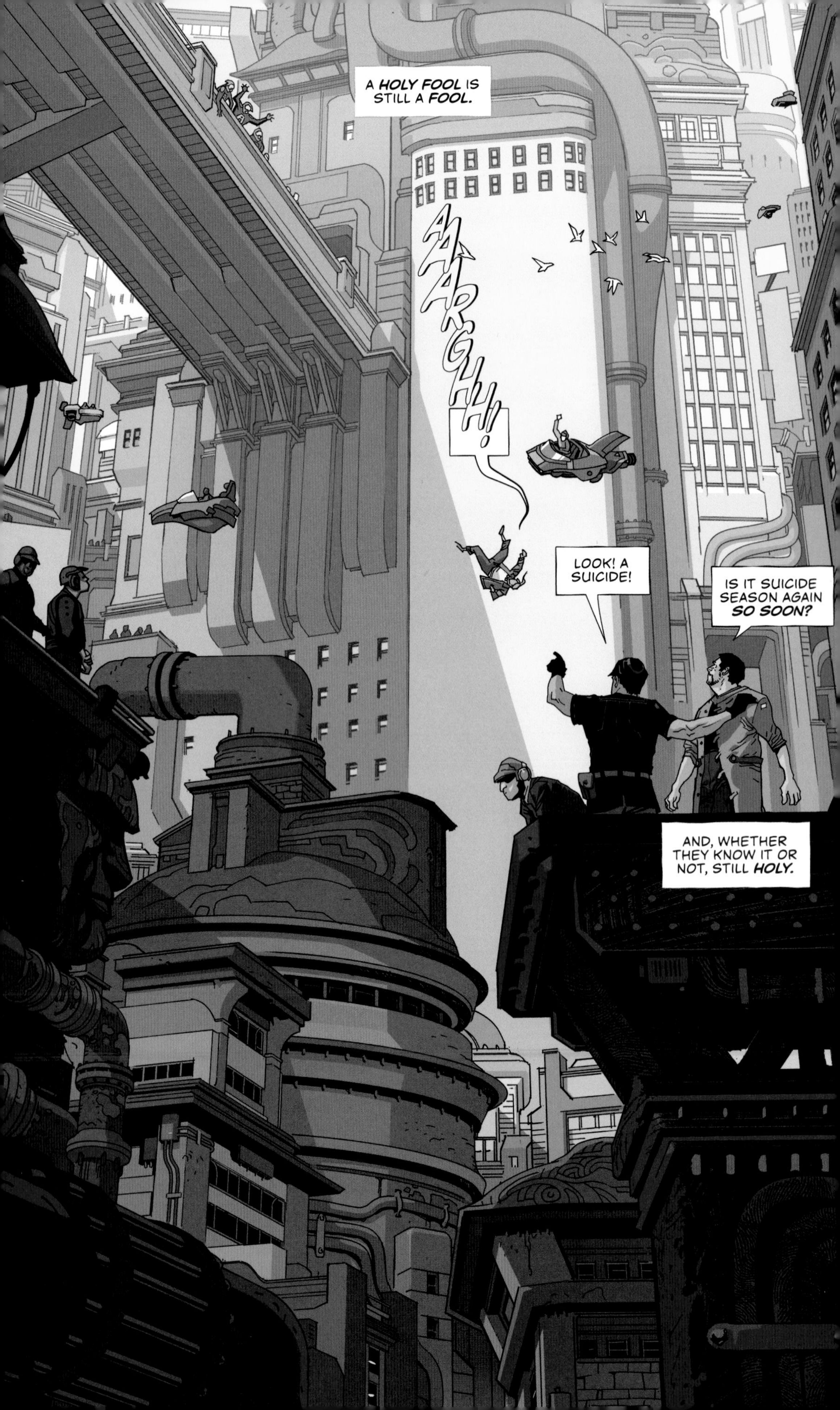
A HOLY FOOL IS STILL A FOOL.
AAARGHH!
LOOK! A SUICIDE!
IS IT SUICIDE SEASON AGAIN SO SOON?
AND, WHETHER THEY KNOW IT OR NOT, STILL HOLY.

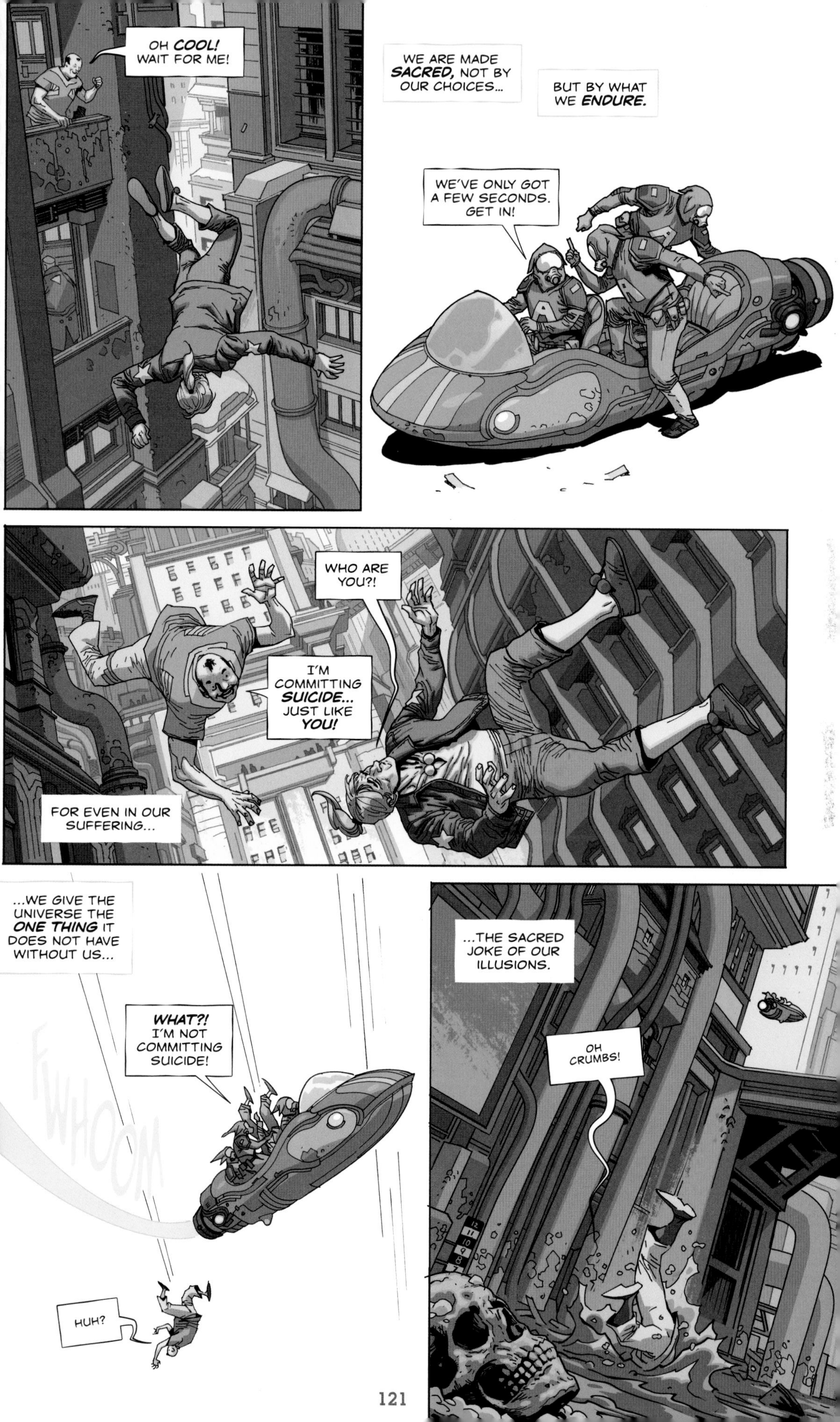
OH COOL! WAIT FOR ME!
WE ARE MADE SACRED, NOT BY OUR CHOICES...
BUT BY WHAT WE ENDURE.
WE'VE ONLY GOT A FEW SECONDS. GET IN!
WHO ARE YOU?!
I'M COMMITTING SUICIDE... JUST LIKE YOU!
FOR EVEN IN OUR SUFFERING...
...WE GIVE THE UNIVERSE THE ONE THING IT DOES NOT HAVE WITHOUT US...
FWHOOM
WHAT?! I'M NOT COMMITTING SUICIDE!
HUH?
...THE SACRED JOKE OF OUR ILLUSIONS.
OH CRUMBS!

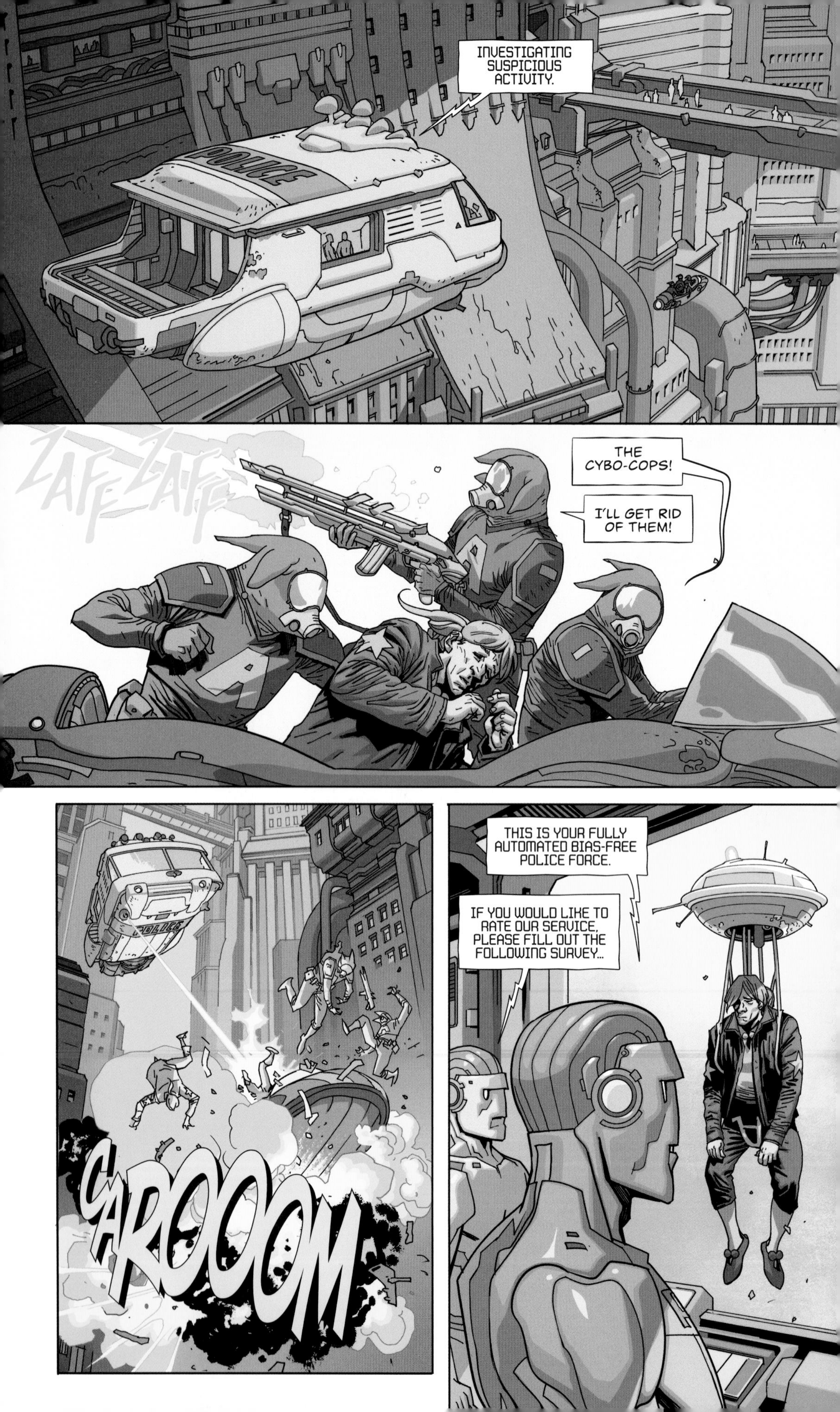
INVESTIGATING SUSPICIOUS ACTIVITY.
POLICE
ZAFF ZAFF
THE CYBO-COPS!
I'LL GET RID OF THEM!
CAROOOM
THIS IS YOUR FULLY AUTOMATED BIAS-FREE POLICE FORCE.
IF YOU WOULD LIKE TO RATE OUR SERVICE, PLEASE FILL OUT THE FOLLOWING SURVEY...

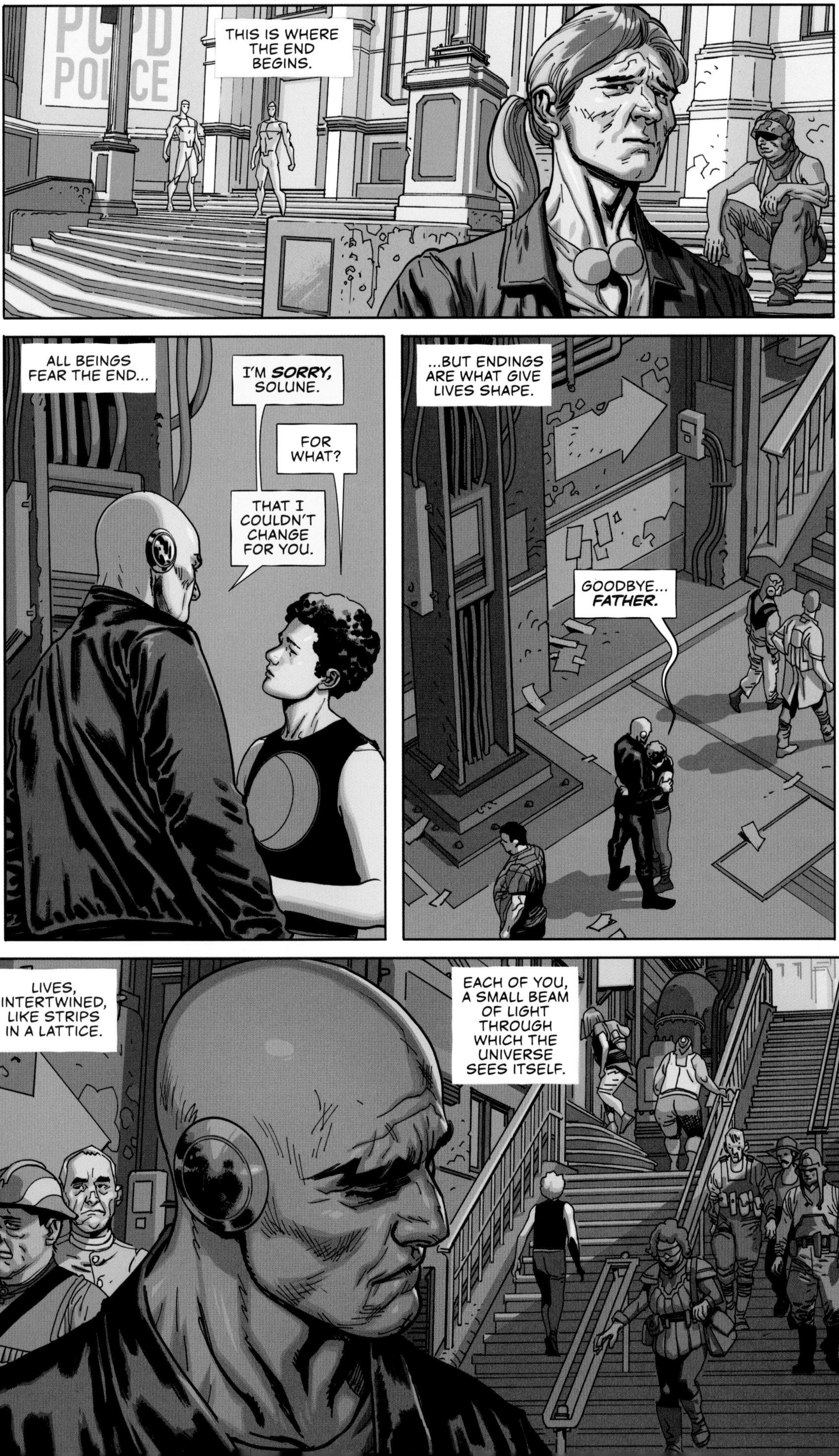
THIS IS WHERE THE END BEGINS.
ALL BEINGS FEAR THE END...
I'M **SORRY,** SOLUNE.
FOR WHAT?
THAT I COULDN'T CHANGE FOR YOU.
...BUT ENDINGS ARE WHAT GIVE LIVES SHAPE.
GOODBYE... ***FATHER.***
LIVES, INTERTWINED, LIKE STRIPS IN A LATTICE.
EACH OF YOU, A SMALL BEAM OF LIGHT THROUGH WHICH THE UNIVERSE SEES ITSELF.

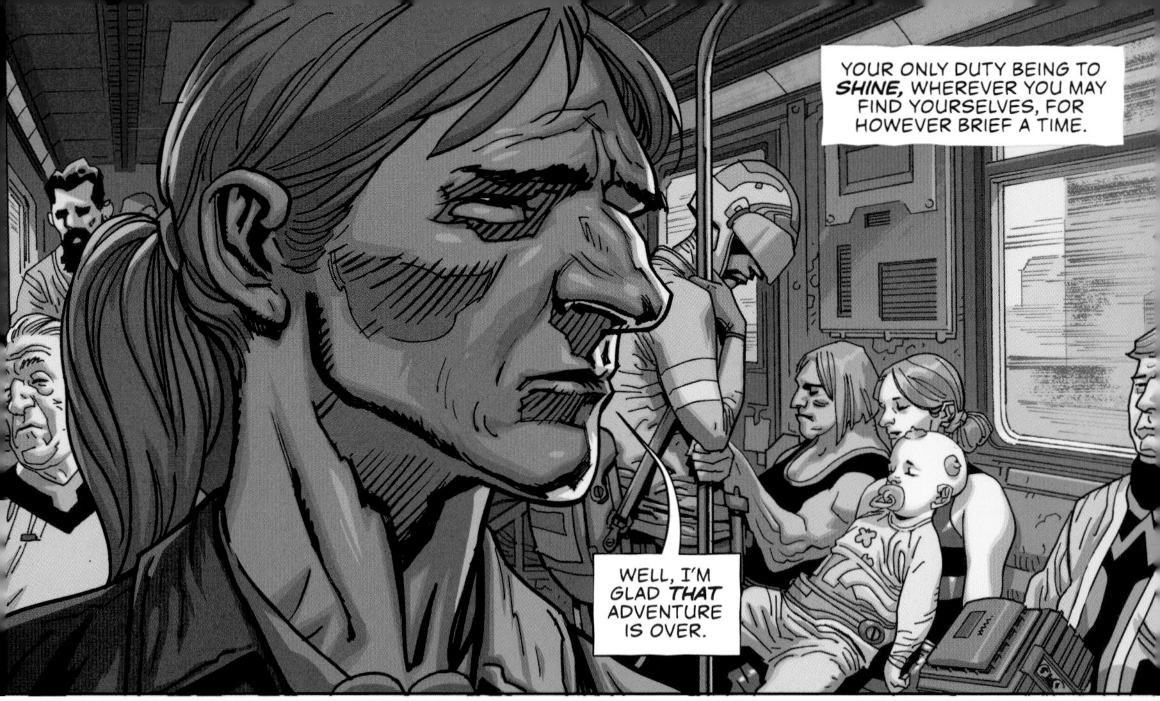
YOUR ONLY DUTY BEING TO SHINE, WHEREVER YOU MAY FIND YOURSELVES, FOR HOWEVER BRIEF A TIME.
WELL, I'M GLAD THAT ADVENTURE IS OVER.

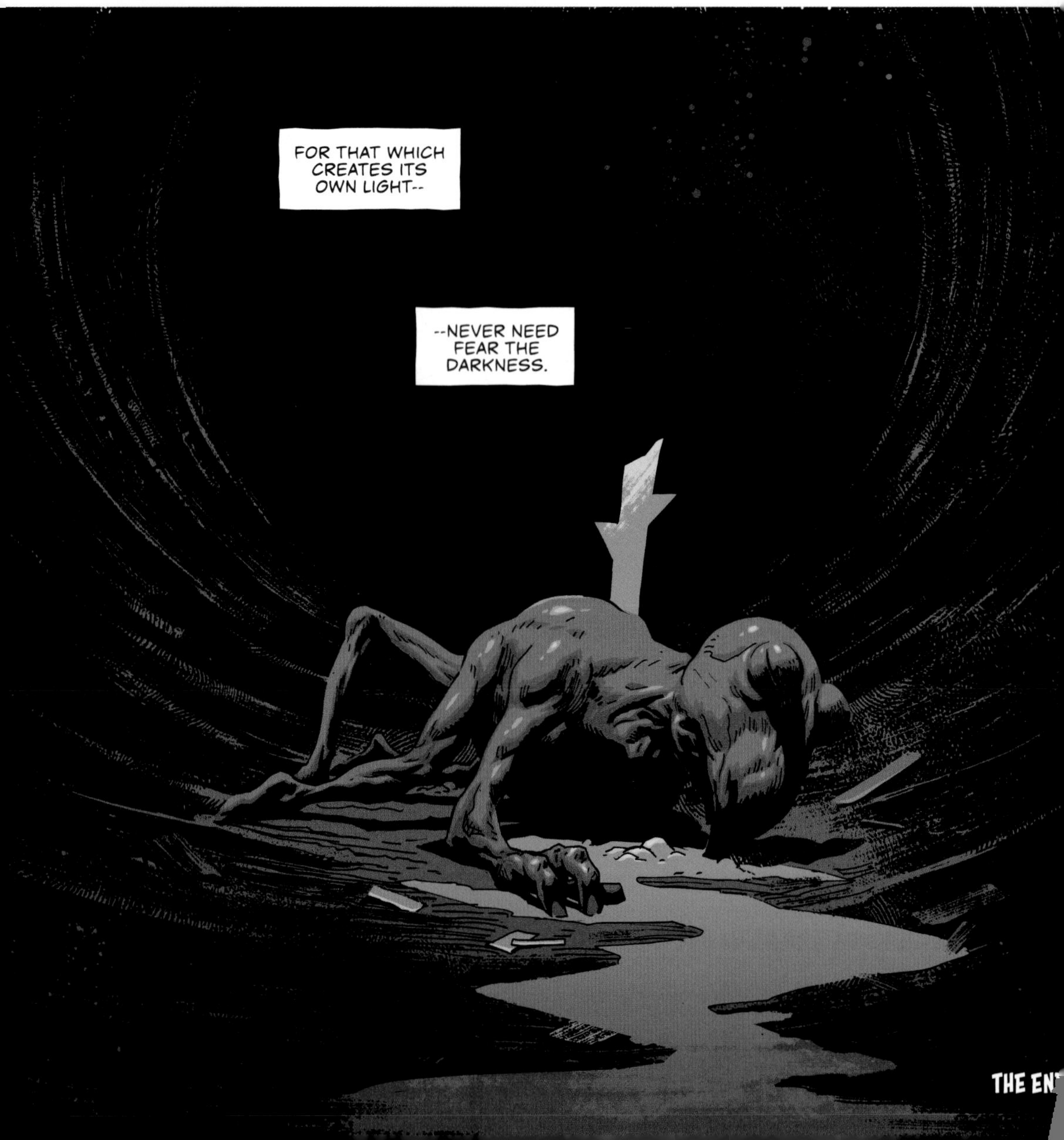
FOR THAT WHICH CREATES ITS OWN LIGHT--
--NEVER NEED FEAR THE DARKNESS.

AUTHOR BIOS

Mark Russell: In 2015, Mark Russell made his debut in comics with his critically acclaimed reboot of the DC comic *Prez* with Ben Caldwell. Russell went on to write highly praised runs on *The Flintstones*, *Exit, Stage Left!: The Snagglepuss Chronicles*, and *The Wonder Twins* at DC, as well as *Red Sonja* for Dynamite and the controversial *Second Coming* at AHOY Comics.

Yanick Paquette: Yanick Paquette began his career as a comic book illustrator in the United States in 1994. He worked for Topps, Marvel, and DC Comics, illustrating titles including *Wonder-Woman*, *Superman*, *Batman*, *Avengers*, *JLA*, *X-Men*, *Wolverine Weapon X*, *Terra Obscura*, *Seven Soldiers*, *Swamp Thing*, and *Earth One*. He collaborates with the biggest writers of the medium, including Alan Moore, Scott Snyder, Jason Aaron, and Grant Morrison.

Dave McCaig: Dave McCaig is a Canadian artist and colorist who also works in the animation industry. He has worked on comics including *Adam Strange*, *X-Men*, *Star Wars*, *Superman: Birthright*, *The Matrix Comics*, *Nextwave*, *New Avengers*, *Northlanders*, *American Vampire*, and *Nemesis*. Animation projects have included key colour design on the first three seasons of *The Batman* (2004) animated series at Warner Brothers and various duties on the fourth *Teenage Mutant Ninja Turtles* film.

Troy Peteri: Troy Peteri started lettering in the late 1900s and forgot to stop. Since that time he's lettered approximately half a squillion pages of comics, many of which include *Batman*, *Spider-Man*, *Witchblade*, and now *The Metabaron*, *Psychoverse*, *Dying Star*, and *Kill Wolfhead* from Humanoids' Incal Universe.

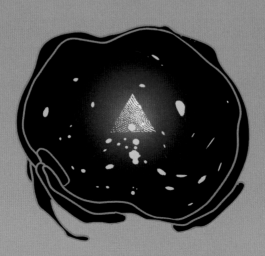

MAPPING OUT THE INCAL UNIVERSE

Since its original publication, *The Incal* has spawned an entire universe of adventures centered around its characters and concepts. The following is a suggested reading order for these various graphic novels, available to order through your local comic book retailer.

1 THE INCAL

Story by Jodorowsky | Art by Mœbius

Start here to avoid spoilers and introduce yourself properly to the expansive Incal Universe. John Difool, a low-class detective in a degenerate dystopian world, finds his life turned upside down when he discovers an ancient, mystical artifact called "the Incal." Difool's adventures bring him into conflict with the galaxy's greatest warrior, the Metabaron, and pit him against the awesome powers of the Technopriests.

jodorowsky · mœbius
THE INCAL
HUMANOIDS

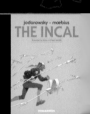

2 BEFORE THE INCAL

Story by Jodorowsky | Art by Zoran Janjetov

The adventures of a young John Difool before he became a famous sci-fi anti-hero. Orphaned at an early age, Difool becomes a "pre-detective" who uncovers a dark secret with serious political ramifications. He's helped along the way by Deepo, a concrete seagull he rescues from the streets.

jodorowsky · janjetov
BEFORE THE INCAL
HUMANOIDS

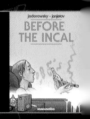

3 AFTER THE INCAL

Story by Jodorowsky | Art by Mœbius

In an alternate-world finale to John Difool's story—and Mœbius's final contribution to the Incal saga—a mysterious, metallic virus has devastated the immense City-Shaft, and Difool once more has to save the day. *After the Incal* was left incomplete due to Mœbius' untimely death, and was later reimagined in *Final Incal*.

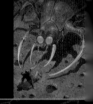

4 FINAL INCAL

Story by Jodorowsky | Art by José Ladrönn

John Difool finds himself in the middle of a galactic war between the Bethacodon and Elohim. The only way to save the galaxy is to find and rescue ***Before the Incal***'s Luz De Garra, prisoner of the Gounas.

jodorowsky · ladrönn
FINAL INCAL
HUMANOIDS

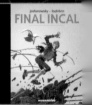

5 METABARONS GENESIS: CASTAKA

Story by Jodorowsky | Art by Das Pastors

The origin of the first Metabaron, Dayal de Castaka. Far from being noble warriors with an inflexible code, we learn that the earliest Metabarons were disloyal, vengeful pirates born out of brutality and war.

METABARONS GENESIS:
CASTAKA
HUMANOIDS

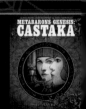

6 THE METABARONS (FIRST CYCLE)

Story by Jodorowsky | Art by Juan Giménez

This collection introduces the history of the Metabarons and reveals the origins of the dynasty's deep-seated principles, their vast wealth, their cybernetic implants, and their most brutal custom: slaying one's own father in mortal combat to become the next Metabaron.

The Metabarons
HUMANOIDS

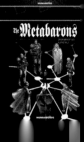

7 WEAPONS OF THE METABARON

Story by Jodorowsky | Art by Zoran Janjetov and Travis Charest

This volume recounts how the mightiest warrior in the universe built his arsenal of war, the galaxy's most powerful and destructive weapons, all in an effort to secure his position as the universe's ultimate warrior.

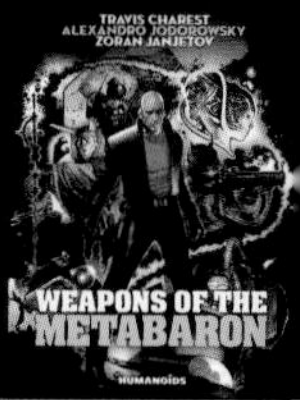
TRAVIS CHAREST
ALEXANDRO JODOROWSKY
ZORAN JANJETOV
WEAPONS OF THE METABARON
HUMANOIDS

8 THE METABARONS (SECOND CYCLE)

Story by Jerry Frissen | Art by Valentin Sécher, Niko Henrichon and Pete Woods

The Metabaron finds himself facing the invulnerable and cruel Wilhelm-100, the Techno-Admiral, agent of the new Techno- Techno regime.

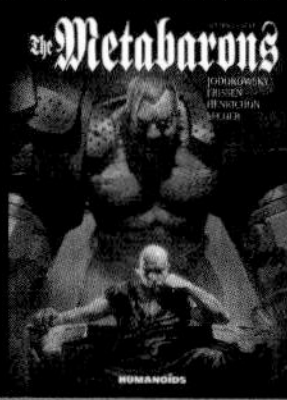
The Metabarons

9 SIMAK

Story by Jerry Frissen | Art by Jean-Michel Ponzio

Phoenix, a gifted but amnesiac policeman, investigates the murder of his partner and finds himself in danger on Solar Corona, the city-planet of non-stop debauchery, facing the Metabaron's enemies, the transhuman Simaks.

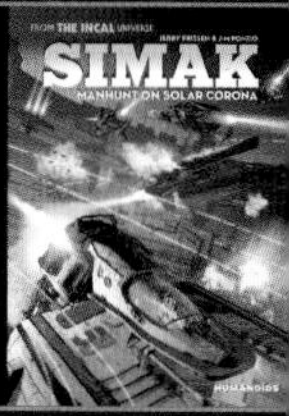
SIMAK
MANHUNT ON SOLAR CORONA

10 MEGALEX

Story by Jodorowsky | Art by Fred Beltran

On the planet-city of Megalex, urban sprawl consumes all, leaving only a few bastions of nature and a mass of drug-addled citizens who are always searching for distractions from their daily drudgery. That changes when a clone, known only as the Anomaly, allies himself with rebel forces intent on dethroning their tyrannical rulers.

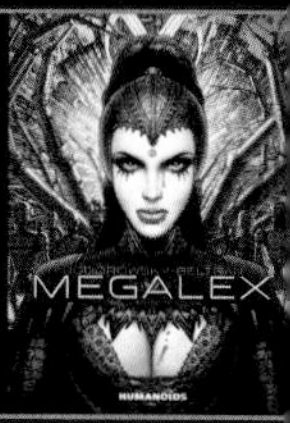
MEGALEX

11 THE TECHNOPRIESTS

Story by Jodorowsky | Art by Zoran Janjetov and Fred Beltran

Albino, the Supreme Technopriest, remembers his childhood, his apprenticeship, and the obstacles that challenged his ambitions in a universe where technological advances are paradoxically matched only by the cruelty and the barbarism of the forces controlling it.

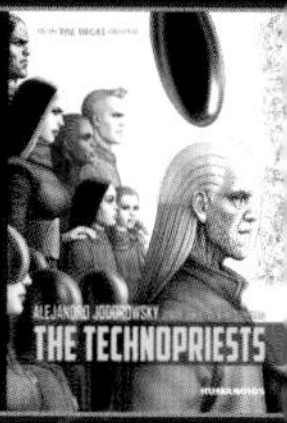
THE TECHNOPRIESTS

12 THE INCAL: PSYCHOVERSE

Story by Mark Russell | Art by Yanick Paquette

In this prequel to *The Incal* all reality hangs in the balance as the Psychoverse wages war against the Matterverse, bringing the heroes of *The Incal* into conflict with the dreaded Psycho-nuns.

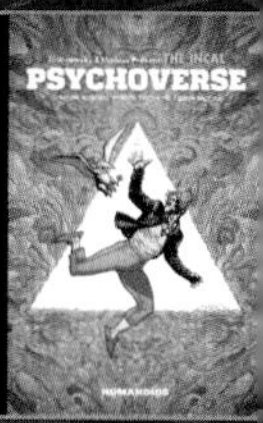
PSYCHOVERSE

13 THE INCAL: DYING STAR

Story by Dan Watters | Art by Jon Davis-Hunt

Commander Kaimann, the great space pirate, has nearly succumbed to ruin when he inadvertently opens a rift in time and space that connect him to Aurora, a nun facing imminent death. Kaimann and Aurora must overcome the very laws of the universe to escape their tragic fates.

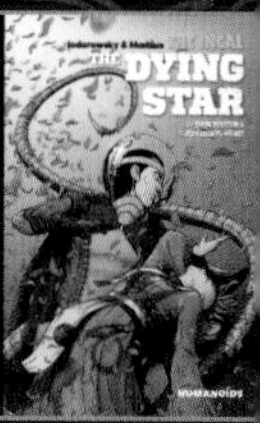
DYING STAR

14 THE INCAL: KILL WOLFHEAD

Story by Brandon Thomas | Art by Pete Woods

Renown lover and mercenary Kill Wolfhead lingers on the brink of death, and the only ones who can save him are a group of his abandoned children. But all is not as it seems, and some may not be acting with the most altruistic intentions.

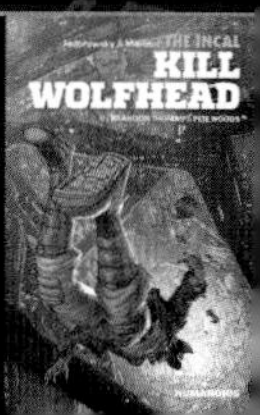
KILL WOLFHEAD

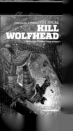

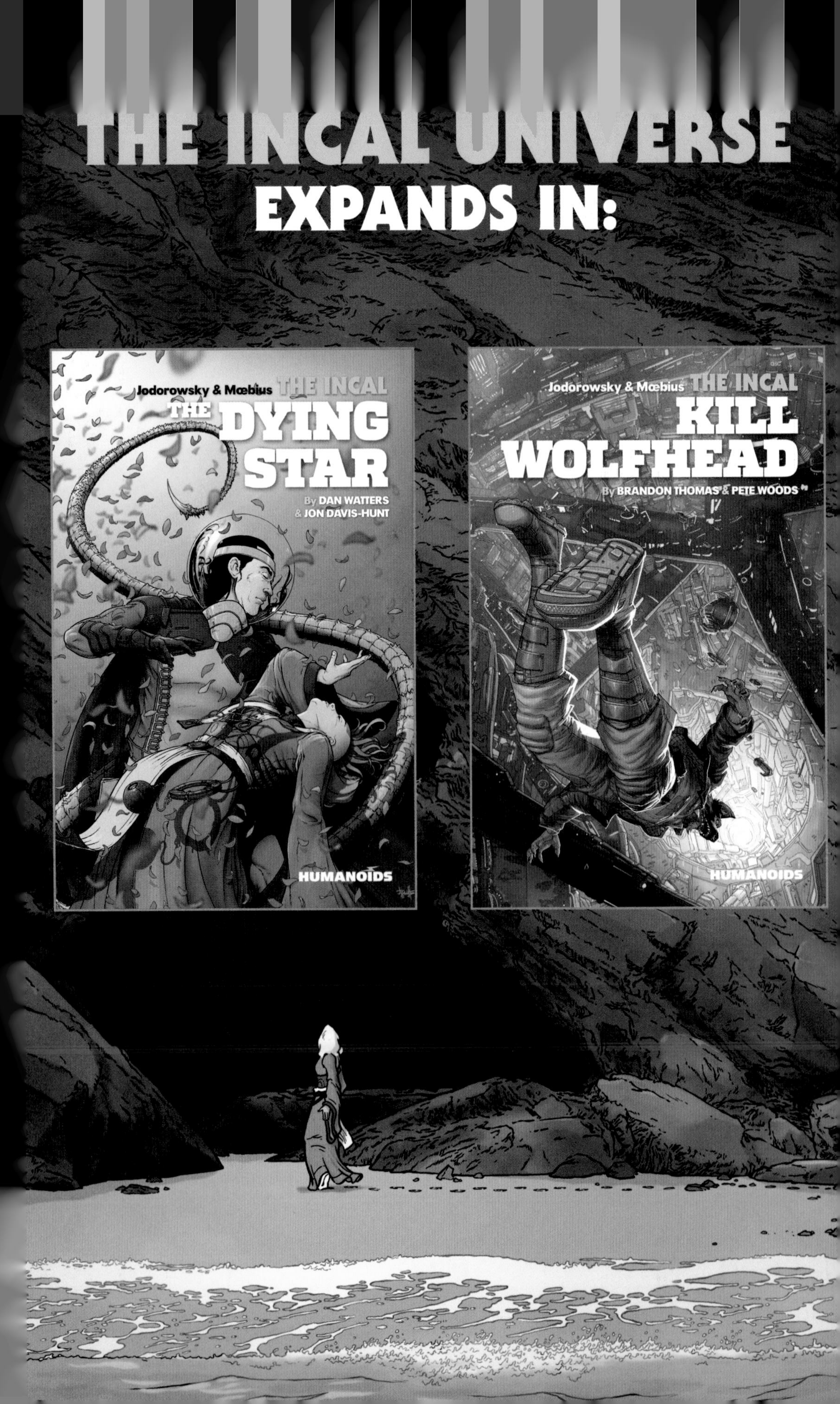

THE INCAL UNIVERSE
EXPANDS IN:
Jodorowsky & Mœbius THE INCAL
THE DYING STAR
By DAN WATTERS
& JON DAVIS-HUNT
HUMANOIDS
Jodorowsky & Mœbius THE INCAL
KILL WOLFHEAD
By BRANDON THOMAS & PETE WOODS
HUMANOIDS